I DRINK THEREFORE I AM

I Drink Therefore I Am

A philosopher's guide to wine

ROGER SCRUTON

continuum

Continuum International Publishing Group
The Tower Building   80 Maiden Lane
11 York Road   Suite 704
London SE1 7NX   New York NY 10038

www.continuumbooks.com

First published 2009
Paperback edition published 2010
Reprinted 2011 (twice), 2012

British Library Cataloguing in Publication Data
A catalogue record for this book is available from the British Library.

ISBN: 978-1-8470-6508-7 (hardback)
       978-1-4411-7067-5 (paperback)

Typeset by Sabon by BookEns, Royston, Herts
Printed and bound in India

Contents

Come – the palace of Heaven rests on pillars of air.
Come, and bring me wine; our days are wind.

(Hafiz)

Preface

This book is not a guide to drinking wine, but a guide to thinking it. It is a tribute to pleasure, by a devotee of happiness, and a defence of virtue by an escapee from vice. Its argument is addressed to theists and atheists, to Christians, Jews, Hindus and Muslims, to every thinking person in whom the joy of meditation has not extinguished the pleasures of embodiment. I have harsh words to say about the health fanatics, about the mad mullahs, and about anybody else who prefers taking offence to seeing another's viewpoint. But my purpose is to defend the opinion once attributed to Plato, that 'nothing more excellent or valuable than wine was ever granted by the gods to man', and I am confident that all those who are offended by this innocent endeavour thereby give proof of their irrelevance.

Previous drafts were read by Chris Morrissey, Bob Grant, Barry Smith and Fiona Ellis, and I have benefited greatly from their criticisms. Previous draughts were drunk with Ewa Atanassow and Thomas Bartscherer, who also made valuable suggestions which I have done my best to recall. I am especially grateful to my wife Sophie, for putting up with the twelve years of research that went into the writing of this book. Some of this research was conducted on behalf of the *New Statesman*, whose editors have shown exemplary patience in tolerating, within the covers of London's otherwise most respectable left-wing journal, a column devoted to tradition, family, hierarchy, hunting and God, with a few hints as to how those insufferable topics might be swallowed. The column has been a source of great enjoyment to me, and I have drawn freely on the observations that occurred to me while writing it.

I have also made use of other published material, notably a chapter on 'The Philosophy of Wine', contributed to Barry Smith's collection on this topic, *Questions of Taste: The Philosophy of Wine*. This chapter was an early version of what is Chapter 6 of the present book. I have also drawn on two memoirs written for other purposes, one of my tutor, Laurence Picken, written for a recent commemorative volume devoted to Jesus College, Cambridge, and one of David Watkin, written for a volume presented to him on his retirement. Some parts of Chapter 5 draw on material first published in MIT's online *Technology Review*.

Sperryville, Virginia;
Malmesbury, Wiltshire;
Christmas 2008

1
Prelude

Throughout recorded history human beings have made life bearable by taking intoxicants. And, while societies differ over which intoxicants should be encouraged, which tolerated and which forbidden, there has been a convergence of opinion around one all-important rule: that the result must not threaten public order. The Native American pipe of peace, like the Middle Eastern hookah, illustrates an ideal of social intoxication, in which good manners, uncomplicated affections and serene thoughts are brought into being by communal puffing. Some people see cannabis in similar terms, though research into its neurological effect sheds another and more disturbing light on its social meaning.

The problem case, however, is not cannabis but alcohol, which has an instant effect on physical coordination, on manners, on emotions and on the understanding. A visitor from another planet, observing Russians under the influence of vodka, Czechs in the grip of slivovitz, or American hill-billies blotto on moonshine, would surely favour prohibition. As we know, however, prohibition doesn't work. For if society is sometimes threatened by intoxicants, it is equally threatened by the lack of them. Without their aid we see each other as we are, and no human society can be built on so frail a foundation. The world is besieged by destructive illusions, and recent history has made us wary of them, so wary that we forget that illusions are sometimes beneficial. Where would we be without the belief that human beings can face down disaster and swear undying love? But such a belief persists only if renewed in imagination, and how can this occur if we have no escape route from the evidence? The need for intoxicants is therefore deeply embedded in us, and all attempts to forbid our habits are bound to end in failure. The real question, I suggest, is not whether intoxicants, but which. And – while all intoxicants disguise things – some (wine pre-eminently) also help us to confront them, by presenting them in re-imagined and idealized forms.

The ancients had a solution to the alcohol problem, which was to wrap the drink in religious rituals, to treat it as the incarnation of a god, and to marginalize disruptive behaviour as the god's doing, not the worshipper's. This was a good move, for it is far easier to reform a god than a human being. Gradually, under the discipline of ritual, prayer and theology, wine was tamed from its orgiastic origins to become first a solemn libation to the Olympians and then the Christian Eucharist – that brief encounter with the sacred which has reconciliation as its goal.

The religious solution is not the only ancient one. There is also the secular symposium. Instead of excluding drink from society the Greeks built a new kind of society around drink. Not, of course, strong drink of the vodka or whisky kind, but drink just strong enough to permit the gradual loosening of the limbs and of the inhibitions – drink that causes you to smile at the world and the world to smile at you. The Greeks were human, and would over-indulge, like Odysseus's crew in Circe's palace. They too had their period of prohibition, recorded in the *Bacchae* of Euripides, which tells the dire story of Pentheus, torn to pieces in punishment for casting out the god of wine. But in the symposium they discovered the custom that brings out the best in wine and the best in those who drink it: the custom through which self-certainty comes even to the timorous. It is this self-certainty, or *Selbstbestimmung*, as the German romantic philosophers called it, that is the subject of this book.

The symposium invited Dionysus, god of wine, into a ceremonial precinct. Guests, garlanded with flowers, would recline two to a couch, propped on their left arm, with food on low tables before them. Decorous slaves filled their cups from a communal mixing bowl, in which the wine would be diluted with water so as to postpone for as long as possible the moment of inebriation. Manners, gestures and words were as strictly controlled as at the Japanese tea ceremony, and guests would allow each other time to speak, to recite or to sing, so that conversation remained always general. One such event, recorded and embellished by Plato, is familiar to all lovers of literature as the scene of the encounter between Socrates and Alcibiades. Plato's *Symposium* is designed as a tribute to Eros. It is really a tribute to Dionysus (or Bacchus, as the Romans called him) and illustrates the ability of wine, when properly used, to set love and desire at a distance that makes them discussable.

The Greek symposium was exclusive and highly privileged – only men could participate, and only men of a certain class. But the principle applies more widely. Wine is an addition to human society, provided it is used to embolden conversation, and provided conversation remains civilized and general. We are appalled by the drunkenness in our city streets, and many are tempted to blame alcohol for the riot, since alcohol is part of its cause. But public drunkenness, of the kind that led to prohibition, arose because people were drinking the wrong things in the wrong way. It was not wine but its absence that caused the gin-sodden drunkenness of eighteenth-century London, and Jefferson was surely right to argue that, in the American context, 'wine is the only antidote to whiskey'.

The social drinking of wine, during or after a meal, and in full cognizance of its delicate taste and evocative aura, seldom leads to drunkenness, and yet more seldom to loutish behaviour. The drink problem that we witness in British cities stems from our inability to pay Bacchus his due. Thanks to cultural impoverishment, young people no longer have a repertoire of songs, poems, arguments or ideas with which to entertain one another in their cups. They drink to fill the moral vacuum generated by their culture, and while we are familiar with the adverse effect of drink on an empty stomach, we are now witnessing the far worse effect of drink on an empty mind.

It is not only drunken brawls that offend, however. So do most dinner parties. Guests shout egocentrically at their neighbours, ten conversations are pursued at once, each leading nowhere, and the ceremonial replenishing of the glass gives way to grabbing and guzzling. A good wine should always be accompanied by a good topic, and the topic should be pursued around the table with the wine. As the Greeks recognized, this is the best way to consider truly serious questions, such as whether sexual desire targets the individual or the universal, whether the Tristan chord is a half-diminished seventh, or whether there could be a proof of Goldbach's conjecture.

We are familiar with the medical opinion that a daily glass or two is good for the health, and also with the rival opinion that any more than a glass or two will set us on the road to ruin.[1] Such counsels are important, though less important than they seem. Whatever the effect of wine on physical health, it has far more significant effects on mental health – both negative, when detached from the symposium culture, and positive, when joined to it. Already in America (in many parts of which the age of consent for alcohol is five years on from the age of consent for sex) wine bottles have to be marked with a health warning. If the purpose is to educate the public, then all well and good, provided the warning tells the truth (which it doesn't). But the same educative goal ought to persuade us to put health warnings on bottled water too, reminding us of the dreary states of mind that come from drinking it, of the need to take time off from hypochondria in order to give food and drink to the soul, and of the ecological madness of transporting around the world in bottles, the stuff that rains from above us and flows beneath our feet.

In his essay on Persian poetry Emerson commends the great wino Hafiz in the following words:

> *Hafiz praises wine, roses, maidens, boys, birds, mornings and music, to give vent to his immense hilarity and sympathy with every form of beauty and joy; and lays emphasis on these to mark his scorn of sanctimony and base prudence.*

It is against sanctimony and base prudence that much of my argument is directed, not in order to encourage vice, but in order to show that wine is compatible with virtue. The right way to live is by enjoying one's faculties, striving to like and if possible to love one's fellows, and also to accept that death is both necessary in itself and a blessed relief to those whom you would otherwise burden. The health fanatics who have poisoned all our natural

---

[1] Those interested in the medical benefits and risks should read Frederick Adolf Paola, 'In Vino Sanitas', in Fritz Allhoff (ed.), *Wine and Philosophy: A Symposium on Thinking and Drinking*, Oxford 2008.

enjoyments ought, in my view, to be rounded up and locked together in a place where they can bore each other rigid with their futile nostrums for eternal life. The rest of us should live out our days in a chain of linked symposia, in which the catalyst is wine, the means conversation, the goal a serene acceptance of our lot and a determination not to outstay our welcome.

In this book I discuss wine as an accompaniment to philosophy, and philosophy as a by-product of wine. In my view wine is an excellent accompaniment to food; but it is a better accompaniment to thought. And by thinking with wine you can learn not merely to drink in thoughts, but to think in draughts. By swallowing premise, argument and conclusion in one full, satisfying stream, you do not merely understand an idea; you fit it to the life in you. You come to gauge not only its truth and coherence, but its value. Wine is something you live by; so too is an idea. And as far as life is concerned, wine is the test of the idea – the preliminary sampling which foreshadows the long-term mental effect. Wine, drunk at the right time, in the right place and the right company, is the path to meditation, and the harbinger of peace.

PART ONE: I DRINK

2

My Fall

Growing up in the post-war England immortalized by Philip Larkin and Kingsley Amis I rarely encountered grapes or their divine by-product. But something called wine was familiar in our family, and the autumn seldom arrived without the gallon jars of sugared elderberry juice congregating before the brown enamel stove, our mother waiting for the day when the frenzied bubbling would dwindle to a whisper and the dark red liquid could be siphoned off and bottled. For three weeks the kitchen was filled with the yeasty scent of fermentation. Little clouds of fruit-flies hung above the jars and here and there wasps would cluster and shimmer on the spilled pools of juice.

The elder grows wild in our hedgerows, and produces the fragrant flowers which are at their headiest on midsummer nights – exhaling the perfume evoked in Act II of *Die Meistersinger*, as Hans Sachs sits before his cottage, meditating the great problem which, in my experience, wine does more than anything else to solve – the problem how to turn *eros* into *agape*, how to give up wanting someone, so as to want her happiness instead. Steeped in water, thickened with sugar and citric acid, the elderflower makes an agreeable summer cordial. The dark red berries are almost sugarless, but rich in tannin and pectin. If you boil them, strain off the juice, add sugar and reduce it, the result is a jelly which keeps for years and which adds a sweet crimson halo to the taste of lamb.

However, it is for its wine that the elderberry has been most esteemed by the English. Plum, redcurrant, apple and gooseberry make excellent fruit-wines, still sold commercially in Austria. But none compares with elderberry wine, which, because of its quota of tannin, will mature for several years in bottle, acquiring its own splenetic English finish. The sugar is not provided by the fruit, but must be added to the initial must of water and bruised berries, three pounds to the gallon – to use the old and forbidden language – if you want the result to be dry. Although there are yeasts on the skins, they cause only a slow fermentation. Our mother would therefore stir in a quantity of brewer's yeast, which instantly caused the stalks of clustered berries to rise up and dance at the brim.

When enough colour had been leached from the berries she would pour the foaming torrent from the bucket into the jars, each sealed with a one-way valve to permit the escape of carbon dioxide while forbidding the inflow of oxygen. And the patter of the bubbles soothed our autumn evenings until bottling time, at the start of winter. We would keep the wine for two years, occasionally visiting it in the cellar under the kitchen and holding it to the light to admire the black deposit. When at last a bottle was opened we would take a glass after supper, much as our ancestors took their claret. And the resulting mixture of appreciative grunts and monosyllabic praise was the most interesting wine-talk that I have heard.

Those were happy days in our family: days before our mother's frail self-confidence had crumbled before our father's inexplicable rage. The bitter-sweet dust of elderberries on the tongue brings to mind her gentle face, her shy concern for her children, and the guilt that we rehearse together now, when we recall with tears her unswerving, suffering love for us. Elderberry wine belongs with her, in an England of quirky privations, of home-grown recipes and self-sacrificing kindness, a world in which the grape had yet to cast its spell over the suburbs. My two sisters and I were raised in the shelter of penury and puritanical restraint. And maybe we would have retained the meek decencies of our childhood, had it not been for the great transformation that our generation underwent when the Portuguese brand called Mateus Rosé burst on the scene, along with other breaches of English decorum, around 1963, 'Between the end of the *Chatterley* ban/ And the Beatles' first LP', as Philip Larkin famously put it (though in another connection). Then

The earnest trumpet spake, and silver thrills
From kissing cymbals made a merry din –
'Twas Bacchus and his kin!
Like to a moving vintage down they came,
Crown'd with green leaves, and faces all on flame;
All madly dancing through the pleasant valley,
To scare thee, Melancholy!

Maybe Keats should not have rhymed 'melancholy' with 'valley';
but he certainly knew something about the effects of wine. We
rushed ignorantly into the stream that had suddenly bubbled up
in our quiet streets; we bathed in its fresh aroma, and gulped
down its gift of dreams. I went up to Cambridge, one of the lucky
few with a college scholarship. And despite this financial
resource, wine kept me in poverty.

But I drank without knowledge, ignorant of the priests that
Bacchus has spread around our world, and who pursue their
calling in places which can be discovered by accident but seldom
by design. During my summer vacations from Cambridge I
sometimes stayed with Desmond, a witty Irishman who had read
everything, slept with everyone, spent whatever he could, and was
recovering in a village near Fontainebleau. It took a little time to
discover that Desmond was an ordained priest of Bacchus, since
his doctor had advised restraint in the matter of alcohol.
Desmond had interpreted this to mean first-growth clarets at
dinner, and maybe second-growth at lunch. His doctor, he felt
certain, would particularly approve of the Château Trotanoy
1945, made from the last grapes to escape the plague of
phylloxera, which had such an improving effect on a frail
constitution when drunk alone after dinner. Desmond held that
such wines would be quite insulting to the medical condition of
his young guest, whose untutored taste-buds and anaemic
bloodstream were clearly crying out for Beaujolais. I gratefully
drank what was offered, and felt sorry for Desmond, that his life
was so bound by dreary medicinal routines.

Still, I couldn't help being a little curious about this bottle
which Desmond would hug to himself in the library after dinner.
The enigmatic name, the faded label, the frail tenacious hands
that closed around the bottle, all emphasized the mystery. Finding
Desmond asleep one day in his armchair, I quietly relieved him of

his treasure and was granted for the first time the indescribable experience that comes when the aroma of a great vintage wafts above the glass, and the lips tremble in anticipation as though on the brink of a fatal kiss. I was about to fall in love – not with a flavour or a plant or a drug but with a hallowed piece of France. That bottle from which I had unfurled the loving hands contained a glinting, mahogany-coloured liquid, an intoxicating aroma, a subtle and many-layered flavour, but also something more precious than all of these, summarized in the ancient and inscrutable names of Trotanoy, the château, and Pomerol, the place. I was overwhelmed by the sense of this drink as the distillation of a place, a time and a culture.

I learned thereafter to love the wines of France, village by village, vineyard by vineyard, while retaining only the vaguest idea of the grapes used to make them, and with no standard of comparison that would tell me whether those grapes, planted in other soils and blessed by other place-names, would produce a similar effect. From the moment of my fall, I was a *terroiriste*, for whom the principal ingredient in any bottle is the soil.

By 'soil' I do not mean only the physical mix of limestone, topsoil and humus. I mean the soil as Jean Giono, Giovanni Verga or D. H. Lawrence would describe it: nurse of passions, stage of dramas, and habitat of local gods. The deities from which the villages of France take their names – whether pagan, as in Mercurey and Juliénas, or Christian, as in St Amour and St Joseph – are the guardians of vines that have acquired their character not only from the minerals that they suck from the rocks beneath them, but also from the sacrificial rites of lasting communities. That thought was intimated by my first sip of Ch. Trotanoy, and it is a thought that has remained with me to this day. But the concept of *terroir* has now become highly controversial, as more and more people follow the path to perdition that I trod those forty-five years ago. Poetry, history, the calendar of saints, the suffering of martyrs – such things are less important to the newly flush generation of winos than they were to us lower middle-class pioneers. Today's pagan drinkers are in search of the uniform, the reliable and the easily remembered. As for where the wine comes from, what does it matter, so long as it tastes OK? Hence the tendency to classify wines in terms of the brand and the grape varietal, either ignoring the soil entirely, or including it under some geological category like chalk, clay, marl or gravel. In short, the new experience of wine is that of drinking the fermented juice of a grape. But that was not my experience on that fatal day in Fontainebleau: with my nose rubbing the nose of Trotanoy I was coming face to face with a vineyard. There in the glass was the soil of a place, and in that soil was a soul.

Wine criticism, as we know it today, was the invention of a literary critic, Professor George Saintsbury, who published his pioneering *Notes on a Cellar Book* in 1920. Not a single grape varietal is mentioned in that book, which dwells on the vineyards, villages and vintages represented in the Professor's cellar over a full drinking life. Saintsbury does not treat his reader to 'tasting notes', which he dismisses as 'wine slang'. A wine, for him, was an individual, not to be assimilated to a type or a brand; each taste was the inimitable signature of a place and the traditions established there, among which the choice of grape is only one. And in my view (which I shall later try to justify) wine should always be approached in this way, if it is to open the way to serious meditation. 'Nothing makes the future so rosy,' Napoleon remarked, 'as to contemplate it through a glass of Chambertin', and we instantly respond to the sentiment. But suppose he had said 'nothing makes the future so rosy, as to contemplate it through a glass of Pinot Noir'? The word 'contemplate' would have lost its resonance, and the remark, no longer associating the greatest risk-taker of his day with a tranquil plot of earth in Burgundy, would have been flushed clean of its pathos and its spiritual truth.

Desmond owned a flat in an inner courtyard off the Rue Molière. The sun never penetrated into this courtyard, and Desmond's windows opened onto dark gullies which would fill each midday with the smell of fried garlic and the shouts of home-coming men. On my visits to Paris I occupied the inner room. It had no windows, and I would spend the day lying on the bed that filled the space, holding under the bedside light one or other of the books that lined the walls. I became as lost in French literature in that darkened room as I had been lost in French wine in the darkened library at Fontainebleau. The literature and the wine seemed to me to be different manifestations of the same idea. The bohemian poet, weaving his *paradis artificiel* in the city garret, was connected by unseen spiritual threads to the walled garden of sun-swollen grapes – the natural paradise from which he had fled. But why had he fled? What did this city bring that the countryside lacked – that countryside so exactingly described by Balzac and Zola? Turning the leather-bound pages of Baudelaire, Verlaine, Nerval and Rimbaud, and then those of Apollinaire, Leiris, Éluard and Ponge in their plain white Gallimard covers – covers so flattering to the reader, in their implication that there is no need to explain what he will find between them – I arrived at an idea of Paris. I associated this idea with Desmond, believing that it had brought him to the city many years before, in search of the thing that can be found only where solitude and society flourish side by side, where erotic dreams compete with weary disillusion, and where the sounds and sights of ordinary bourgeois life prick the observing consciousness with sudden sharp regrets – and that thing is the self. Desmond had come to Paris after the war, with the remains of a squandered fortune, and an omnivorous sexual appetite, in order to waste his inheritance and confront himself. And, because for all his profligacy he had a heart of gold, he was rescued by the good woman who could care for him, who took him down to Fontainebleau, to make a home for him and the children of his failed marriages – and a home too for me, who had fallen for one of those children and then been dumped by her.

And maybe that was what I too would find in Paris – this elusive thing, myself, the thing that Rimbaud sent in his *bateau ivre* across imaginary seas, though in fact to Paris and into the arms of Verlaine, the thing that Desmond had confronted in that sombre, windowless closet in the city's heart, and which I too hoped to confront, maybe while reading Baudelaire in that very closet or through some encounter achieved in the zinc-topped bar by the *porte cochère* below.

And then one day a living poet came to stay in Desmond's flat. His name was Yves de Bayser:[1] a distillation of the erotic and the aristocratic that ought to have marked out a place for him in any literary circle. He was still young, tall and good-looking. He had been befriended by René Char and Albert Camus. But his *Églogues du Tyran* had attracted no notice from the critics, his love-life was in disarray, and he sat motionless in the corner,

---

[1] Pronounced *baisère*, not *baiser*, for obvious reasons.

wearing dark glasses from under which the tears made snail-tracks down his large red cheeks. It was clear that Yves had come to stay and, on my visits from Fontainebleau, I did my best to talk to him. When at last I broached the question of his troubles, he responded with a description of his childhood in the Valois, imbuing it with the claustrophobic atmosphere of Chateaubriand's *Mémoires d'outre-tombe*. He got as far as the quarrel between mother and father and then said '*mais tout ça c'est bien loin*' and left off with a sigh. Each time I broached the topic the response was the same: a careful narrative, breaking off at that impassable point, with the words '*tout ça c'est bien loin*'. After a while I began to think of him as the soul of Desmond's flat. He did not read or write, but sat among the books as though personifying their meaning. He acknowledged all my opinions with a gentle nod of the head, as though he had for a long time struggled against the orthodox view of Baudelaire, Rimbaud, Aragon or whoever and finally admitted defeat. He was a symbol, to me, of literary suffering; and if anyone was on the way to discovering himself, in the peculiar circumstances made available by Paris, it was surely Yves, who seemed to have everything needed for the task. He had suffered and was suffering; he was absorbing the ineffable Parisian loneliness in the quality darkness of Desmond's *echt*-bohemian flat; he was in the middle of the city, surrounded by the cries and rumbles of bourgeois normality; and he never ventured into the street. He had published a book of poems, in one of those plain white covers which are such incontrovertible proof of a distinguished soul. He had loved, and been loved by, both men and women. And he had created his childhood on the models of Chateaubriand and Proust. Yet there was something missing.

It didn't take much to understand what it was. I had seen Yves make himself a sandwich or a cup of coffee. But I had never seen him drink a glass of wine. I reported this to Desmond, who informed me that Yves was a reformed alcoholic, who would not touch the demon drink in any form. In consequence his melancholy had become static, congealed, an immovable deposit in the base of his mind, with all ideas and longings trapped beneath it.

By now I had advanced my apprenticeship to the point of rounding off each day in Paris with a glass of white wine, and developing a certain taste for Muscadet. I kept a bottle of it in the refrigerator at Rue Molière and, visiting the flat one day, Desmond was appalled to discover me pouring this slug-coloured liquid into a glass. He hurried to the nearest Nicolas, returning with a bottle of Puligny-Montrachet, and some ice to cool it. This wine proved as great a revelation as that stolen glass of Trotanoy, rising to meet me like a flower in the glass, its buttery petals enclosing a crystal radiance of apple-flavoured fruit. And once again I associated this complexity and clarity of flavour with the soul of the soil. The name of the wine too had charm, though it was a long time before I learned the meaning of that hyphenated 'Montrachet'. All other white wines that I had encountered seemed insignificant in comparison with that simple Puligny from Nicolas, and indeed my nose-to-nose encounter with the village of Puligny-Montrachet was far more influential even than my visit in the glass to Trotanoy. On returning to Cambridge I brought with me a love of white Burgundy and a belief in its attributes which was in no way diminished by my ignorance of the grape, the way of life and the viticulture inherent in the place to which I was attached. Like one who has fallen in love at first sight, I had full and privileged knowledge of the object of my affections, and needed no information from any source beside my own intoxicated senses. And if, in my subsequent travels in France, I have never visited Burgundy this love of mine is the explanation. I know the place too well to be able to face what it has no doubt suffered from the trampling of affluent tourists.

Desmond was an affectionate roué, who did much to loosen in me the restraints of a puritan upbringing. But during my undergraduate years I encountered another of Bacchus's priests who was, by contrast, as buttoned up as a priest can be. Coming from our local grammar to a college dominated by self-confident boys from Eton and Harrow, bearing a scholarship in a subject that I abhorred, and finding myself in a suite of chill bare Victorian rooms at the start of the coldest winter on record, my first instinct had been to run away. It was an instinct that I could not act upon since there was nowhere to run to, I having already run away from home nine months before in one of those definitive adolescent gestures which I was planning at some stage to revoke, though I never in fact got round to it. There was nothing for it but to go to this old geezer who had been appointed *in loco parentis* and to tell him that I was not going to read natural sciences, that the thought of crystallography, biochemistry and microbiology filled me with disgust, that there must surely be some other subject – Chinese, for instance – that would answer to my bohemian yearnings without damaging my brain, and that in any case if he didn't come up with something better I was leaving the college that night, so there.

My agitated knock was greeted with silence. Listening carefully I discerned a faint, mouse-like scraping somewhere behind the door. After a while I realized that the sound was music – though music played so softly that it was like music remembered, rather than music heard. I knocked again and, after a short pause, was greeted with a quiet 'come in'. Bursting through the door like the proverbial bull I found myself in a china shop, surrounded by precious vases, delicate musical instruments and a hundred polished and fragile things, among which none appeared more fragile or more polished than the *loco* himself – a large porcelain head which turned faint blue eyes in my direction from behind a clavichord, on the keys of which his beautiful ivory hands were resting.

'You are my tutor,' I blurted out, overcome with confusion.

Dr Picken looked at me silently.

'I feared as much,' he said at last.

'I need to talk to you.'

He got up from the clavichord and quietly closed the lid. With slow studied gestures, like a bomb-disposal expert, he turned and tiptoed to his desk, from where he gestured me towards an armchair. I stood by it, not sitting, and delivered my prepared speech. He winced every now and then at some particularly coarse turn of phrase, but otherwise remained seated, motionless behind a neat array of pens, papers and green jade dragons. When I had finished and after a moment's silence during which he studied me apprehensively, he quietly addressed the problem, as though speaking to himself and in a voice so soft that I had to strain to overhear him.

'I cannot recommend Chinese,' he said. 'It is a language I happen to know, collection of languages I should say, and requires an immense amount of work and dedication. We can rule out English since obviously you will read those books in any case, and that really leaves no choice save history or moral sciences. Not that I approve of either.'

'What,' I asked, 'are moral sciences?'

'Well may you ask. It is the traditional Cambridge name for philosophy.'

'Moral sciences, then,' I instantly decided.

Dr Picken sighed reproachfully.

'We admit you young men to read the natural sciences, which are, you know, the greatest legacy of this university, and you can never stay the course.'

'Would *you*?' I asked, looking around at the books and instruments, the scrolls and vases, and assuming myself to be in the presence of a distinguished orientalist.

'I did,' he replied.

'You mean you are a scientist?' I asked incredulously. He nodded.

'I branched out a bit,' he added. 'But I stayed the course.'

I eagerly accepted the glass of sherry which he poured from a decanter. He told me about his work in cytology, concerning which he had written a large book. I asked to see it, and turning over the pages I saw that the last chapter was entitled 'Envoi', a word that I knew from Ezra Pound's Cavalcanti translations. I looked across at Dr Picken with renewed interest. This old geezer was clearly not *loco* at all; nor was he so very old. I asked him what he thought of Ezra Pound. He responded with a shy but authoritative lecture on the Confucian Odes. Pound's inaccuracies in the translation, he told me, were off-set by some real felicities in the feeling. He went on to talk about the Noh plays, indicating without stating it that he knew Japanese as well. And when at last I was convinced that this man was quite the most learned person I had ever met and that I ought to take his advice, he got up slowly, and said,

'Moral sciences it is, then. I will send you to Dr Ewing.'

His manner was somehow precarious, and it became clear to me that I was intruding, that I had been intruding all along, that only a carefully nurtured veneer of politeness had enabled him to carry on a conversation with me, and that his interrupted session at the clavichord had probably been going on in his mind throughout our talk. I left with a note for Dr Ewing, and so began my career as a philosopher.

Dr Picken was a conscientious tutor, who refused quite categorically to make favourites of his pupils, and who invited us all to dinner, five at a time, once a year. I know that I was a trouble to him, often visiting him at unauthorized hours for an emergency *exeat*, which he would grant while looking at me from distant and fearful eyes, as though not sure whether I was tricking him into complicity in some crime about which he would rather not know. He retreated from emotion, and would not allow me to express it. And sometimes, passing his room in the evenings, and seeing him seated at the clavichord, or at the lovely old chamber organ on which he played the Chorale Preludes of Bach, I would have the sense of a creature so fragile that merely to touch him would cause him to fall in fragments to the floor.

I can still remember the conversation with which Dr Picken advanced me to the next stage of my career as a wino. He had cheered me up with some Burgundy left over from one of his dinners and we were standing in his little kitchen, as neat and clean as every other part of his museum-like rooms, as he carefully washed up – it being intolerable to him to see a dirty glass polluting the chair-side table. He turned to look at me – which he rarely did – and all of a sudden his round face shone with a divine radiance.

'I should tell you,' he said, 'that the Burgundy you have just drunk was not very good. In fact commercialization has more or less destroyed the region, and people of your generation will probably never know Burgundy as we knew it. With one exception. There is a small Domaine in Vosne-Romanée called Domaine de la Romanée-Conti. If you ever come across it you should drink it. It has the perfect balance of stalk and fruit, and the soil speaks through it too. Nobody else now knows how to make wine like that.' And after holding my astonished gaze for a moment, he as suddenly looked away, clearly wondering whether he should have made so blatant a display of his apostolate.

This opinion was delivered to me in 1964, when Romanée-Conti was probably twice as expensive as other *grands crus*. In this as in everything Dr Picken's opinion was also knowledge.[2]

---

[2] Saintsbury was of the same opinion as Dr Picken: 'It is the fashion ... to put Clos-Vougeot at the head of all Burgundies, and very delicious Clos-Vougeot can be; but I never drank any specimen thereof equal to the 1858 Romanée Conti for the combination of intensity and delicacy in bouquet and flavour, for body, colour and every good quality of wine'. *Notes on a Cellar-Book*, London 1920, pp. 54–5.

The Domaine, whose 4 acres of ancient vines have been prayed over for centuries by the monks of St Vivant, is now recognized, following seven centuries of mortal determination and divine intervention, as the greatest vineyard on the Côte d'Or. I remembered Dr Picken's little speech, and was able to repeat it at all kinds of gatherings where knowledge about good wine was rewarded with a glass of it. But it was forty years before I tasted Romanée-Conti, and by this time it was fifty times the price of other serious Burgundies.

I found myself at a professional tasting organized by Corney and Barrow, the London merchant with exclusive British rights to the Domaine's wines. I stood among silent, long-faced Masters of Wine, in a room of hospital aspect, with clean white shelves, decanters, glasses and each wall lined with taps and sinks. I watched the expert Adam's apples trembling on the expert necks, and listened in awe to the wine as it slurped and gurgled around those distinguished palates, to be suddenly and peremptorily spat into the sink – a hundred quid's worth with every gob!

I encountered for the first time the real suffering of the wine writer. For how can you swirl something around in your mouth with a beatified expression on your face, knowing that its going price is £1,500 a bottle, and then just scribble 'damned good' on your note-pad? I saw the crumpled brows as they strove to lengthen their paragraphs, to Parkerize here and cauterize there, and in one way or another to excuse the horrible crime of throwing the entire monthly cost of the family mortgage down the sink. I struggled for a long time to describe the Grands Échézeaux, and eventually came up with: 'Saint-Saëns's 2nd cello concerto: deep tenor notes behind a sylph-like veil'. I looked at the description for a while, and then crossed it out, revolted by its affectation, and wrote 'damned good' instead. And whether those paragraphs of flimsy winespeak, with their mixed metaphors and far-fetched analogies, ever mean more than that is one of the deep and difficult questions that I address in Chapter 6.

How can anyone afford this wine? 'Easy,' said Corney and Barrow's Adam Brett-Smith, 'Romanée-Conti is the only wine you can reliably drink for free: just compare the *en primeur* price with the price today.' Sure enough, it was on sale in 2003 for £3,500 for six, and a year later, on the day when I drank it, for £8,400. You could have bought a dozen in 2003, sold six in 2004, keeping six bottles for yourself and £1,400 profit. And you would have the added comfort of knowing that you were robbing the rich. The only problem, of course, is to find that initial £7,000.

Dr Picken, I am sure, could never have spent on wine the money needed to buy the last extant example of the Anatolian reed-flute; and in any case, in his day Romanée-Conti was affordable (sort of). Dr Picken was, in fact, frugal in his habits, and the very image of the bachelor don, who had retreated from life in order to immerse himself in learning. Wine was part of that learning, and the pleasure that he took in it was inseparable from the knowledge that shone from the meniscus. For those who have dedicated their lives, and who have put *eros* to one side, wine provides a solace that endows the hard-edged armour of scholarship with a soft lining of pleasure.

Dr Picken typified the osmotic process whereby a cultural and intellectual inheritance was transmitted within college walls. Provided you approached him with a humility equal to that which he constantly displayed, you could pick up from him any amount of knowledge on any number of subjects – from the wave structure of the benzene ring to the translation of Dante, from Frazer's theory of magic to the chronology of the Upanishads – and the very irrelevance to the surrounding world of everything he knew made the learning of it all the more rewarding. He justified, in my eyes, the rigorous monasticism that had been nurtured by the Cambridge colleges, living as he did in permanent retreat from ephemera. His attitude to learning was the very opposite of that which has come to dominate the schools and universities today. He did not believe that the purpose of knowledge is to help the student. On the contrary. For Dr Picken, the purpose of the student is to help knowledge. He was throughout his life the willing and self-sacrificing trustee of an intellectual inheritance. Young people mattered to him because they had the brains into which his reservoir of learning could be poured, along with the wine. He looked at us students sceptically, but always with that underlying hope that, in this or that undisciplined young face, there was yet the outward sign of a brain large enough and dispassionate enough to capture some of the accumulated knowledge of mankind, and which could carry that knowledge through life without spilling it, until finding another brain into which it might be discharged.

I learned from Dr Picken, therefore, that wine is not just an object of pleasure, but an object of knowledge; and the pleasure depends on the knowledge. Unlike every other product that is now manufactured for the table, wine exists in as many varieties as there are people who produce it. Variations in technique, climate, grape, soil and culture ensure that wine is, to the ordinary drinker, the most unpredictable of drinks, and to the connoisseur the most intricately informative, responding to its origins like a game of chess to its opening move. And precisely because there is nothing – nothing *immediate* that is – to be done with the knowledge contained in wine, Dr Picken had acquired it, just as he had acquired knowledge of Japanese *gagaku*, of the semantics of modal logic, of the metrical structure of the Andalusian *qasida*, and of quantum effects in the pre-frontal cortex. He taught me not just to think without relevance, but to drink without it too. Only in that way do you subvert the rule of mere opinion, and place knowledge on its throne.

It is thanks to people like Dr Picken that Bacchus has been duly honoured in our colleges, and it was to one of those colleges, Peterhouse, that I proceeded in due course as a Fellow, bringing with me, however, the disreputable baggage of a bohemian life that included everything, from guitar to girlfriend, that Dr Picken would have observed with distress. Peterhouse had an excellent cellar, where classed-growth clarets lay dreaming through the years, to be made available to the Fellows at a fraction of their market value. I arrived there in 1969, fresh from the *événements de mai* which I had witnessed in Paris, and in response to which I had discovered my vocation as an intellectual pariah. The long march through the institutions was proceeding apace, the Marxizing of the curriculum had been more or less achieved, and the only good thing remaining about collegiate life, so far as I could see, were the cellars – though these too were threatened, the office of Peterhouse Cellar-Master having been bestowed on a cheery American leftist who was rapidly auctioning off these symbols of class privilege and capitalist decay.

At the end of my first year there arrived among the Fellows another pariah called David Watkin, an architectural historian notorious for his habit of wearing a collar and tie. He had been described to me as an evil reactionary, an enemy of social progress and enlightenment, who would do his best to thwart the ambitions of those Fellows who were striving to meet the educational challenges of the twentieth century. This description so warmed me to the unknown Dr Watkin that I immediately went to call on him in the rooms which he had been assigned in St Peter's Terrace, on the staircase next to mine. I was astonished to discover that he had already transformed the day-quarters of the dingy don who had previously occupied them to the chambers of a Regency gentleman, with furnishings, prints and ornaments that might have been rescued from a great estate, and a great disaster. It had the air of someone who had fallen from the heights of inherited affluence and who was struggling to maintain himself in elegant decline.

The impression was enhanced by the presence of my third priest of Bacchus, the former Catholic chaplain to the university, Monsignor Gilbey, meticulously dressed in the style of an Anglican clergyman of Jane Austen's day, crouching forward in a bergère chair as though interrupted in the course of a confessional. Dr Watkin himself was dressed in a three-piece suit and starched collar, from which his thin neck rose like a fluted column, bearing a head of Doric severity which, however, on my explaining my identity, broke into a thin Ionic smile. I was introduced to the Monsignor, who confined his adverse judgement of my bohemian dress to a rapid sweep of the eyes, and then rose to take me by the hand as though welcoming the Prodigal Son. The two of them began to talk with a kind of Firbankian allusiveness of the appalling nature of Dr Watkin's new surroundings, and the dialogue between them, in which I was included as a sympathetic audience, could have been conducted by two out-of-work actors, consoling themselves with their favourite Noel Coward roles.

And indeed, as I came to know them better, I came to understand both of them as accomplished thespians, who had chosen their roles and chosen to be meticulously faithful to them. To say this is not to make a criticism. On the contrary, it is testimony to their great strength of character that, having understood the moral and aesthetic chaos of the world into which they were born, they each of them recognized that there is only one honest response to it, which is to live your life as an example. This is what Alfred Gilbey was to David Watkin; and it is what David Watkin has been to me. As I got to know him, and as the smile with which he greeted me advanced from that original Ionic thinness to a positively Corinthian gaiety, I found myself roused first to admiration and then to wonder that a person should be able to live as David lived, his deeply romantic sensibility confined in a dramatic role entirely devoted to the classical idea. He had absorbed that idea from the Monsignor, who taught that chaos lies all around us, and that our first duty is to impose upon it whatever order – spiritual, moral, aesthetic – it can bear. The alternative to order is not freedom, which is a form of order and its highest purpose, but disorder, randomness and decay. This was a thought that I too had retrieved, though from the smoke-filled, glass-spattered streets of Paris in 1968 rather than the country mansion, now an estate of council houses, in which the Monsignor had been raised. When David and I sat down – as we often did thereafter – over a bottle of claret, it was to drink to the divine orderliness that sped from the bottle, and to lament the chaos all around. David's room was a refuge from the modern world; and no refuge, he believed, is complete without claret: a theorem which we proved conclusively, and many times over, from the premises provided by Peterhouse cellar, which included a sublime Château Palmer 1962, a Château Léoville-Lascases from the same year and a Grands Échézeaux 1961 which David would drink only if there was no claret on offer, believing that gentlemen do not drink Burgundy after dinner.

David was one of many friends made in my brief time as a don. However, in all respects relevant to the donnish life I was abnormal: right-wing, proletarian, heterosexual – any one of those defects would have raised suspicion, but to possess them all suggested a reckless disregard for proprieties. I left as soon as I could for London, taking with me a few cases of 1961 claret. But I kept in touch with Monsignor Gilbey, and would sometimes dine with him. And under his tuition my understanding of wine took another great leap forward.

Although the Monsignor was a priest of Bacchus, he was also an apostle of Christ and a devotee of order in all its forms. He spent less time seated at his special table than kneeling in his private chapel (both situated, as it happens, in the Travellers' Club in Pall Mall). Convinced that it is in the nature of truth to give offence, he lived in a small, charmed circle of recusants, secure in the belief that 'in my Father's house there are many mansions', so that death would not, after all, be a social disaster. Two sounds above all, he remarked, attach us to this vale of tears: the cry of beagles on a lively scent, and the pop of claret from the bottle. He was as unmusical as he was politically incorrect; but he was right about claret. The shape of the bottle combines with the texture of the wine to produce a sibilant bubbling, somewhere between a murmur and a kiss. Maybe this justifies claret's otherwise peculiar English name (applied to the wines of Gascony when Gascony was the merrier part of England, and when it was only the light red *clairet* that was shipped).

Gilbey held that claret is to be drunk for preference after a meal. The wine should fall onto a full stomach, and rise again as discourse. This idea originates in the symposium of the Greeks, to whom we owe the proverb *oinos kai aletheia*, wine and truth, which became *in vino veritas* when the Romans took over. Claret still has this aura for me, of a wine to be not swilled but meditated, and always in good company – which does not, of course, preclude drinking it alone, if your own company reaches the required standard (which, after a glass or two, I find, mine does).

The Gilbey family is famous for its gin; but they also own Château Loudenne, a bourgeois growth in the Médoc, acquired in 1875, a few years after the Rothschild family acquired Château Lafite and a few years before the whole region was devastated by phylloxera. The Monsignor, in dedicating his life to Christ, had never doubted that his soul had also been improved by claret, and by the civil dialogue that claret induces in its devotees. His second priesthood therefore fitted naturally behind the first. He knew exactly how to choose from a wine list the unassuming claret which, like his own Loudenne, would make no boastful claims for itself, either on the label or in the glass, which would suggest neither wealth in the purchaser nor ignorance in the guest, and which would rise from the glass with that fresh savour and smiling address that is never more evident than in the better *crus bourgeois* – not Loudenne only, but the exquisite Château Villegeorge or the robust Château Potensac, with their simple *appellations* of Haut-Médoc and plain Médoc. It is, Gilbey taught, in the inner landscape created by these modest clarets, that the soul of the drinker most often encounters the soul of the drink. They are conversational wines, wines to be listened to; and they provided the 'third that walked beside us' when the Monsignor explained to me the orthodoxies of the Catholic faith, and the hierarchies which they seemed, in his beatific vision, to demand of us. I did not go along with what he said, but I wrote of his character and philosophy much later, in *Gentle Regrets*, remembering with gratitude and affection a man who, on the narrow path marked out for him, went always forward, his bright eyes fixed on the horizon where his Saviour stood.

Of the 1961 clarets that I brought with me to London, I drank only a single bottle. Following marital breakdown they accompanied me, my sole capital, to a flat in Notting Hill, to be stored in the damp cellar beneath the road. The labels fell off, so that it proved impossible to auction them when divorce and the taxman required it. Luckily, however, a good friend and fellow lover of white Burgundy, Antonia Fraser, was at the time initiating her husband to be, Harold Pinter, into the higher liturgy of Bacchus. She was able to persuade Harold that no cellar would be complete without a stock of 1961 clarets, even if their identity had to be taken on trust from a far from trustworthy philosopher. Harold bought the lot, and generously invited me to share the first of them – a Croizet-Bages. We sat together for an hour, on either side of the only thing we ever agreed about, our thoughts fixed on the ambrosial liquid in which we hid our awkward smiles.

One treasure from my Cambridge years, however, remained with me. Somehow I had managed to acquire a bottle of 1945 Château Lafite – the greatest year from the greatest of clarets. I judged it too good to share, except with that special person whom I had never met, and too good to drink alone unless to mark some new beginning, some break in the scheme of things which I could hardly hope to recognize before it was past. So the bottle accompanied me through life's turmoils like a talisman. I sank often, and drank much. But at a certain point began the steady upward climb that I describe in *On Hunting* – the climb which led from my initial position, as an arrogant outcast in a university whose name I disgraced, to my final destination as a contrite and undistinguished follower of foxhounds. I learned of a tiny sheep farm in Wiltshire, whose lady owner wished to sell. It was autumn when I visited the place. Before the hearth sat a woman with a gentle face and quiet demeanour, tending the gallon jars that stood by the cast-iron stove. I listened to the bubbles as they danced in the valves, and studied the wasp-edged puddles on the tiles. I had come home.

A month later the farm was mine, and I celebrated this unexpected good fortune by sitting alone to drink my treasure, looking in amazement across an ancient pasture towards Sam the Horse, the one creature whose opinions were reliably more conservative than mine.

It is fruitless to attempt to describe the flavour of Lafite. Its effect on the nose, the tongue and the palate cannot be captured in words, nor should we view with anything but contempt the new habit, associated with American wine critics like Robert Parker, of assigning points to each bottle as though in a hard-run race to victory. To assign points to a claret is like assigning points to symphonies – as though Beethoven's 7th, Tchaikovsky's 6th, Mozart's 39th, Bruckner's 8th all hovered between 90 and 95. So let me conclude this brief survey of my apprenticeship with the real reasons for esteeming that bottle of 45 Lafite. Not only was it priceless and irreplaceable, so that pulling the cork was a final goodbye to a mistaken path. It also prompted me to order and unfold my thoughts, to take things gently and in proper sequence, to look back over failure in a spirit of forgiveness and to face the future with no thought of success. The wine catalysed those thoughts, but it did not cause them: for they had their origin in me, and in all that I had been holding within myself and forbidding, until this moment, to take shape as *Selbstbestimmung*. I came to see that we receive by giving, and that my good fortune would be incomplete if not shared. I needed to shake myself free of pettiness and resentment, and to count my blessings, whose flavour was distilled in the glass from which I sipped. And I was permitted, now, to cast my thoughts back, beyond the years of foolish self-assertion, to those evenings of peace and penury, when the fruit flies hung above the gallon jars, and our mother busied herself with the small rituals of home. Was it surprising that, with my mind so softened, I was soon to meet the special person with whom this bottle might have been shared?

3

Le Tour de France

The ancient view that saw happiness as the by-product of virtue, and virtue as suspended from the four 'hinges' of courage, temperance, prudence and justice, does not exhaust the precepts of morality. It tells us how we should care for ourselves and for others; but it does not tell us how to care for the world. Discovering the extent of our trespass on the natural order, we have come face to face with the categorical imperative to live in another way. The message that Rilke read in the headless, legless torso of an antique statue of Apollo, we read now in every portion of our mutilated earth: *you must change your life.*

To do so we should follow the example set by the Slow Food movement in Italy, and by the wine industry of France: in everything necessary to human life, we should champion the local over the global; and in everything superfluous we should allow the global to enjoy its empty triumph. While the globalization of luxuries will undermine their value, the globalization of food and drink will undermine everything else. The case for this has been put so powerfully in recent years, that I am surprised to discover politicians, economists, WTO apologists, Eurofreaks and other unscrupulous optimists, who are still able to pooh-pooh it. We may not agree with George Monbiot, that globalization can be controlled only by global democracy.[1] But we must surely accept the premise from which his argument begins, which is that our local human resources – material, geographical, social and spiritual – are being depleted

---

[1] George Monbiot, *The Age of Consent: A Manifesto for a New World Order*, London 2003.

by processes that have no need to answer for the damage they cause and no ability to repair it.

To say that is not to endorse the view of the whiners, who blame human consumption for global warming, and who use this to mortify our pleasures. I don't know whether they are right; but they don't know either: if they did know, they would speak the language of science, and not that of a millenarian religion. Unlike the eco-whiners I don't oppose travel because of the energy consumed by it. I oppose travel when it causes people to wander where they do not belong, unsettling those who are settled there, and dispersing the spiritual capital that is stored in every place where love has been invested.

Around Malmesbury, I discovered, there is still a local food economy. That is because farmers live by barter, and can ignore the laws that tell them not to sell unpasteurized milk, unstamped eggs, home-killed pork or freshly strangled chickens. When it comes to local wine, however, the regime of insane regulations begins to bite. An enterprising neighbour planted vines at nearby Noah's Ark, where he made a crisp dry white from Riesling, Scheurebe and similar varietals. He worked seriously and scientifically and named his product 'Cloud Nine', in honour of the crows, ninth pair of creatures to enter Noah's Ark, who chattered contentedly in the clouds around the mast. And he proudly put his product on sale as 'English Table Wine'. A European Directive told him to pour the stuff down the drain or risk prosecution.

The offending word was not 'table' or 'wine' but 'English'. This bottle laid claim to a locality not recognized by our rulers, the locality that shaped me, the object of my visceral attachments and subject of my collective memories. Just as the English are not to be allowed their own Parliament, their own law or their own historical homeland, so are they not to be allowed their own wine. Sure, the UK is still recognized – it has an aseptic, bureaucratic sound to it, is not a place but a concept, and shares a letter with the ruling power. Officially, however, there is no such region as England, and the person who sets out proudly to show that the English can make wine now, as they did in Saxon times, and who announces this on the label, is committing a crime.

George Monbiot wouldn't worry about this, for he sees national loyalties as obstacles to the global democracy which is to rescue our birthright from the predators. I see the EU's directive in another way: as an invitation to re-assume English sovereignty over Gascony, and to sell the English Wine that Chaucer sold, grown on the banks of the Gironde.

For me, therefore, ideological rectitude coincides with personal taste. I can champion the local against the global by exploring, in my glass, the country which I have adopted as my spiritual home. I can treat with suspicion those globe-trotting bottles which bear the names of grape varietals, and head for the villages and vineyards of France, which refuse to be anything but a place enshrined in a name.

Before drinking France at home, however, I used to travel there – all other ways of enjoying the country being far too expensive for a student. Paris was a long day's journey by train and boat. In those times nobody thought of the environment as a victim of abuse: they were too busy thinking the same of the *classe ouvrière*, and brewing vengeance against the bourgeois oppressor. The slow journey to Paris, rewarded at the Gare du Nord with a *kir* sipped at a café table, was sufficient proof of distance; no language was spoken in the places that I knew save French, and only one or two *quartiers arabes* gave a premonition of the disintegration that we witness today. Nevertheless, France was in trouble. Those who spoke for its culture and identity were vilified as 'racists', 'fascists' and *poujadistes*. Sartre was busy writing his anti-bourgeois poison in the *Nouvelle revue française*, Foucault was about to publish *Les mots et les choses*, and 68 was in the air like 'the breeze from other planets'. Soon France was to go under, as the children of the elite seized their inheritance and took it off to the pawn shop.

Often in those days of transition, I would sit beneath the roof of an old *immeuble* on the Rue de Bérite, watching the antics in the street below, as the mood of rebellion intensified. From time to time I would visit Desmond, but I was no longer dependent on his hospitality, having built a world of my own on the edges of that destructive student society so brilliantly invoked by Louis Pauwels in *Les orphelins*, his great novel about 1968. I surrounded myself with the literature of the real France; I struggled to acquaint myself with the Catholic Church and its dying rituals; I cooked authentic French meals on the little stove beneath my window; and when I could afford it I went down to Nicolas for a bottle, with which to travel to the parts of France that my old scooter had never reached. Looking back on it, and with a little bit of censorship, I can fairly say that 'bliss was it in that dusk to be alive'.

When Desmond poured my first ever glass of Puligny-Montrachet he opened wide the door unlocked by the Trotanoy that I had liberated from his sleeping hand. I knew then that France was not a political entity – or only superficially so. The *pays réel* and the *pays légal* were, as Charles Maurras had notoriously written, in conflict.[2] And for me the *pays réel* is a thing of the spirit. The tiny vineyard of Le Montrachet straddles the communes of Chassagne and Puligny and produces, from the Chardonnay grape, a wine that is equalled only by the adjacent vineyards of Chevalier-Montrachet and Bâtard-Montrachet. Materialists, oenologists and wine-nerds have an explanation for this: a little outcrop of Bathonian limestone protrudes through the regional marl into the topsoil right under these vineyards. But this recently discovered fact is of little real significance. A great wine is a cultural achievement, not available to Protestants, atheists or believers in progress, since it depends on the survival of local gods. One of the greatest goods bestowed on France by the Catholic Church is to have offered asylum to the battered gods of antiquity, to have fitted them out with the clothes of saints and martyrs, and to have cheered them with the drink that they once brought down from heaven to us all. That, in a nutshell, is why French wines are the best.

Each acre of soil in Puligny has its own fertilizing mulch of history, in which saints and sinners have conspired to consecrate the grape. You don't have to go to the expense of a Montrachet or a Chevalier-Montrachet to prove this. In recent years I have explored the village of Puligny in the glass. And although I have

---

[2] See Charles Maurras, *Mes idées politiques*, Paris 1937. As the principal intellectual force behind French nationalism between the wars, and as a supporter of the Vichy régime, who did not trouble to conceal his anti-Semitic sentiments, Maurras has been struck off the register of legitimate thinkers, something that rightly happens to an author who is crazy, vindictive, malevolent and right-wing like Maurras, but alas never happens to an author who is crazy, vindictive, malevolent and left-wing, like Sartre. See Appendix.

never set foot there, I can fairly say that I know every acre of it – and obstinately use that measure which the European Commissioners, who have the death of Europe in their hearts, are about to make illegal. For it describes the *terroir réel* beneath the *territoire légale* of the bureaucrats.

This returns me to the dispute between the *terroiristes*, for whom wine should be understood as an 'expression' of the soil, and the *garagistes*, who believe that it is the grape, not the soil, that matters – a dispute recently popularized in Jonathan Nossiter's film *Mondovino*. As I shall later argue, this is not a dispute that can be easily resolved. What we read into a wine, by way of meaning, is not determined by an 'aspect': it is not like the story told in a picture, which is directly there in what we see. Nor is it clearly detachable from our own cultural attainments. That first face-to-face encounter with the soil of Trotanoy did not occur without preparation. The education that made this experience possible was delivered to me by Balzac and Flaubert, by the villages around Fontainebleau, by the Debussy Preludes and Berlioz's settings of Gautier. And of course by Proust. Whatever I was to taste in the glass, I knew in advance that it was a part of France – the France that was already my spiritual home and to which one part of me has ever since belonged, even if it is a France that is now buried under a multicultural *pays légal*.

This suggests that it is not just an exaggeration but fundamentally misleading to describe a wine as an *expression* of the soil. It stands to the soil rather as a church spire stands to the village beneath it: a *reaching out* towards a meaning which it acquires only if we have the culture and the faith to provide it. It is one reason why blind tastings are so misleading: it is not the taste, considered in itself, that we hold to our lips, and you can no more understand the virtues of a wine through a blind tasting than you could understand the virtues of a woman through a blindfold kiss. My judgement of the wines of France should not be taken, therefore, as definitively refuted, just because blind tastings have so often left the wines of France behind.

Thirty years ago, Steven Spurrier, a British wine merchant, presented Californian wines side by side with French classics at a blind tasting in Paris. The assembled French experts were horrified to discover that they had preferred the American intruders. One judge asked for her score cards to be returned;

others complained that Mr Spurrier had deliberately biased the procedure. For a while Mr Spurrier was *persona non grata* in the French vineyards. There is, however, a revealing coda to that story. The thirtieth anniversary of that event was recently celebrated with re-runs. Three of the original French producers, led by Paul Pontallier of Château Margaux, refused to join in. Nor was the anniversary a cause of uniform rejoicing in California, James Barrett, the owner of the winning Chardonnay, having quarrelled with his former winemaker, a tough nut of a Croatian with the biting name of Grgich, who had become Barrett's competitor. Barrett and Grgich cannot be invited to the same event, and refer to each other with a quantity of *ressentiment* that would have confirmed Nietzsche's view of the democratic culture. Indeed the whole episode has been an object-lesson in resentment, and proof of the sinful pride of human nature.[3]

Now it seems to me that the best of all remedies for pride is wine, and I am baffled that it has not worked on Messrs Pontallier, Barrett and Grgich – surely proof that they lack what is required to understand the real meaning of their product. After a glass or two, I find myself able to do what we all should do, and which only pride forbids, which is to rejoice in the success of our rivals. After all, a world that contains success is better than a world without it, and under the influence of wine all success casts credit on the drinker. Wine offers a glimpse of the world *sub specie aeternitatis*, in which good things show their value, no matter who possesses them.

One of those good things is history. Blind tastings assume that wine is addressed solely to the senses, and that knowledge plays no part in its appreciation. To think you can judge a wine from its taste and aroma alone is like thinking you can judge a Chinese poem by its sound, without knowing the language. And just as words sound different to the one who knows their meaning, so do wines taste different to the one who can locate them in a place and a time. The Cabernet Sauvignon that beat Mouton-Roths-child into second place in 1976 was 'Stag's Leap', made by a Mr

---

[3] The story is told by George M. Taber, *The Judgement of Paris*, New York 2005. See also Appendix, under 'Strauss'.

Winiarski with young vines from a new vineyard in a winery founded in 1972 in a state whose wine industry was invented in the nineteenth century by a self-styled Hungarian count. Ponder all those matters carefully, and you will allow the motto that used to grace every bottle of Mouton before it was reclassified as a *premier cru*: *premier ne puis, seconde ne daigne, Mouton suis.* This motto, adapted from that of the proud ducs de Rohan (*Roi ne puis, prince ne daigne, Rohan suis*), captures that elusive quality known as 'breeding' – a quality which has only something to do with ancestry, and much more to do with culture, settlement and *pietas*.

My defence of *terroir*, in other words, is not merely a reference to that outcrop of Bathonian limestone under the marl of Le Montrachet. It includes the Duchy of Burgundy as a moral idea; it includes the Latin name of Puliagnicus, and the other name, Montrachet, in which both t's are unpronounced, and the many names around it – Les Chalumeaux, Les Referts, le Clos des Meix, Les Folatières – names not so much bestowed as discovered in the long encounter between man and soil; it includes the centuries of viticulture under the watchful eye of the Cistercian Abbey of Maizières; it includes the vineyards, with their dry stone walls and wooden gates, and the plateau of Mont Rachet, which catches every drop of sunlight, dawn to dusk. All this and more goes into that wine, which, in the opinion of Alexandre Dumas, you should drink on your knees, with head bared in reverence – a wine which is the very distillation of the virtue that the Greeks called *aidōs*, the candid recognition that the other is more important than yourself.

Visitors to Burgundy (including those like myself who visit the region only in the glass) will be enchanted by the medieval towns and villages, and by the monasteries and churches whose shadows fall across the land like benedictions. They will sense all around them the history and religion that made the Dukes of Burgundy into such great medieval potentates, and they will know that this soil is hallowed soil: it has been blessed and cajoled and prayed over for centuries, many of the vineyards being worked by monks for whom wine was not just a drink but a sacrament. Burgundy was for many centuries the heart of the Christian mission in Europe, with the Benedictine Order centred at Cluny, and the Cistercian at Cîteaux and Clairvaux. Even in this sceptical age their vine is, for the Burgundians, something more spiritual than vegetal, and their soil more heaven than earth.

The active involvement of the Church in replanting and restoring the old Roman vineyards was matched by the keen financial interest of the Burgundian rulers. The fourteenth-century Duke Philip the Bold made red Burgundy into a luxury item, by banishing the 'treacherous' Gamay grape, and forbidding all but the Pinot Noir. So rigorously did he protect the reputation of his wines that his own wife Marguerite, Duchess of Flanders, was refused the right to brand casks from her vineyard with the coveted 'B'. A century later Duke Philip the Good made an equally important step, by forbidding his subjects to plant vines in the valleys, so confining the vineyards to the Côte d'Or and the Côte Chalonnaise, where the soil is well drained and impoverished, as vines require. It was Philip's tax collector, Nicolas Rolin, who – having destituted the Burgundians in his lifetime – founded the famous Hospice de Beaune on his death, endowing it with vineyards whose products are auctioned in the hôtel de ville of Beaune at every vintage. This auction is also a festival, when the Burgundians renew their attachment to their history, their product and their saints. It brings home to the visitor that Burgundy is not a drink but a culture, and one that renews itself each year like Dionysus, the god of wine.

The Revolution destroyed the Church's hold on the landscape and led to the abandonment of the priories. Church lands passed to local bourgeoisie and peasantry. Then the Napoleonic inheritance laws came into force, so that with each death the *terroirs* were divided. Tiny adjacent patches of land might be cultivated by neighbours who disdain to imitate each other's ways, and today the 125 acres of the Clos de Vougeot are divided between 80 owners. True, the big *negociants* are moving into the wine trade, and many estates have become the property of '*sociétés anonymes*'. But most vineyards are not anonymous at all, being owned and worked by local families, many of peasant stock and each proud of the viticultural traditions that distinguish it. Hence there is no wine that I know of that comprehends so many varieties of taste as red Burgundy – so many varieties, indeed, that you can hardly believe that it is all made from a single grape. To appreciate Burgundy as it really is, you must leave it to mature for at least five years, after which time a strange transformation occurs in the bottle. The grape gradually retreats, leaving first the village, then the vineyard and finally the soil itself in the foreground. Historical associations come alive as tastes and scents, ancestral traits appear like submerged family features, and that peculiar Burgundy nose, as distinctive as the nose of Cleopatra, sits at the rim of the glass like a presiding god. The aroma of old Burgundy is the slowly rotting leaf-mould on a grave: a soft, sweet, musky fermentation, last breath of life from the sinner who lies decomposing below.

The most important thing to remember when exploring Burgundy is that the world is full of people who are both very rich and very stupid, who can be relied upon to spend virtually unlimited sums of money on products about which they know nothing except that other people as rich and stupid as themselves are spending unlimited sums of money on them. These people are extremely useful to the rest of us, since they put a premium on knowledge. Thus you can know immediately that you won't be able to afford Le Montrachet, but that it might be worth visiting the place next door.

Take the famous hill of Corton, on which is grown the other truly great white Burgundy, the famous Corton-Charlemagne, unaffordable to you and me. This hill lies between Aloxe-Corton and Pernand-Vergelesses. Those names tell you that Le Corton is the most famous vineyard in Aloxe, and the Île des Vergelesses the most famous (though hardly known for all that) in Pernand. Le Charlemagne (a vineyard given by the Emperor Charlemagne to the Abbey of Saulieu in 775) is situated on a favourable slope of the hill of Corton, not above Aloxe but above Pernand. The Île des Vergelesses lies below it, planted with Pinot Noir. In between the two, however, is a tiny vineyard called 'Les Noirets', which is neither a *grand cru* like Le Charlemagne nor a *premier cru* like the Île des Vergelesses, but a simple commune wine of Pernand, planted with Chardonnay and producing a wine with the fine clean aromas and deep nutty richness that are the hallmarks of a noble white Burgundy. Few of those who pay a fortune for a bottle of Corton-Charlemagne have ever heard of Pernand-Vergelesses, fewer still of Les Noirets. I am very sorry to be telling you about it. But what would be the point of this chapter if I didn't?

Fermentation proceeds in stages, some fast, some slow, and

each with its peculiar by-products. Two stages are particularly important in the case of white wines – the malic and the lactic. Malic acids (from Latin *malus*, an apple) impart freshness, while lactic acids (from Greek *laktos*, milk) impart a more buttery character. The use of oak casks adds the vanilla flavours of the oak, while encouraging lactic fermentation. The art is not to overdo it – an art that is practised in Burgundy but bungled just about everywhere else, though not, it should in fairness be said, in the best of the Californian wineries. The greatest of white Burgundies have all the freshness and acidity of the first fermentation, harmonized by the deep soft horn-calls from the cask.

This does not mean that we should ignore those greener wines in which the freshness of the grape still lives and tingles. The most famous of these have their own *appellation*, that of Chablis, which lies to the north of the Côte de Nuits and whose wine is a Burgundy only in name. Even when matured in old oak barrels, Chablis resembles glass, through which the bright minerals of Jurassic marl and limestone shine like polished pebbles in a stream. There is no better wine to accompany shellfish, or chicken in white sauce, or the trios of Haydn. But the best accompaniment to Chablis is more Chablis, sipped quietly at the desk as night draws in.

Chablis tends to occupy the malic end of the Chardonnay spectrum but, unlike other wines which share its tang, it can combine absolute purity with a rich and shadow-filled personality, like Jane Austen's Emma. It should always be kept for a few years, so as to grow up, as Emma did, by being bottled up. The wine comes in four grades: Petit Chablis, Chablis, *premier cru* and *grand cru*, the last being luscious, aromatic wines from the right bank of the Yonne, which have great staying power and may take ten years or more to mature.

Two lesser white Burgundies have helped my thoughts in times of transition, and deserve a mention in this place. For they illustrate a truth that will occupy me in later chapters, that what we learn from wine we also bring to it. I have learned from Michelangelo about the pathos of mother love and the divinity of suffering; I have learned from Mozart about the hope that turns the deepest sadness to joy; I have learned from Dostoevsky about forgiveness and how the soul is cleansed by it. And those gifts of understanding were brought to me by art. But what I have learned from wine has welled up from within me: the drink was the catalyst, but not the cause, of what I came to know. It was not long after that celebratory bottle of 45 Lafite that I had a great decision to make. Should I leave the half-time professorship at Boston University, which had kept me with one foot in the academic world? The question coincided with a new routine of solitude, in the broken-down sheep-farm near Malmesbury which it was now my business to restore. My affirmative answer drew on thoughts that congregated like eager ghosts around the glass, whenever I treated myself – which I did each evening – to the Montagny *premier cru* that I had discovered through the tiny family firm of Châteaux Wines in Bristol. This wine is grown at the Domaine des Moirots in the hamlet of Bissey-sous-Cruchaud, and those names brought me back to my spiritual home, far from my new home in rural Wiltshire. A *moirot* is a marshy place, and those damp patches below the terraced fields are pictured in the freshness of the wine, whose depths are cool and clear. Domaine des Moirots has an alert address like a pointer: and it was pointing to the solution that I had already in my heart concocted, as I watched the cows chewing the cud beyond my window, and meditated on past mistakes and future hopes. Ever since that time I have ensured that a case of the Domaine des Moirots lies ready in the cellar.

Ten years later I found myself back in America. My wife had inherited a cottage by the sea; we had sold it, and spent the money on acquiring a farm in Virginia. It was a crazy move, since the house – an eighteenth-century mansion – had been abandoned for a quarter of a century, and stood vast and bleak and crumbling above its pasture, like a monument to the Confederate dead. For a month I sat alone in the adjacent cabin and contemplated this – the newest and biggest of my self-imposed tasks. By night I heard the lugubrious howling of the coyotes and the occasional scream of what might have been a mountain lion; by day I heard the plaintive call of the vultures as they circled above the scraps that those predators had left. The Hazel River bubbled over stones in the valley and every now and then one of the black Angus heifers that grazed there pushed a damp muzzle against the window and stared at me, curious to discover life in this cabin that had been empty for years.

Sometimes I walked over to the barn to observe the white owl in the rafters. He would study me down his solemn beak, offended by my casual manner. When the sun shone a groundhog, red with dirt, sat out on the stump before the cabin steps; I would open the door to see him roll lazily into his hole. In the streams across the meadow I found minnows, snakes, frogs and crayfish, while snapping turtles would thrust their Thumbelina faces from their shells like moralizing priests in dog-collars. I was reminded of the England of my childhood, when a jam-jar dipped in a stream would provide instruction for hours. I was reliving experiences that I had all but forgotten, listening, looking, and occasionally starting in alarm at the creatures whose territory I shared and who rightly but ineffectually made moves to exclude me. And I began to believe in the future that I had carelessly snatched from the vast reservoir of possibilities.

In those strange new circumstances, I had to confront decisions of an entirely new kind, concerning an adventure which, but for my unforgiving need to be master of my fate, would never have been inflicted on my innocent wife and children. How to take the next step, how to understand America as a home, far from my life-place in England and my soul-place in France – this was the question that troubled me. And meanwhile what on earth could I drink? This second question was answered when I discovered, in the village store in Washington, Virginia (not to be confused with Washington, DC), a supply of white Marsannay.

Situated just south of the suburbs of Dijon, Marsannay grew from the trade in *grands ordinaires*, which French cities require every bit as much as the trade in *grandes horizontales*. Since 1987, however, it has enjoyed its own *appellation*, and is unique in being registered for all three colours: red, white and rosé. It is also unusual in another respect: very few white wines are produced on the Côte de Nuits, yet that of Marsannay has, in replica, the qualities of the Côte de Beaune whites, and is usually far cheaper. The 2001 from Bruno Clair had ended up in Little Washington at 18 dollars a bottle – affordable, and also necessary, if the clouds that hurried across my mind were to be dispelled.

Only a refugee from cheap Californian Chardonnay can fully appreciate the merits of white Marsannay, which is like the synopsis of a masterpiece, enhancing the appetite for what it does not quite provide. I sipped it on the porch of the old house, looking across to the hills down which the blood-red fall was marching, conquering tree after tree. And from my little corner of old France the contours of America stood out suddenly sharp and clear. America is not, as England and France have become, a set of instructions. It is the by-product of the myriad decisions made by people who are free to choose. Judged from some elevated perspective many of them ought to be less free than they are. But that is the nature of the place. And only a fool or a wimp would retreat from decisions in a place where nothing happens without them. That glass of straw-coloured Marsannay pointed the way down a long path which I subsequently took, finding new employment, new friends and a new home for my family, in a society where affection is immediately offered, and seldom runs deeper than that implies.

Between Marsannay at the top and Montagny at the bottom, the Côtes abound in places where some version of the refined white wine of Burgundy is produced. Some of the villages are well enough known: Auxey-Duresses, St Romain, St Aubin on the Côte d'Or and Rully and Givry on the Côte Chalonnaise. But it was the all but unknown village of Ladoix that first set me thinking about the matter that most troubles me today, and which I discuss in Chapters 5 and 8 of this book: the problem of contingent being. And in the course of reflecting on this topic I have received help from two other places, one all but unknown, the other known for its red wine but hardly at all for its white. The all but unknown place is Maranges – the marshy nowhere beneath the Côte d'Or, which is neither a village nor a religious precinct, but simply a place into which the winemaking energy of the Côte has spilled.

The other place is one where an old god has kept not only his local habitation but also his name. Mercury was a latecomer to the Roman Pantheon. His name derives from *mercari* – to trade – and he was the god of merchants, represented with the attributes of the Greek god Hermes, to whom, however, he was only superficially related. There was a temple to Mercury on the Aventine and, as the Romans spread across Gaul, the god's temples sprang up among the settlements, places of urgent prayer as tense with human greed and divine mischief as the stock exchange today.

One of these temples gave its name to the village on the Côte

Chalonnaise which, after a brief period of eclipse, is now, along with its neighbour under the same *appellation*, St Martin sous Montaigu, an important place on the wine-lover's map, and a source of the kind of bargain for which the god was famous in the days when he listened to prayers. Of the three million or so bottles of Mercurey produced each year about a tenth are white, and about a tenth of those again are entitled to call themselves '*premier cru*'. But if your eyes have alighted on a bottle so labelled, you should thank the god of bargains for your luck. With all the harmonies and apple aromas of a true white burgundy, a first growth Mercurey Blanc will provide you with the perfect accompaniment to metaphysical difficulties at a price you can afford.

I faced, in the wilds of the Blue Ridge, the primordial loneliness that is banished from the American cities, and which stalks the crew-cut lawns beyond suburban windows without showing its face. This loneliness is simply the default position of a society in which freedom is the ruling principle. In France equality and fraternity have extinguished liberty, and the loneliness in France is therefore *real* loneliness, not the default position from which you move by exercising your freedom of choice, but a position outside society, cut off from the comforts of community, powerless, helpless and without recourse. Such was my situation in the year that I spent in France, having left Cambridge to take up a position as *lecteur* in the Collège Universitaire at Pau. I lived high above the Gave de Pau, in an old farmhouse called Le Bué, which is the equivalent in the now dying language of Béarnais of *les brouillards*. And indeed the house was often cut off by mists, and for days drenched in unceasing rain as the winter drew on. I was alone there, and with neither piano, radio nor gramophone, none of which I could afford. All I had were a few scores – Beethoven quartets, Wagner operas and Schubert *lieder*.

Being cut off from music, however, I began to think about it. Soon I was convinced that there is no harder or more important philosophical question than that of the nature and meaning of music. I tried to get my mind around the problem of expression: what does it mean to say that a piece of music expresses grief, how can we justify that judgement, and why does it matter? I wrestled with the concept of melody: what is it, and how is it that melodies continue when the sound has stopped? And the problem of harmony: what is the difference between a chord and a 'simultaneity'? When two voices harmonize, is the result two things together, or one thing alone? And the problem of musical depth: why do we say the late Beethoven quartets are profound, and what is missing from the world of the person who doesn't understand them?

Wine had a small part to play in getting me started on those questions. Le Bué was situated on the Côteaux de Jurançon, the incomparably beautiful foothills of the Pyrenees, which begin above the village of Jurançon across the river from Pau, and roll for 30 miles until breaking in a white surf of scree against the mountains. On wave after wave of pasture the broad-roofed farmsteads bob like covered fishing boats. On the rare fine days of winter I looked down from my window on terraced vineyards, which furrowed the hillside in their own little wavelets, before disappearing over the horizon in a precipitous rush.

Peace comes when people plant vines, and ends when they dig for oil. Hence when oil was discovered beneath the Côteaux their tranquillity vanished. Fumes from the refinery at Lacq blighted our vineyards, and only the more distant reaches of the *appellation* escaped. Now the gas has run out, and Jurançon is beginning to re-emerge as a great wine-producing area, with a dry white made from the local Gros Manseng and a long-lasting *vin moelleux* made from a blend of the Gros and Petit Manseng. The latter wine owes its sweetness to *passerillage* – that is, pinching the stalks at the end of summer so that the grapes are deprived of sap and shrivel in the sun – and is unusual in combining luscious sweetness with a razor-sharp acidity. Hence sweet Jurançon can accompany the most savoury dishes; indeed there is no wine more suited to cut the grease off a *confit d'oie*. Locals will drink sweet Jurançon throughout a meal. And those who know this wine will surely agree with the judgement of Colette, who described it as 'a dazzling imperious prince, as treacherous as any great seducer'.

Pau was a centre of humanism under the angelic Queen Marguerite of Navarre, author of the *Heptameron*, and became a Protestant enclave under her grandson Henri. Obliged, on becoming King of France, to embrace Catholicism Henri IV nevertheless issued the Edict of Nantes, legalized Calvinism, and created in his birthplace a kind of haven of eccentricity. When Wellington's peninsula campaign finally brought him to Pau, many of his mad-dog officers felt sufficiently at home there to settle on the Côteaux de Jurançon – my landlady was descended from one of them. Characters in Henry James often spend parts of their useless lives in Pau, and even in my day the town contained an English shop where two old geezers sold Heinz baked beans, PG Tips and HP sauce, in containers whose labels had faded to a uniform parchment yellow. It came as no surprise to learn that the current Mayor of Pau has decided, in response to the outrage committed by our Parliament, to establish a municipal pack of foxhounds.

Sweet Jurançon was served at the baptism of Henri IV and subsequently at all the royal ceremonies of the house of Navarre, and praised by Lamartine as an accompaniment to religious thoughts. I have looked in recent years for a sweet Jurançon to match the dusty bottles of the 53 and 55 which my neighbour, old Monsieur Boulet, would open after his *cassoulet* on Sunday afternoons. Those oily, caressing syrups, with their incense-laden aroma, would change M. Boulet's monologue in the space of half an hour from a peasant grumble to a hymn of praise. Somehow, no Jurançon since has equalled M. Boulet's. But it was a bottle of the 55 sec that helped me to see why I should apply myself to the philosophy of music.

A party of students arrived one day in a Deux Chevaux, bringing cheese, wine and guitars. I was teaching them to sing English Christmas carols in two-part harmony; they were teaching me to appreciate *Dans l'eau de la claire fontaine/Elle se baignait toute nue*. This was a bargain and, *enfin, bref*, we had a good time together, even though it troubled me that they showed so little interest in the classics. In rural France in the 1960s music meant traditional songs, with a bit of Piaf, Greco, Prévert and Brassens thrown in, and here and there the puzzled appreciation of Buddy Holly, Elvis Presley and Chuck Berry.

I began to lecture them, and quickly ran into a slough of questions. Just why does taste in music matter? What is it that they are missing, after all, in knowing none of the Beethoven sonatas? Why are symphonies so important? Why should they be interested in this group called the Beatles and what was so special about the English folk songs that I tried to foist on them as the high point of popular inspiration? I talked myself into a cul-de-sac and just stood there, with the beautiful girl from Martinique called Lotus showing her enamel teeth in a laugh. It was then that Pierre took from his rucksack the bottle of 55 Jurançon, stolen from his father's cellar, and held it out, saying that it was for me alone. I opened it and filled a glass. The Manseng makes a sharp, citrous, long-lasting wine, which, after ten years in the bottle, is wonderfully aromatic and lively, with a golden yellow colour. It attacks with sweet, frothy flavours, and then goes clean on the palate like sand from which a wavelet has withdrawn. And that clean taste rescued my thoughts. Like M. Boulet I stopped grumbling at the things I disliked and began instead to praise the things that I liked. I looked for words which made sense to me and would make sense to them, to say why I had remained sane on the Côteaux de Jurançon by playing the symphonies of Beethoven in my head, and how I walked in the mists with their sunshine always inside.

The nearest red wine district to Jurançon is Madiran, and this too I would drink during my apprenticeship, appreciating its deep virile character almost as much as its absurdly low price. During the Middle Ages Madiran was the wine of the pilgrims to Santiago de Compostela, who took it with them rather than suffer the wines of northern Spain – in which matter they were entirely misled, as I shall suggest in the next chapter. Madiran is a generous, flavoursome product of the local Tannat grape: purple, spicy, long lived and – after a few years' bottle age – as soft and yielding as a mother's cheek. Throughout my year in the Pyrenees Madiran was my red wine of choice, and it was only later, on returning to Cambridge, that I fell under the spell of Bordeaux.

Meanwhile I would travel on my scooter around the villages of the Béarn and the Pays Basque, sometimes going further afield into the Languedoc and always stopping at churches, to absorb their damp, prayerful silence, and to be for a moment at one with the people who lay buried all around. France has been worn down by Revolution and repeated military defeat, by indigenous treason, hostile immigration and the rise of the socialist state; but its landscape is a sanctified landscape, and in the years between Charlemagne and St Louis, when the vineyards began to take root, every inch of France enjoyed its saintly protector, whose name would often become the name of a place, and become smooth and polished over time like stones in a stream. Thus the steady flow of piety and dialect has smoothed Sanctus

Sidonius into Saint-Saëns. From the earthy St Gengoux to the seraphic St Exupéry these names express the archaeological reality of a nation rooted in a place, a faith and a tongue. All this is beautifully conveyed by Proust, the *curé* of Combray being a symbol, for me, of the *pays réel* beneath the débris.

Some of the village names are surprising, like that of St Amour in the Beaujolais, from Amor, a Roman soldier, who was martyred as a Christian. Readers of Proust will remember the young and charming Marquis de St Loup, who, by offering both manly protection and feminine submissiveness to a narrator who has done nothing to deserve either, comes across as the supreme fantasy object – the impossible recipient of an impossible desire. But many will be surprised to learn that there was a real Saint-Wolf, and that a real place is named after him. And although you cannot buy a kiss from Proust's cuddly Marquis, you can drink the place whose name he bore.

Thieri Loup was one of three brothers, contenders for the hand of a woman who lived near Montpellier in the thirteenth century but who would not commit herself to anyone. Thieri joined the Crusaders in order to prove his virtues, returning to find that she had proved hers by dying. Instead of selling his story to the tabloids Thieri retired to a hilltop hermitage, and devoted his remaining years to prayer. His brothers did the same. In due course Thieri was canonized and the hill named in his memory.

The Pic de St Loup is the northernmost part of the Côteaux de Languedoc, which is itself the northernmost area in the winegrowing region of the Languedoc. Here the aromatic Syrah, Mourvèdre and Carignan grapes distil the herb-laden air of the region into liquid essences. The combination of cool nights, hot days and chalky subsoil impart a finesse unusual for the Midi, and the Pic de St Loup has become the epicentre of the Languedoc revolution. A region once devoted to the production of industrial alcohol is rapidly becoming a wino's paradise.

The Languedoc is a place of experiment – not merely because the *appellation contrôlée* rules have allowed this, but also because that is the nature of the people who live there. They have been heretics, Templars, Albigensians, people who as Thieri Loup discovered will not say '*oui*' but at best only '*oc*': enough to send the most ardent admirer to the Holy Land. It is a place on the margin of officialdom, for the most part allowed to call its wines *vins de pays*, but with a few *appellations contrôlées* springing up at the edges. A *vin de pays* is not an industrial product, like the *vins ordinaires* which were often all I could afford in my youthful tramps around France, but a carefully nurtured attempt to capture local soil and local character. There are producers of *vins de pays* who rival those of the *appellations* grown to either side of them, and for whom the lack of official recognition is a spur to competitive zeal. Such, for example, are the *vignerons* of the Côtes de Thongue around Pézenas, makers of red, white and rosé wines who have been egging each other on to adapt new varietals to their ancient soil, and to rival the famous wines grown to the east, west and north of them. And all over the Languedoc the experiments are proceeding, with new varietals and new combinations growing under the protection of a *vin de pays* label.

The wine-based economy of the Languedoc was devastated by phylloxera. Only growers in the renowned exporting vineyards could afford the costly business of grafting onto stocks imported from America, and whole areas of the Languedoc suddenly found themselves grapeless and – what is worse – wineless. The first effect of this was to produce a grim and unforgiving peasantry, intent on punishing the officials of the Third Republic and if possible gaining access to their cellars. In 1907 the people of Béziers, Perpignan, Carcassonne and Nîmes rallied behind one Marcellin Albert and induced mayors all across the Languedoc to send back their mayoral sashes and close the town halls. The obvious remedy was to release enough wine from the cellars of the Assemblée Nationale to quench the thirst of the protestors. Instead Clemenceau sent in the troops. Five people were killed and over a hundred wounded, and Albert was imprisoned in Montpellier. The peasants got the message and the vineyards of Languedoc remained unplanted for half a century.

It is only since the war that the region has revived, to work towards those few *appellations contrôlées* that I mentioned. One, granted for red and rosé in 1982, and for white in 2006, is that of Faugères, an area north of Béziers, incorporating villages with deeply rooted names like Cabrerolles and Caussiniojouls. The population of the Faugères *appellation* is around 3,000, down from 4,750 a century ago, and the wine production is still under 100,000 litres. That's less than 330 litres per person, which, at a litre a day, doesn't leave much room for exports. Still, you can occasionally find the reds washed up on distant shores by the global entropy, and you should certainly do your duty by the long-suffering peasantry of Faugères and purchase them. A complex blend of Cinsault, Carignan, Syrah, Mourvèdre and Grenache, the red has the bony structure of a *vin de garde* beneath a costume of summer fruit that flutters charmingly in its own endogenous breezes.

Encircling the Languedoc, however, are the older wine-growing regions, with long-established routines and settled plantings: the Rhône to the east, Cahors, Bergerac and Bordeaux to the west, the Loire to the north and nestled against the Pyrenees, St Mont, Madiran, Corbières and Collioure. It is because of long settlement that the varietals have, so to speak, disappeared in these regions behind the saints and their shrines. Sometimes it took a deliberate decision to bring this about. For the most part, however, the nature and proportions of the varietals have been settled as the land has been settled, by adjustment and compromise, and by the invisible hand that moves in the wake of human enterprise.

A telling illustration is provided by the wines of the Rhône Valley, which in some places are the product of a single and locally entrenched grape, and in other places produced from blends that are without explanation other than the one that tradition supplies. Before the re-emergence of the Languedoc it was indeed the Rhône Valley that supplied the zinc-topped bars of Paris. First planted by Greek colonists in the fourth century BC, the vineyards are an epitome of French history, and the best northern Rhône wines are now as expensive as Burgundy. The reds are made from the Syrah grape, sometimes mixed with a little white Viognier. Those of Hermitage, the saddle-shaped hill carved from the Massif Central by the Rhône, and of the adjoining Côte Rôtie, are of an incomparable finesse, which can be fully appreciated only when they have been kept for a decade or more. The longevity and charm of red Hermitage is well captured in the following extract from George Saintsbury's *Notes on a Cellar Book*, describing a forty-year-old Hermitage, the 'manliest' wine he had ever drunk:

> *It was browner than most of the Hermitages I have seen; but the brown was flooded with such a sanguine as altogether*

*transfigured it. The bouquet was rather like that of the less
sweet wallflower. And as to the flavour one might easily go
into dithyrambs. Wine-slang talks of the 'finish' in such cases,
but this was so full and so complicated that it never seemed to
come to a finish. You could meditate on it, and it kept up with
your meditations. The 'gunflint' which, though not so strong in
the red as in the white wines of the district, is supposed to be
always there, was not wanting; but it was not importunate and
did not intrude too much on the special Hermitage touch . . .*

It is many years now since red Hermitage has been easily
affordable, and to find a red Rhône that reconciles the quantity
currently required with the expenditure currently available you
must travel further south, into the Ardèche, home to the vineyards
of St Joseph.

Mallarmé frequented the Ardèche because its name encapsu-
lated the two greatest influences on his life: *l'art et la dèche* – art
and penury. St Joseph is not in fact a poor man's wine, but it is
cheap for what it is: smooth, soft and fruity, relatively light, but
with the subtle peppery bouquet of Syrah at its best. As we go
south the oenological confusion increases. A great many
communes are entitled to the *appellation* Côtes du Rhône
Villages, but few of them have an *appellation* of their own.
Many villages are indignant about this, and some have
successfully lobbied for recognition, including Crozes-Hermitage,
Cornas, Lirac, Vacqueyras, Gigondas and most recently Rasteau.
The first two lie at the southern end of the northern Rhône
Valley; the remaining four are adjacent to the most famous (and
most overrated) vineyard of the southern Rhône: Châteauneuf-
du-Pape. Besides these there are many villages which, while
obliged to sell their wine under the generic label, will nevertheless
affix their own name beneath it – excellent examples being Sablet,
Brézème and Saint-Gervais.

Vacqueyras, like all the southern Rhônes, is made from a
mixture of grapes, from which it acquires the regional *accent du
midi*. It is usually sold far too young; but when mature, after six
years or so, it will waft from the glass like a soft chorus of horns.
As for Châteauneuf, its variable quality is a reflection of the
varied position of the vineyards as much as the varied intensity of
the prayers that are uttered there. Each Châteauneuf is an

individual blend of the many permitted varietals, and each reflects
a particular aspect of this sun-drenched *climat*, whose red-clay
terraces rise height over height above the left bank of the Rhône.
One of the best remedies to a gloomy winter's evening in the
Wiltshire claylands is the Rasteau produced by the house of
Tardieu-Laurent, convinced and self-declared *terroiristes*, who
look for their wines among stingy, prune-faced *vignerons* with old
and withered vines, on the assumption that the trickle of juice
that will emerge from them will contain the very essence of sin,
sun and soil. Their wine is a rich, inky blend of Cinsault, Syrah
and Grenache with the power of a Châteauneuf, and a date-and-
almond spiciness that might have been carried by the mistral from
the shores of Tunisia.

Among the dry white wines of the northern Rhône, none is so
widely esteemed as that of Condrieu. Its history, however, is an
unhappy one. Following a local rebellion the Emperor Vespasian,
who blamed the trouble on the habit of drinking too much of the
local wine, had all the vineyards torn up. His successor, the
Emperor Probus, saw matters more clearly, and recognized that if
the wine is good and freely available, then rebellion will occur
only in a state of incapacity. In the year 281, therefore, he
replanted the vineyards, importing the white Viognier grape from
Dalmatia. It is a difficult grape to manage, prone to diseases and
flowering when there is still a threat of frost. The granite soil of
Condrieu and the steep slopes on which the vines are planted add
to the problems faced by the local *vignerons*, and the effect of
post-war migration to the towns meant that, by 1965, there were
only 8 hectares remaining under vines.

All that has now changed, as reverse migration, farm subsidies
and social mobility have combined to replace the withering limbs
of rural France with prosthetic extensions from Paris. More than
100 of the available 200 hectares are now planted, producing half
a million bottles a year. The wine is justifiably famous for its
delicate apricot aroma, for its fine combination of opulence and
citrous acidity, and for its robust attitude to even the most
impertinent foods. It is as refined and evocative as anything
grown to the north of it, and owes to the Viognier its wonderful
floral kisses and wicked waspish sting. But it is appallingly
expensive, sometimes rivalling the first growths of Burgundy,
especially when guaranteed by a famous producer like Guigal.

Across the river in the Ardèche, however, the Viognier has been successfully planted on soil not entirely dissimilar to that of Condrieu, and enjoying a comparable climate. The resulting *vin de pays des Côteaux de l'Ardèche* is now exported by several growers, and some versions of it can be meaningfully compared with Condrieu, even if they do not equal it. I do not mean to imply that the quality of this wine should be attributed purely to the grape, as though the same effect could be achieved in South Africa, New Zealand or Argentina. The Ardèche version shows the virtues of climate and soil, and its trellises of perfume are raised on stone foundations that cannot be matched save by the greater wines from across the river. Strictly comparable to Condrieu, however, is the wine of Château Grillet, a single vineyard also devoted to the Viognier which, despite having its own *appellation*, is a mere 8 acres in size. The Château was visited by Thomas Jefferson during his bibulous spell as ambassador to France and described by the famous 'Prince Curnonsky' (Maurice Edmond Sailland, *prince des gastronomes*) as one of the five greatest white wines of France.

Hermitage produces a white from the Marsanne and Roussanne grapes. This wine lacks acidity, but acquires after a few years in bottle a fragrance and fleshiness that set it in a class by itself. Its dense and complex flavour answers well to spicy seafood dishes, like stewed octopus. If truth were known, however, the best accompaniment to a bottle of fine old white Hermitage is a clay-baked hedgehog, and it is a pity that the law governing protected species compels us to use char-grilled squirrel instead.

In the past I have usually turned for white Rhône to Berry Brothers, partly on ecological grounds (Berrys went on importing their white Hermitage in casks for as long as the law permitted), partly because of their long-standing relation with the firm of Chapoutier, whose white Hermitage, blended from many different vineyards and called 'Chante Alouette', has comforted me in darkest times with its cigar-box aroma and autumnal taste. It is also from Berry Bros that I have obtained a most remarkable white St Joseph: Les Oliviers, made by the Domaine Ferraton. The Domaine, now run by the fourth generation of the Ferraton family, is characterized by meticulous craftsmanship, contempt for short cuts, and a deep love of the Rhône Valley and its *terroirs.* This wine is bottled unfined and unfiltered, and has a golden clarity and an almond aroma that keep your eyes, your lips and your nose firmly attached to the glass. The very opposite of industrial Chardonnay in its soft-spoken tones and intensely local character, it is nevertheless full bodied, rich and mellow, an excellent accompaniment to boiled fowl, and also to more delicate dishes, such as itself. Indeed it is a wine that should not be wasted on food, but sipped in a flower-strewn meadow beside your favourite companion.

The Rhône is probably the most ancient of the wine-growing regions of France, and its vineyards have been stitched like sequins to the map. This has been the long work of small producers, some cultivating only an acre or two, discovering by slow and sacrificial labour exactly how to coax the soil into the fruit and the fruit into the aroma. These small producers were once acknowledged as national heroes, who had done more for their country's reputation than any football team. In 1990, however, under pressure from the health fanatics, the Loi Evin was passed, making it impossible for producers to advertise the merits of their wines. This has been a boost to the big booze barons, who don't depend on advertising since they have a guaranteed market share. The advertising ban in France is the first step towards the globalization of a product whose greatest virtue is precisely that it puts a premium on locality, and invites you to stay where you are. As always, however, the whiners prefer to forbid our pleasures, rather than to discover the virtuous forms of them.

As yet the smaller *appellations* have escaped the global maelstrom. And one in particular deserves mention here, since it featured in a moment of profound meditation. Tucked away below the eastern tip of the Pyrenees, its vineyards running up to the Mediterranean coast, in the last pocket of Catalan France before the real Catalonia, lies one of the smaller of the French *appellations* – just 800 acres of vineyards, making red and rosé wines from Grenache Noir, Carignan and Mourvèdre, with Syrah and Cinsault for spice. The red wines of Collioure are full, rich, round, fruity and smooth like the luscious female nudes of the sculptor Aristide Maillol, who lived in the region and whose tomb stands by the vineyard of Clos Chatard. Roll the name 'Maillol' in your mouth while imagining well-shaped buttocks and well-matured wine, and you won't be far from the taste of Collioure. It is the serene, established, robed and pontifical version of a flavour distantly imitated by those recently ordained candidates from the Languedoc. Its soft tannins, deep ruby colour and cherry-brandy aftermath ensure that, if anything can revive you, you will be revived by Collioure.

It was a glass of Collioure which sparked off my meditations on the death of my noble, generous, ever-to-be-mourned horse Barney, who had collapsed beneath me a few days earlier in Badminton Park. As I sipped the wine I recalled Barney's mouth, opening as though to beg for some such potion. Finding no relief, he neighed twice from the encroaching darkness and died. No drink now revives Barney's memory as vividly as the Collioure that might once have revived his heart. Whenever I have a bottle before me I recall his virtues, and his determination to go on, half blind, arthritic and yet still a leader of the herd, to the very end.

The best of the Collioure vineyards is the tiny Domaine La Tour Vieille, whose Puig Ambeille 1998 was allotted three well-deserved stars in the Hachette wine guide, and whose La Pinède 2002, which fed my thoughts of Barney, is every bit as smooth, rich and fruity. At 14.5 per cent this comes close to the strength of a fortified wine, but with none of the burned beetroot flavours of those subtropical gut-busters from Australia. Indeed Collioure combines strength with gentleness, boldness with grace, just as Barney did.

All that Barney did for me, some other horse could do – though it is fair to say that I have looked for that other horse in vain. Mourning him, however, I reflect on something else, over and above his qualities. I attribute to him an individuality that is *substantial* – not derived from or dependent upon his qualities, but the seat in which those qualities inhere. At the same time, this individuality is not like that of a person: it is not located in some centre of thought and action which is the self-referring 'I'. I do not mourn, in Barney, the loss of a personal relation, or a truly sacrificing love. Such a love is not available from a horse, nor even from a dog, whose dependence on his human master always falls short of the real metaphysical endorsement that occurs when I meets I.

Reflecting on this, I came to see that the metaphysical predicament of the human being – the deep clash contained in the words 'I am', the one affirming transcendence, the other denying it – entirely transforms our affections, and puts us in the way of mourning not people only but everything that captures our affections. Sophie's horse Kitty did not mourn, though when Barney died she stopped, as though she had heard those neighs, uttered so faintly and imploringly 3 miles away. Yet the next day she had transferred her affections, as a vine might clamber on to another branch.

Although those very English meditations were sparked by a glass of Collioure, it should be acknowledged that the natural accompaniment to thoughts of old England are the wines of Bordeaux, a town still counted among the titles of our crown, whose product is peculiarly suited to the English temperament in its restrained and phlegmatic fruitiness. Centuries of obstinate English eccentricity are contained in the peculiar name 'claret', bestowed on wines that are as deep in colour as the wine that Homer had in mind, when describing the 'wine-dark sea' (though they say that Homer was blind). Recall that

> *We shall not cease from exploration,*
> *And the end of all our exploring*
> *Will be to arrive where we started*
> *And know the place for the first time.*

T. S. Eliot's famous description of our spiritual journey applies equally to our journey into wine. Beginning from claret, we venture out in search of strange fruit, exotic landscapes, curious lifestyles and countries with nothing to recommend them save their wines. And after punishing body and soul with Australian Shiraz, Argentine Tempranillo, Romanian Cabernet Sauvignon and Greek Retsina, we crawl home like the Prodigal Son and beg forgiveness for our folly. Claret extends a warm and indulgent embrace, renewing the ancient bond between English thirst and Gascon refreshment, soothing our penitent thoughts with its quiet and clear aroma, sounding its absolution in the depths of the soul. This is the wine that made us and for which we were made, and it often astonishes me to discover that I drink anything else.

For, apart from the classed growths, claret is cheap. This is not the place to reflect on that extraordinary classification undertaken in 1855 for the Great Exhibition in Paris, except to note that, with a few adjustments, it is as accurate a guide today as it was a century and a half ago, despite all the changes in ownership and technique – sure proof of the *terroiriste* philosophy. Returning from Jurançon to Cambridge, so as to know the place for the first time, I found myself enjoying dining rights at King's College, at the time a fiefdom of the Labour aristocracy, and not much better today. On Sunday nights the wine at dessert was Ch. Latour 1949 – bottles that would sell for my monthly income, poured down the throats of sneering sociologists! I would huddle in a corner with the ageing E. M. Forster, sharing his dismay at the realization of his old liberal dreams, listening to his reminiscences of Alexandria and Cavafy, and conjuring into the glorious scent of that never-to-be-forgotten claret, an image of my future, far from this place where Forster and I were exiles, I temporary, he for the remainder of his days. 'Only connect!': his famous words were often in my mind, as he and I sat radically disconnected from the rest of the dessert table, jealously watching the decanter as those undeserving hands poured out its treasure. Morgan Forster was a gentleman, who strove to look kindly on the things he deplored. And his very kindness showed that he had repudiated the spirit which had been born among the Cambridge 'apostles', which had explored the drawing rooms and bedrooms of Bloomsbury, and which had come home at last, not to know the place for the first time, but to destroy it.

I left Cambridge, after my brief spell as a don, firmly associating claret with the great question that was to occupy me for the rest of my life – namely, what remains of England, and how can the remnant be saved? This may not look like a philosophical question; but in due course it led me along a fascinating philosophical path, through the spooky wood where Hegel's Owl of Minerva flits in the branches, towards the clearing made by the English common law. I had discovered the idea which leftist orthodoxy had censored out of all discussions – the idea of corporate personality, or 'the soul of the *polis*', as Plato described it. The corporate soul of England glimmered at the bottom of the claret glass, and I have associated my old country ever since with this wine grown in my spiritual home.

Bordeaux is both one and many: a myriad *terroirs*, each with its own personality and its unique spiritual fate, sharing the format of a bottle, a history, and a long-standing customary law. And in this it resembles England, that place in which eccentric individualists spontaneously combine as a single club. The bottles of Bordeaux stand side by side in my mind in regimented order, their ranks spelled out in the great edict of 1855, itself, however, no more than a summary of what custom and tradition had sanctified. And each bottle, claiming as a 'château' what may be in reality no more than a garden shed (though sometimes a shed with knobs on), has its own eccentric dignity, refusing to melt into the hierarchy in which it plays its own individual part. Even the names might be English: Talbot, Cantenac-Brown, Léoville-Barton, Smith-Haut-Lafitte. And it has always seemed to me testimony to a palate blighted by a New England youth, that Henry James should praise Pontet-Canet for its 'touch of French reason, French completeness', in *A Little Tour through France*. True, it was a bottle of Ch. Pontet-Canet 1959 that sealed the bargain that sent me to Jurançon. But I drank it with Nico Mann in his rooms in King's, from which we could look from Gothic windows over the quiet waters of the Cam. And as the Pontet-Canet went down from my mouth, so did my heart come up to meet it, knowing that this room, this friend, this view and this taste, were part of my farewell to England.

There is little that I can say of the many contented hours of meditation and good will that I owe to the wines of Bordeaux. But one point deserves mention, which is the social and cultural consequences of the classification of 1855. Since that great event the wines of Graves, St Émilion and Pomerol have also been awarded ranks, while to the list of classed growths has been added the long coda of *crus bourgeois*. Thus the French wine trade perpetuates the leading myth of French culture – the myth of the 'bourgeois' as the second-class citizen, the dull, small-minded foil to the flamboyant sensibility of the aristocrat and the artist. Wine snobbery has added its force to Flaubert, Sartre and Foucault, in the great effort to make the ordinary Frenchman look small.

This presents us *bourgeoisie* with a familiar problem. How do we sneak into the upper echelons without looking ridiculous? How do we grab some of the rewards appropriated by the land-owning and brain-owning classes, while holding on to our hard-won cash and maintaining our attitude of honest self-sufficiency? One answer is to go in search of 'second wines'. The classed growths of Bordeaux now issue some of their product under this label, allegedly taken from younger vines, or matured in a more 'forward' style – but serving in any case to maintain the ludicrously inflated prices of their siblings. Many of these wines are indistinguishable from the official article, and sold at less than half the price. I would recommend the second wines of Ch. Branaire Ducru and Ch. Mazeyres – the latter offering stunning and affordable proof that Pomerol is, at its best, the greatest of all the clarets, and reminding me of that greatest of all Pomerols, the 1945 Trotanoy, which tempted me to my original sin, and whose theft was the cause of my fall.

However, it is for the most part the *petits châteaux* which have made life interesting for me. First have been the minor growths of St Emilion, which achieved a sketchy classification in 1954, identifying *premiers grands crus classés* which as a result became unaffordable. The *grands crus*, by contrast, which may lose and gain that title from year to year, are often within my price range, and one of them, Ch. Barrail du Blanc, has brought both consolation and friendship, being the wine that I drink with my fellow santaphobes on Christmas Day. This combination of Merlot and Cabernet Franc, from a tiny vineyard no bigger than the field occupied by Sam the Horse, has a full harmonious fruit and a delicate nose without warts or hairy cavities. Pour this wine after dinner, and you will observe a warm evening light in the glass, with nymphs and satyrs swimming in a pool of purple. And its effect on Christmas is like the effect of pure spirit on a stain.

Equally important have been the wines of Châteaux Cissac and Potensac, both *crus bourgeois* from the Médoc, which produce lovely dark clarets from blends in which Cabernet Sauvignon predominates. Because the plain Médoc *appellation* is without snob appeal, these wines are affordable, and for balance of fruit and tannin, and delicacy of scent, they deserve to be far better known. Their Roman names, which demand scholarly decipherment, add to the pleasure of drinking them.

From the Haut-Médoc and benefiting likewise from the absence of a village *appellation*, is the deep purple wine of Château Villegeorge, the 1961 of which I was fortunate to drink during my penitential period as a Cambridge don. For some reason I recall the flavours of these three so vividly that it is as though I were rolling them on the tongue as I write.

It is as true of Bordeaux as it is of Burgundy, that you should always look for the property next door. If you are an enthusiast for Graves, then you should buy the ridiculously cheap Château Picque-Caillou, a property built in 1780 which lies on sandy gravel close to Château Haut-Brion, and which produces a wine with the pebbly cleanness suggested by its name and the clear garnet colour and perfect balance of its expensive neighbour. But perhaps it is in the matter of sweet Bordeaux that the next door principle is most rewarding.

There is a first-growth Sauternes called Ch. Lafaurie-Peyraguey, known to every reader of *Brideshead Revisited* as the wine that sets the tale in motion. 'Don't pretend you have heard of it,' Sebastian admonishes as he delivers a bottle to that fatal picnic, and as a result we all have. Lafaurie-Peyraguey is comparable in a good year to nearby Ch. d'Yquem, and a third of the price or less. There are those who are distressed when rich people spend hundreds, sometimes even thousands, of pounds on a bottle of wine, while others are obliged to drink water. But if you have a lot of money, throwing it away is best – best for you, since it frees you of a burden, best for the recipient, who needs it more than you do (else why are you throwing it away?), best for all of us, who are somewhere downstream from your folly. And the more perishable and pointless the thing on which your money is squandered, the more worthy the act. The worst use of money is to add to the junk pile of old cars or kitsch houses. The best use is to buy mega-expensive wine, so turning your money into biodegradable urine, and returning it to the primordial flux.

But then, you ask, who would want to drink sweet wine in any case? Well, there is a noble precedent. The adventures of Odysseus and his crew have a single form: ordeal, escape, sacrifice, feast and then the *glukon oinon* that restores the world. If you like sweet wine then follow the Homeric example: drink it on its own, after dinner, with no wine before. And if you can precede the meal with some Cyclops-blinding, Charybdis-skimming or Siren-resisting, so much the better. For people like myself, with chivalric but conservative values, life abounds in hair-raising adventures. So why shouldn't we reward ourselves, after a day of dragon-slaying, with a bottle of sweet Bordeaux?

Unfortunately, in this as in everything else, fashion goes against us. The habit has arisen of drinking Sauternes and Barsac with a meal; they are even called 'pudding wine', by those who wish to suggest a deliciously untroubled childhood in a large country house. Yet worse than this Mitford-like affectation is the habit of drinking Sauternes with *foie gras* – as though excess becomes success if you double it.[4] Far better to finish your dinner (roast pork and crackling, no dessert), and then put the wine, cool, clear and golden, on the table. You could even decant it, since old Sauternes has tartar crystals which dance like bottled fairies in the lees.

The vineyards that produce the great sweet wines of Bordeaux are all clustered around the place where the Ciron joins the Garonne. The chill waters of the Ciron cool the vapours of the warm Garonne, creating a micro-climate of 'mists and mellow fruitfulness'. The *Botrytis cinerea* – 'noble rot' – then settles on the grapes and shrivels them. The grapes are harvested one by one, so that the vines must be picked several times, and the quantities are tiny. Vintages depend on long warm autumns, and if the noble rot does not appear, the wine is written off entirely. It is not surprising if the result is expensive – though no more expensive than it deserves to be.

Which brings me back to Lafaurie-Peyraguey. The classed growths of Sauternes suffer from the comparison with Yquem. For Yquem has absolutely no market among real wine lovers. If they have enough money for a bottle of Yquem, they will buy half a dozen Ch. Suduiraut (an exquisite first growth) or Lafaurie-Peyraguey instead. Yquem can maintain its price only because the world is full of stinking rich vulgarians who know nothing about wine, and therefore buy the best. But as with women and horses, the real best is second best.[5]

Just behind Suduiraut, unknown to most Sauternes addicts, is a

---

[4] Barry Smith interestingly adds that 'the most magnificent accompaniment to Sauternes is Roquefort. The salty, acidic tang of the cheese and the sweet burnished flavours of the wine blend into something greater than both.'

[5] Another angle on to this interesting phenomenon is provided by the theory of 'Veblen goods' in economics – i.e. goods (named from Thorstein Veblen, theorist of 'conspicuous consumption') that become more desirable as their price increases. See Justin Weinberg, 'Taste How Expensive This Is', in Fritz Allhoff (ed.), *Wine and Philosophy: A Symposium on Thinking and Drinking*, Oxford 2008.

third best wine which, in a good year, is comparable to its illustrious neighbour. This wine – Château Briatte, the pride and joy of M. Roudes, its proprietor – is neither a classed growth, nor anything else that might inflate its price. But it produces a rich elixir from old vines, and has received a gold medal in the Paris Concours Général. If you appreciate the honeyed flavour and meadowsweet nose of Suduiraut, you can find versions of them at half the price in Briatte. This too is a wine that I keep in constant supply, since it was when sharing a glass of it with Sam the Horse one evening that I stumbled on what still seems to me to be the most plausible theory of musical expression. It is no more true that we understand the expressive content of a work of music by finding the words for it, than we gather the meaning and virtue of a wine from our attempt to describe its taste. On that evening in the stables with Sam I was prompted by Château Briatte 1991 to recall *La fille aux cheveux de lin* in Debussy's first book of Preludes, without for a moment supposing that this girl was contained in the wine as a face in a portrait or a thought in a sentence. Nor is she contained in the music. Debussy puts the title at the end of the piece, preceded by three dots, to show that it is an association, not a meaning, that he has in mind. You can understand the music, and never have a thought about a girl with flaxen hair.

This observation prompts another, namely, that evocation and expression are quite distinct. Both wine and music can evoke things; but only music can *express* them. Expression is what you understand when you hear or play with understanding. It is not a cloud thrown up by the music but a thread that binds it. The tenderness of Debussy's Prelude is contained in its pentatonic theme, and unfolds through the music: the modal harmonies emphasize the feeling, presenting the melodic line with a flesh-like softness of touch. In describing this tenderness we are not referring to an evocation but to something that is part of what the music means – something which gains, from the music, an intelligence and identity of its own. Someone who missed this tenderness would have failed to understand the notes that contain it. And we will have a clue to the concept of musical expression if we can show just when the words that a piece of music calls from us describe a *process in the music*, rather than a process in us, and a process that we must grasp if we are to hear or play with understanding.

The comparison between wine and music helps us also to understand why wine is not an art form. The notes in music are also gestures, marked by intention. In listening to them we encounter an act of communication, an intentional *putting across* of an imagined state of mind. We also hear a process of development, a logical argument from note to note, so that form and content advance together, as in a sentence. Other things that we produce intentionally are not *marked* by intention as works of art are marked. The lettuces that grow in my garden were grown intentionally, and I worked to ensure that they had the shape and flavour that they have. In that sense their shape and flavour are intentionally produced. But the taste of the lettuce is not the taste of my horticultural intention, in the way that the sound of the kettledrum at the start of Beethoven's violin concerto is the sound of a musical intention. We don't taste intention in a lettuce as we hear intention in music. And that goes also for wine. However much the tastes in a great wine are the result of an intention to produce them, we don't taste the intention in tasting the wine, as we hear the intention in music. Wine results from the mind, but never expresses it.

I first came to understand the rottenness of British industry in France, as I toured the villages on the old 500cc AJS which had replaced my scooter. Everywhere I went this machine was caressed by admiring hands and eyes, and there was not a *gars du village* who wouldn't have exchanged his mother for its likeness. But no British motorcycles were on sale in that wide-open market, no manufacturer had opened an office or taken out an advert, and not a spare part was to be had. When the front tyre split near Libourne in the Dordogne, I was forced to leave the bike in a garage, and go back to England for a tyre.

Having been told that there were no trains until the morning, I settled with my sleeping bag under a tree. In the last rays of the sun a farmer was working in the neighbouring field, and he came across to enquire what I was up to. My story must have touched him, for he came back an hour later carrying bread, pâté and a bottle of wine: Entre-Deux-Mers, he explained, from his neighbour's newly rescued vineyard, which he swore was the equal of any white wine in the world, now that the vines had been replanted. The partiality of the true patriot always persuades me, and I eagerly set out to confirm the judgement. On that calm summer night outside the village of Vayres, with the Dordogne river glinting in the distance and a heart full of gratitude, I was easily converted to this wine which I had known previously only as the cheapest white in Jesus College buttery.

What I did not know then was that Vayres is not a white wine village at all, but the centre of a district which has been known since the nineteenth century for its reds, and allowed its own *appellation* in 1931. Not to be confused with the more famous Graves on the left back of the Garonne, Graves de Vayres produces full, flavoursome wines, rich in minerals from the gravelly soil that is acknowledged in its name. Château Bel-Air is an excellent example: a Cabernet-based wine full of character, with bright minerals shining through its canopy of fruit, and a hint of iron and leather, like the wine in which Sancho Panza detected the taint of a bunch of keys. It needs some years in the bottle to smooth away its rough edges, but is well worth the wait. Impossible to confuse with the velvety wines of Graves proper, Graves de Vayres is made for big rough dinners, like those we serve to our farming neighbours in Wiltshire. And it goes roaring down the tube in pursuit of a hog roast, just as I roared through the vineyards that produced it all those years ago.

Going further north-east from Bordeaux we enter Bergerac, which produces cheap but well-made wines from the Bordeaux varietals. Bergerac used to be known as the poor man's claret, the favoured drink of Labour campaigners as they attempted to imitate the patrician lifestyle, if not the empty flatulence, of Roy Jenkins. Fortunately human memory fades, even the memory of those sofa-shaped bores who hobnobbed their way to the top by pretending to be socialists. Nor need we recall the raw supermarket blends that bore the name of Bergerac and which were rightly driven to extinction by the Australians. Bergerac has matured, and all winos should take an interest in a drink that welcomes you home from your campaigns, whatever their causes, and whatever their effects. I have a soft spot for Château Grinou, which, in good years like 2003, has the depth and fruit of a St Emilion, with a spicy aroma and a round, full sweetness on the tongue. You could drink this every day and never tire of it, even when you waste your days on political campaigning. The same estate's white is also exemplary, achieving a perfect marriage between the rich fruit of the Sémillon grape and the grassy freshness of Sauvignon. La Tour Monestier, the estate next door to Grinou, illustrates the diversity of white Bergerac, polishing up the Sémillon-Sauvignon blend with 20 per cent of Muscadelle, adding its apricot scent and clinging flavour.

I have a soft spot too for the wine of Cahors. This beautiful town, situated on the Lot, which it graces with a spectacular bridge of stone, was able, during the Middle Ages, to send its wine downriver to the sea. By the fourteenth century 'the black Cahors' was being exported all over Europe. Its reputation stood as high as Bordeaux, and its murky colour – caused by baking the grapes or boiling the must prior to fermentation – made it seem like the perfect replacement for blood lost in a royal tournament.

Modern methods of vinification have lightened the colour; but Cahors remains, nevertheless, one of the darkest of wines. It owes this feature to its dominant grape varieties – the Tannat and the Malbec (known locally as Auxerrois), which are sometimes blended with Merlot to make the deep, tannic, prune-flavoured wine that is nectar to those who enjoy it, and gall to those who don't. I belong to the former class, and I approve of Cahors all the more in that, like so many wines from the south-west of France, it is undetachable from a place and its soil. Malbec and Tannat are only now being globalized by the quaffing trade, the first having gained a foothold (after misguided attempts to eradicate it) in Argentina, where it produces soft, rich wines that are among the best products of South America. The concentrated tannins of these grapes are intensified by the iron-rich subsoil of the Cahors region, to make slow-maturing inward-looking wines that need to be coaxed from the glass with long quiet spells of meditation.

Friends who live in nearby Fronton, just north of Toulouse, dismiss Cahors as an austere, gaunt and ungenerous wine. This judgement does not, in my view, reflect badly on Cahors, but rather emphasizes the peculiar virtue of Fronton, which has a plush, ripe, juicy quality, like a lovely neck in the teeth of a vampire. Fronton is yet more locally rooted than Cahors: the Negrette grape is unique to the region, supposedly brought from Cyprus nine centuries ago by the Knights Templar. The red-stone soil, poor in nutrients but rich in minerals, perfectly suits these small, spherical grapes with their blackberry flavour, and the wine, when mixed with Syrah or Cabernet for added perfume, is as supple and as cheap as Bergerac.

In my early pilgrimages to the temples of Dionysus my journey from Paris to the south-west took in the left bank of the Loire, slipping through the vinous villages and skirting the walls of castles where *claquemurés* old aristos were still holding out, staring from high windows at the dreaming fields. Architecture, landscape, vegetation, even the strong broad flow of the river, seemed to glow with the idea of France, and Orléans, lying on the northern apex of the Loire, endowed the river with a mystic air of nationhood. The right of France to exist had been fought for and won in these parts – won in defeat, through the martyrdom of St Joan. The Loire recalled that most shameful of English crimes, and stirred the impossible hope that one day I might become a Frenchman. I wore a *beret basque*, smoked Gitanes, and travelled with a pocketful of symbolist poetry. But the AJS was a giveaway, and my French pretensions followed all my other pretensions, waving goodbye through a drunken haze somewhere in the region of Aux – whose name is commemorated in the excellent Médoc called Patache d'Aux, after the stagecoach that plied between there and Bordeaux.

Since those days tourism has besieged the châteaux and ransacked the villages; roads have been unconscionably widened and high-speed trains have abolished distance – that precious commodity without which people no longer belong where they are. Nevertheless, some local loyalties remain, and the first among them is the *têtu* attachment to the Cabernet Franc. We all know the white wines of the Loire – from the snail-coloured Muscadet to the green and glittering Sancerre. But the locals have a greater fondness for their reds, to which the Cabernet Franc imparts its special violet-brown colour and musky aroma. Red Loire produces some of the last genuine bargains in the new wine economy, and most of them are to be found along the stretch between Saumur and Tours.

After World War I the vineyards were neglected and the Loire's reputation has gained nothing from the global market, which prefers new wine to old, and varietals to local saints. Cabernet Franc has no reputation apart from that bestowed by the Loire (though there are excellent examples in Hungary); and it produces wines that need keeping if their shy and subtle aromas are at last to steal from the bottle. The best, in my experience, are made in Bourgueil and neighbouring St Nicolas-de-Bourgueil, some on the yellow tufa slopes above the Loire, others, of a smoother and fruitier character, on the gravelly soil beneath them. The vineyards are cooled by the Atlantic winds, which blow west to east along the river's corridor, resulting in wines more notable for their fruit than their body, though with surprising depth and character and, at their best, a civilized style that matches that of the most distinguished clarets.

There are two schools of thought regarding Bourgueil. One holds that these should be light wines, pale in colour, with forward fruit and tannins, to be drunk young, possibly chilled, and at any rate without the sniffing and snorting that are called for by deeper and more complex bottles. The other school of thought holds that Bourgueil should be so crafted that all the fruit and flavour is distilled from the grape, to form a deep blackberry-coloured must and a wine rich in tannins, needing several years in the bottle before it gives of its best. Such a wine is the Bourgueil La Petite Cave made by Yannick Amirault, whose 40-acre estate lies between Bourgueil and St Nicolas and who vinifies under both *appellations*. The Cabernet Franc is known in the region as 'Breton', and M. Amirault's Breton first name might imply some special intimacy with a grape that can thrive in temperate zones.

The heart of red Loire is the 5,000 acres around the old fort of Chinon, amid country described by Rabelais in *Gargantua* and *Pantagruel*. Chinon is by no means standardized; indeed it as prodigious as Rabelais, producing smooth wines for every day and also bottles of great depth and subtlety which will, when mature, match the leading growths of any other region. At a certain point in Rabelais's *Pantagruel* Bacbuc offers Panurge a silver book, having first filled it from a fountain of Falernian. 'Swallow this philosophy,' he commands. Thereupon Pantagruel's entourage, having drunk the contents of the book, assail each other with rapturous hymns to the god of wine. In outpourings of philosophical nonsense, they celebrate the power of Bacchus to turn an arse into a face and vice versa, the versa being the usual product of the vice.

Rabelais's own face, slim, witty and compassionate, was as unlike an arse as a face can be. And the wine of Chinon, of which Rabelais was a native, resembles him. This cool, clear red has the luminous forehead of the great philosopher. And Rabelais's face appears on the labels of the best Chinon that I know – that of his fellow philosopher, Charles Joguet – and Joguet's wine carries the eternally valid message of Gargantua and Pantagruel: enjoy what you are, and others too will enjoy you.

Joguet was studying painting and sculpture in post-war Paris when his father's death called him back to the vineyard. Charles was not the normal French intellectual, despising fortune, faith and family for the sake of some *paradis artificiel*. His greatest desire was to belong to the territory that now belonged to him. He and his mother began to restore their meagre patrimony and he applied himself to the deep question of why the Cabernet Franc has never been valued at its worth. The error, he concluded, has been the failure to localize. A product can have a price however freely it roams; but it can have a value only when attached to somewhere definite. This is as true of wines as it is of people. In Burgundy every enclave competes for eminence. But, while the Chinon *appellation* has existed since 1937, the habit has been not to distinguish the *terroirs*, but to blend them. Chinon lovers have their private sources, but the world knows of no favoured hillsides or treasured clumps of vines.

Charles inherited several such clumps, and set about cultivating their distinctiveness. In 1983 he went into partnership with the appropriately named Michel Pinard, and two more friends soon joined them. Today the wines that the Joguet venture produces are marked not merely by the serene love of the soil that caused Charles to begin his experiments, but by the years of family love and faithful friendship that are the natural result of settling in the place that made you.

The virtuous life of settlement, embellishing and sanctifying the place that is ours, is the life to which Bacchus invites us. And that life was everywhere to be witnessed in the France that I knew. The global tide is now washing away the sacred places, and the saints who gave their names to the villages, the vineyards, and the children of France have been taken from their shrines. But something lives on in the bottles that remember them, and it is with a glass of St Nicolas de Bourgueil that I bring this chapter to a close. St Nicholas, fourth-century Bishop of Myra, allegedly emerged from the womb already praising God, and as a result of this and other acts of piety in his early years became the patron saint of children. Hence his rebranding as Santa Claus, the most hateful of all the by-products of Christian culture. However, the real St Nicholas deserves to be rescued from his later desecration. Although, when present at the first Council of Nicaea, he struck the heretic Arius in the face – for which affront he was briefly defrocked by his fellow bishops – this seems to have been the only act of aggression in a life of exemplary gentleness, and the wine that bears the saint's name is gentle in its turn, with a delicate aroma and a lingering benediction on the palate. My thoughts return to 1968, when the iconoclasts broke open the shrines of France and took the sacred statues to the pawnbroker, where they have since stood in the window gathering dust. Is it possible to redeem these icons, who were once trusted to redeem the French? Maybe St Nicholas – who is patron saint of pawnbrokers too – ought to be petitioned to intervene. Meanwhile, however, the godless and disenchanted France of the iconoclasts remains, and the *pays réel* can be visited only in the glass.

4

News from Elsewhere

The grape vine, *Vitis vinifera*, has been cultivated in the Old World at least since 6000 BC, when it was grown in Asia Minor. Cultivation began just south of the Black Sea or even (according to one archaeologist) under it, before the natural dam of the Bosphorus gave way and the Black Sea basin was flooded, drowning those martyrs to whom so much happiness is owed. You could say that wine is probably as old as civilization; I prefer to say that it *is* civilization, and that the distinction between civilized and uncivilized countries is the distinction between places where it is drunk and the places where it isn't.

It should not surprise us, therefore, if wine is still grown throughout the Middle East, in just about every place where the sun doesn't shrivel the vinestocks or the Wahhabists shrivel the balls. In Turkey, Lebanon, Syria, Israel and North Africa we find the vestiges of a trade which once spread south through Assyria, Mesopotamia and Palestine, and which brought to the court of the Pharaohs that magical drink which they knew as *Irp* – a name that doesn't say much for the Egyptian way of swallowing it. The Biblical lands, both before and after the Israelite migrations, were colonized by the grape, which served as a kind of advanced guard of the human hordes, taming the landscape and making it possible to celebrate victories in style.

The city states of Greece and Persia took over the tradition, and with characteristic chauvinism the Greeks concocted the myth of Dionysus, attributing the invention of wine to one of their own late-coming deities, though one born, according to the myth, in Arabia. Chauvinism notwithstanding, the Greeks knew that the best wines came from Byblos on the Levantine coast, and

69

when they transported wine from the Levant to their colonies in Syracuse and Thrace they called the product 'Wine of Byblos' – the first example in the wine trade of a global brand-name, mentioned already by Hesiod in the sixth century BC.

Byblos was the home of the Phoenicians, who traded wine all over the Mediterranean and took the vine with them to their colonies – notably to Carthage and southern Spain. Wine is still grown in Byblos, and also elsewhere in Lebanon, and the wines of the Beqa'a Valley are deservedly celebrated, thanks to Château Musar, made there by the Hochar family.

The Romans destroyed Carthage but kept the vineyards, which flourished until the Muslim conquest. Grapes were grown thereafter for the table and for drying into raisins. And winemaking returned to the Carthaginian shores with the French colonists, who displaced the local muscat grape in favour of Chardonnay, Syrah and Cabernet Sauvignon. The wines of Morocco and Algeria had a certain following in the France of my youth, notably the rosé from the Trappist monastery near Algiers. Alas, the monasteries, which administered to the needs of the poor across the region, have been driven out, and in one famous case – that of Tibhirine – violently destroyed, by Islamist fanatics determined to mount an irrefutable case for the re-colonization of North Africa. In Morocco, however, a vestige of French civilization remains, in the form of a ripe and appetizing Chardonnay obtainable in the bars of hotels, and flowing secretly elsewhere – just ask for a *finjân abyad*, and it will be served up in a tumbler, sometimes with a plate of pickled vegetables.

The cultivation of the vine did not cease with the Roman Empire. The great Burgundian vineyards were already famous in the time of Charlemagne, and those of Dalmatia and the Danube basin have been in continuous cultivation under Roman, Mongol, Hungarian, Turkish and Austrian rule, losing their reputation only when the communists made their relentless war on agriculture. Although the Romans brought the vine to Britain, it was not until the Saxon era that wine became a serious item of agricultural produce. Thirty-eight vineyards are recorded in Domesday book and in about 1125 William of Malmesbury describes the Gloucestershire hillsides as thickly planted with vines, comparing the product favourably with the French. A sparkling wine from Kent was recently judged, in a blind tasting, to be more than a match for Champagne, and who knows, English tourists in France may soon be lamenting the wines of their homeland, as did the Saxon poet Alcuin in the court of Charlemagne.

At the time when the wine trade moved south from Mesopotamia to Egypt it began a journey northwards, into Georgia and Armenia. These regions too deserve the attention of winos, and the black wines of Georgia – which are both light and sweet and somehow suited to the pudding-faced hilarities which until recently tended to accompany their consumption – are among the most intriguing curiosities that the region has to offer. Sweet red wine was popular in the ancient world, where fermentation would be arrested by heating, or the wine sweetened with syrup made from boiled grape-juice. The masking effect of the sugar made this wine palatable to the Islamic conscience, a fact recorded in the Arabic word which the Turks borrow to describe their wine, and which we borrow to describe our fruit-juice – *sharap* as opposed to the Arabic *khmar*. The Georgian wines, along with the sweet Mavrodaphne of Greece, are the last reminiscence of the antique taste in wine, and of the noble compromises which enabled Christian and Muslim to drink to each other, as once again they should.

The Lebanese claim that wine came into the world with their Phoenician ancestors. The point is disputed; maybe it was a little further to the north, in the as yet uninundated Black Sea basin. Maybe it was a little further east, in the Fertile Crescent, or a little further south in the hills of Palestine. But maybe it really was as the Lebanese claim, that their forebears were first to make wine, as they were certainly first to establish a wine-growing and wine-trading economy, exporting their product all over the Mediterranean, and helping the Egyptians to step down from their flat frescoes and dance for a while in 3D.

Lebanon has, for all that, been for two millennia off the wine-lover's map. Ch. Musar apart, its wines are hardly exported; and inside the country a mere three million bottles are drunk each year. The first commercial winery in modern Lebanon was that of Château Ksara, founded by Jesuit monks in 1857 near the Christian town of Zahleh in the Beqa'a, and still Lebanon's biggest and most popular producer. Between the Phoenicians and 1857 wine was certainly produced in Lebanon, since Christian communities had the right under the Ottoman *millet* system to produce sweet wine for Communion, and all communities, Christian, Druze, Sunni and Shi'ite, were in the habit of fermenting grapes for the production of *araq*. The Château was sold in 1972 when the Vatican ordered its foundations to dispose of any profitable enterprises, profit being at the time as politically incorrect as plainsong. After years of rough management compounded by civil war and multiple invasions, Ch. Ksara has now regained its reputation. The red and rosé, made from Rhône varietals like Carignan and Cinsault, will justify a visit to any Lebanese restaurant that serves them. And the most important of those restaurants are still in Lebanon itself.

It was with a bottle of Ksara rosé that a great change came over my thinking. During the Lebanese civil war I visited Beirut with a friend, in order to write about the conflict there. Crossing into West Beirut was difficult; but it was necessary. Nobody was prepared to accompany us save a small wiry nun from the convent of St Vincent de Paul, whose order operates all over the Middle East, often in perilous conditions, bringing relief and education to Muslim and Christian alike. At every point in our journey between shattered redoubts we found suffering: mute, helpless and often terminal. And everywhere, around this suffering, were the arms of love.

After a day visiting people who had lost everything save the miraculous ability to believe in a loving God, we found ourselves in a broken-down area of the city where the Chaldeans congregate and the language of Christ is still spoken. Here stands the convent of Mother Teresa, in which the hopeless cases alone are received. Later that day, in the comparative safety of East Beirut, with a glass of Ksara rosé beside me on the table, I began to reflect on what I had seen, and made a few jottings in my diary:

'We knock at the door; a crippled child drags herself along the floor from a dark recess and howls at us like a dog. A German nun comes to receive us. She is young, pretty, fresh, serene, pleased to be spoken to in her own language. She takes us to her room, past deformed children, gesticulating senile women, and half-human creatures who stare at us from distended eyes like curious birds. There is a general air of excitement at our arrival, and at one point the crippled child drags herself all the way to the sister's threshold in order to cluck at us. The nun clears away her lunch with embarrassed gestures: two radishes, an orange, unleavened bread, and a glass of water. The Mother Superior arrives – a small, cheerful Bengali, who speaks English. She shows us her collection of sleeping creatures: mongols; children with paralysing deformities; others who cry and crawl like animals; but none of them really animals. In each is a carefully nurtured person, planted in this unpromising soil by the good Bengali nuns, and gently tended into lank, distorted but nevertheless eager life. The word "witness" is constantly on the lips of people here. The influence is less Greek than Arabic – *shahada* being always in the minds of Muslims, and taken up by their Christian neighbours, though not in the sense that is all too familiar. For you do not bear witness to the Christian faith by announcing it, still less by killing its enemies. You bear witness in works of charity and forgiveness. Nothing in the world can really overcome the beauty of this idea – and even when I look at the work of the sisters through my most Nietzschean spectacles, seeing this tending of the unfit as a waste of human energy and a defiance of the real interests of the species – even if I seek to protect myself from pity as Nietzsche did, by discarding all leftovers from the evolutionary banquet, I also see the work of the sisters as necessary, and charity as part of the communal will to live. These good nuns have one all-dominating project, which is to light, in whatever human tallow might present itself, the lamp of a human soul. This too serves the species, and far more effectively than the presumptuous will to choose the survivors. And if there is such a thing as God's work, this is it.'

I had been shocked out of the Nietzschean attitudes through which I vainly sought to protect myself from compassion, and been brought face to face with the mystery of charity – the mystery contemplated by Péguy in the person of Jeanne d'Arc, and by Geoffrey Hill in the person of Péguy.[1] I had witnessed the descending love called *agape* by St Paul, and it had filled me with an uncomfortable wonder. Until that moment it was the

[1] Charles Péguy's influential poem *Le mystère de la charité de Jeanne d'Arc* was published in 1910, paving the way for Jeanne's canonization, a decade after Péguy's death in action in World War 1. Geoffrey Hill's poem *The Mystery of the Charity of Charles Péguy* was published in 1983.

ascending love called *eros* which had dominated my life. I was
being turned in a new direction and the taste of that simple rosé,
when I drank it in a London restaurant on my return, brought
back the thought on which Christian witness is based: the thought
of everything, yourself included, as a gift. The Sisters of Charity
had a message of the utmost simplicity: you have been given
much, but what have you given in return? And if you have given
nothing, how will you atone for it? Years later, coming back to
that question, I tried to live in another way, even though suffering
from the 'dark night of the soul', from which Mother Teresa too
suffered – not encountering the necessary being who is God, and
stumbling over the merely contingent beings that clutter every
path to Him. It is precisely because the source of that descending
love is hidden from us, that we pin so many hopes on the
ascending love which has its source in us.

Indeed it can fairly be said that Western philosophy begins
from the study of that ascending love. *Eros* is the phenomenon
that fascinated Plato, and which turned his heart, and his head
too, towards his most famous theories: the theory of the soul and
its aspiration towards the sphere of eternity; the theory of the
forms and the form of the beautiful; the theory of the light that
shines beyond the cave of our mortality; the theory of the *polis*
and its institutions, designed for 'the care of the soul'. At every
point in Plato's philosophy we encounter arguments whose
hidden agenda is to abolish our ordinary, downward-turning,
mortality-accepting affections, and to put the spark of *eros* in
their stead. Hence his hostility to the family, his desire that
children be raised collectively, and his paean to the 'bloom on the
cheek of a youth'. The agonizing sight of a beautiful youth
wrenched the heart of Plato, and tormented him with desire. He
saw no solution to this, other than to turn away from lust and
ascend, through love, to the heavenly region where it is not the
individual boy on whom we gaze but the form of the beautiful
itself, the eternal idea of which the boy is but an instance, and in
the contemplation of which we find our own eternal destiny.

Wine helps us to meditate on charity as on all other deep and
difficult things. But it does not stimulate charity as it stimulates
desire. Bacchus and Eros, according to certain ancient authorities,
are close companions, and work together for the worship that is
due to both. We should remember that Bacchus had an awkward

start in life, being rescued as a foetus from his mother's ashes and transplanted into the thigh of Zeus. But his education on the isle of Naxos overcame whatever disadvantages attached to his birth (which wasn't a birth so much as an amputation). He became the lover and instructor of mankind, who eases our sorrows and also ensures that the spoilsports will be brutally murdered as they deserve. In tribute to this god who is a stickler for piety we should visit from time to time the place of his first mission on earth – a place much changed since the woods have been felled, the rivers dried and the dream-homes built, and therefore much better visited in the glass, where it remains as it was when Hesiod invoked it. And it is not long before you discover that the love that lives in the wine of Greece is not the *agape* that I will always taste in Château Ksara, but *eros*.

At least this is what you learn from Retsina. The use of resin to flavour wine has been practised in Greece since ancient times: early Greek amphorae were lined with pine resin in honour of Dionysus, who was associated with the pine-cone, a symbol of fertility. The sterilizing effect of the resin made Greek wines exportable, hence Pliny's encounter with them, and his disgust at their resinous taste. However, even if producers take advantage of the resin to conceal the defects of the grape, this is a tribute to Dionysus, who never intended his lesser gifts to be rejected. And the very uniformity of Retsina – which remains as much the same from year to year and batch to batch as HP sauce or Marmite – reminds you of the aspect of *eros* that Plato most feared: its rootedness in a general appetite, which gazes on the body of the other, and ignores the soul. Served cold with a plate of olives Retsina is the right way to begin a meal in a Greek restaurant; and almost always it will turn your thoughts in an erotic direction. And if at the end of the meal you order a glass or two of the sweet elixir from Cyprus called La Commandaria, after the Venetian fortress where it is grown, then Eros will certainly take charge of the proceedings. This is surely the wine referred to by Sappho, in one of her great invocations of Aphrodite, mother of Eros:

> *Come Cyprian, into golden cups,*
> *Pouring nectar, gently*
> *Mixed with desire ...*

On the other hand true erotic love arises only when desire has been contained and focused. Plato was therefore right to fear that generalizing appetite, even if he gave false instructions for transcending it. Erotic love ceases to be love when it becomes transferable; and *eros* owes its great power and its real vindication to the fact that it focuses on the other as a free and responsible individual. I have found this thought confirmed, not only in the bawdy brazenness of Retsina, but also in the refined and modest white wine of Crete called Xerolithia. Named after the dry stone walls with which the vineyards around Peza are terraced, and produced from the indigenous Vilana grape, this delicate yellow-green wine is young, lively, slightly *pétillant*, with balanced acidity and an aroma of sweet hay. It is a wine that opens the heart to affection, and dispels those sultry thoughts which will otherwise spoil a courtship – or at least, any courtship worth the pains. The same might be said of the unique and exquisite white wine called Thalassitis from the Isle of Santorini (not to be confused with Thalassemia from the Isle of Cyprus, though probably an effective cure for it). The cry with which Xenophon's weary band, in the *Anabasis*, greet the sight of their salvation – *Thalassa! Thalassa!* – The Sea! The Sea! – resounds in the name, and strangely in the taste, of this island wine, and it has the clean, virginal saltiness of the island girls, as I knew them from my travels, forty years ago. Theirs was a sexuality held in reserve, retained just out of reach, so as to be offered at last as a gift of the whole self. And that is what real sex consists in, and why I differ in my account of it from Plato.

In one respect, however, I agree with Plato's great attempt to vindicate *eros*. He was surely right to believe that the morality of sex derives from the *desire*, rather than from its social and biological consequences. Even if sexual desire had nothing to do with the bearing of children, nothing to do with the formation of families and the reproduction of society, it would still be a moral problem to us, still a source and an object of shame and blame, still something to be withheld until rightly directed. For Plato desire is legitimate when it is directed not at the individual, but *past* him, so as to target the stars. This is crazy, and a glass of wine with the beloved is the best possible disproof of Plato's theory, since it puts you at once into that position which only rational beings know, of looking not *past* another, but *into* him or her. This experience can be understood, once we put concrete particulars in the place of abstract ideas. I look into my beloved's eyes because I want to shine my light into the place from which she too shines on me: that very centre of her being which she denotes as 'I'. And this experience, when 'Our eyebeams twisted, and did thred/ Our eyes upon one double string' – as John Donne puts it – is made legitimate not by that hunger for abstract knowledge of which Plato writes, but by our readiness to give ourselves to the individual, here and now. The twisting of eyebeams is a prelude to the uniting of selves, and seeing things in that way is the foundation of any sexual morality worth the name.

That suggestion highlights both the similarity and the difference between *agape* and *eros*. Both come to fruition in a gift. But in *agape* the gift is repeatable, renewable, and always in search of some new recipient, while in *eros* the gift is focused on another, is jealously withheld until the moment is right and given only on condition of mutuality. While charity asks for nothing in return, erotic love gives only what it aims to receive. Hence *eros* is hemmed in by jealousy, is infinitely vulnerable to rejection, and must protect itself through shame.

Those observations are Old World observations; Plato could have made them, and almost did. New World writings about sex make no mention of the twisting of eyebeams or the pulling of heart-strings. They dwell on pleasure, and even place the whole thing in a framework of cost–benefit analysis, as in the ridiculous book by Judge Richard Posner, entitled *Sex and Reason*, a book which illustrates just how far the malicious description of sex given by the charlatan Alfred Kinsey has penetrated American culture. Just when sex went wrong in America it is hard to say – though James Thurber warned against what was happening fifty years ago, in *Is Sex Necessary?* I venture to suggest that it began rather earlier, with Prohibition, when the puritans, having triumphed in one area, withdrew their vigilance from another and rather more important domain of temptation. Within a decade Americans came to see sex as they saw the next drink: something furtive, to be snatched while you can, mixed from the strongest ingredients. There followed the usual aftermath of puritanism: why forbid it? Why control it? Why be furtive? Let it all hang out! And then, after the briefest of harvests, came pornography, and the addiction which eliminates the other entirely, and destroys the last remnants of erotic love.

Deprived of grapes and other sources of sweetness, with only rye and barley to provide their sugars, the ancestors of the American tribe, who came to the fertile hills and valleys of the Appalachians from the wind-swept moors of Scotland and the Irish bogs, began mashing, malting, distilling and casking, eventually hitting on the drink which Sir Walter Scott, relishing the sound of a word in which we hear the flames and fumes of the distillery, calls by its Gaelic name of *uisgeah* – the water of life. Once in America they hit on a further refinement, which was to store the fiery liquid in casks that had been burned inside. Charcoal absorbs unwanted gases, and also projects a dark mysterious flavour, like big black eyebrows on a clear young face. Thus was created bourbon, which has become a part of the settled, middle-class culture whose icon is the 'real America' of the suburbs, where people sit at home reading about that other America which exists in the novels of Nathaniel West, William Faulkner and Kurt Vonnegut – the America where people get drunk. Bourbon is a refuge for the American soul, to be understood not as a drink but as a 'shot', injected through the mouth into the stomach. In this consensual society negotiations can be measured in terms of the shots necessary to accomplish them. Most business deals are two-shot affairs; but those who know the deep loneliness of America will be familiar with the four-shot or five-shot collisions, from which the human atoms bounce off along new paths of exploration, always cheerful, always alone.

Praising bourbon in *Esquire* magazine, the American writer Walker Percy wrote that it reduces the *anomie* of the modern world. But the four-shot and five-shot encounters with women that he describes show another aspect of the 'real America': not so much *anomie* as an emotional dearth. Not yet the dearth that we witness in the new forms of screen addiction and narcissistic sex, but a growing fear of giving all the same. This fear has produced its own ingenious invention: the cocktail, in which bourbon is stirred with kitsch ingredients and addressed to the female palate. And it works: those suburban marriages are renewed on the lawn each afternoon, as he takes a shot and she a sip, and the anguish slips back into the shadows.

However, I would not disparage the land of the free. There you can fulfil Marx's prophecy, announced in *The German Ideology*: hunting (yes, hunting!) in the morning, fishing in the afternoon, and practising literary criticism after dinner, and all with no CCTVs to keep a record of your misdemeanours. You can wander through the suburbs relishing the silence that emanates from the Disneyland castles in their 3-acre plots. You can indulge your fantasies in burger-bars and shopping malls, and watch the half-ton cubes of human flesh as they propel themselves on invisible and unguessable undercarriages from nowhere to nowhere, blessing with Whitmanesque largesse whatever is placed before their eyes, mouths and nostrils, always smiling, always greeting, and yet with that sweet, sad loneliness that nothing really can cure.

But what do you drink, apart from those lethal shots of spirits – lethal, at least, to the art of meditation? The locals, whose annual intake of 145 pounds of sugar requires perpetual sipping from the cans that armour their midriffs, are guided in this as in most things by a stubborn sense of patriotic duty. Coke is American, so Coke must be drunk. Their brief flirtation with French wine was abruptly ended by a patriotic huff, and although they drink copious amounts of Budweiser, it is only under the impression that it is an all-American product, and in ignorance of the lawsuit whereby the Czechs are striving to reclaim the name, and the beer, of Budějovice.

So what do you drink? The answer is simple: American wine. The discovery of America brought phylloxera to Europe, but the grafting of our vines onto native American stocks saved them from extinction. This story illustrates a general truth, namely that when diseases come from America so, as a rule, do their cures. The lesson is not to avoid the disease, but to press on to the cure. This goes as much for free trade, fast food and feminism as for phylloxera, and if it were not for the fact that I am trying to write about the philosophical aspect of wine I would provide many more instructive instances.

The Zinfandel, brought from Hungary by the self-styled Count Harasthy in the mid-nineteenth century, grows better in California than anywhere else in the world except Apulia in Italy (where it is known as the Primitivo), and 'white Zinfandel', which is actually pink, is a 'blush wine' that has no real equivalent among European products. And the Pinot Noir can rival the middling Burgundies when planted and properly tended in the Napa and Sonoma valleys. On the other hand, those are Old World grapes grafted onto New World stock, and they bear the same relation to the wine of Europe as the MacMansions of the suburbs to the English country house.

Indeed, although in ancient time the feet of Bacchus walked upon England's mountains green, they did not walk upon the mountains of North America until the thirsty colonists cried out for rescue. What is not generally known, however, is that their prayers were answered. From time immemorial grapes had clung to the rocky hillsides and wound along the valleys, waiting the god's visitation. Small, tight and hardy, they yielded a foxy product that did not at first seem to justify the effort of vinification. But hybridization and selective cultivation led to varietals that took their place for a while in the repertoire, before being displaced in the twentieth century by grapes imported from the Old World. And here and there, hemmed in by the global tide, you can still find native grapes salvaged from the flood and carefully coaxed into wines that taste of the soil that shaped them and the history they shaped.

It is in Virginia, settled by civilized gentry rather than by the sour-faced puritans of New England, that serious wine-growing began. Already in 1619 the Colony of Virginia passed a law requiring every man to plant and maintain ten vines. And first among the grapes to be used was the Norton, native to Virginia, cultivated by Jefferson at Monticello, and subsequently planted on many Virginian estates by the god's disciples. 'We could in the United States make as great a variety of wines as are made in Europe, not exactly of the same kind, but doubtless as good.' So wrote Jefferson in 1808. Uniquely suited to the Old Dominion's humid climate, the Norton gave rise, in the late nineteenth century, to a serious 'claret', produced by the Monticello Wine Company and entered successfully for international competitions. Jefferson had ardently defended wine, as 'the only antidote to the bane of whiskey'. But such fine distinctions make no impression on the closed minds of puritans, and wine – far harder to conceal than whiskey – was all but eliminated from the American diet in the days of Prohibition. The Norton took a further beating, at the time of the god's shy return, from the globaglug products of

California. But enough of the old vineyards remained, and in recent years pious disciples have devoted their efforts to restoring them. The result is a remarkable wine that devotees ought to drink whenever they hear the cry of the god as he wanders through that still haunting landscape.

Just down the road from the house that we acquired in the Blue Ridge Mountains is the Horton wine company, and shortly after I had arrived in America, having already acquired the habit of comforting myself each evening with that white Marsannay from the store in Little Washington, a friend brought round a bottle of Horton's Norton. Its inky contents stormed from the bottle like a cloud of hornets, clinging to nose, lips and palate and stinging us with intense flavours of cobnut, cranberry and molasses. Then, as we reeled away, the wine began to sing its great after-song on the palate. The barely discernible foxiness of the American grape sounded like a deep organ-note beneath the choir of summer perfumes. A spicy glow filled the mouth and a deep murmur of fruit echoed in the belly. I recognized the authentic taste of Old Virginny – the red rocky soil, the humid air, the insect-laden breezes, all squeezed into this deep black bottled-up grape, and then released in ecstatic clouds across the table.

It is fair to say, however, that, while the best products of California bear comparison with the wines of Europe, selling for prices that match the prices of the first and second growths of Bordeaux, it is only rarely that American wine achieves the kind of authentic taste of the soil that is achieved by the Norton. It is a soil that has few martyrs, other than the dead that lie buried on the battlefields of the Old Dominion, and no saints or gods to match the saints and gods that lie in the fields of France. The vineyards are recent creations, many of them the work of Italian immigrants, whose life among the vines is beautifully evoked by Vikram Seth in his neglected masterpiece, *The Golden Gate*. The descendants of the old tribe drink moonshine in the long shadows of the Appalachians and sing of Jesus, who is calling them home. And the home he promises is a little wooden cabin like the one they were born in, with apple pie and cider on the table, and maybe, when the Lord comes to visit, a shot of rye. The old tribe of America has settled in a place that it has also sanctified. But somehow it has been done without wine.

Although wine is not necessary for holiness, however, holiness is a wonderful addition to wine. The greatest wines grow in sacred places – the temples of Roman gods, the gardens of monasteries and the terraced hillsides where calvaries parcel out the land. This has always made me suspicious of the wines of Australia and New Zealand. Australia is a wonderful example of a consecrated landscape – but consecrated by people who lived there as hunter-gatherers, and whose culture has since been destroyed. Some part of their spiritual response to the landscape has been captured by Bruce Chatwin in *The Songlines*, and it is a response that is violently contradicted by the serried ranks of beefy Chardonnay and gay Shiraz, and by the million-strong armies of bottles that clank their way to the city, on the first leg of their journey to nowhere, from the nowhere they have been made.

Of course this is the global economy, and we have to live with it. So the WTO has decreed, and who am I to stand against the tide of history? (Come to think of it, I am the only person I know who *does* stand against the tide of history.) Still, there are two points to be made before relenting. The first is that the Australasian harvest comes six months before the European. Hence, in the modern grape-to-sewage culture, Australasian wineries gain a six-month advantage over their Northern competitors, and they make the most of it. No sooner did I begin writing about wine in the autumn of 2001 than I was being asked to discuss wines made in 2000, brought to my table at some cost to the planet but very little cost to the producer, and often with labels boasting of their desecrated origins: Back End, Railway Turning, Wide Bottom, Lone Gum, The Other Side, Over the Hill. Only occasionally, in names like Hunter Valley and Coonawarra, do you glimpse the sacred prehistory of Australia. And then there is Wirra Wirra, one of the oldest and most beautiful wineries in Australia, located in the McLaren Vale; and if ever a wine tasted of Australia, it is their Grenache and Shiraz mix – so strong that it resembles a fortified wine, combining the guilty excesses of port with the playfulness of the Australian outback. More orthodox, with the liquorice flavours and deep purple colours associated with rustic Australian Shiraz, is that from the Brokenwood winery. If I were to describe this wine, I would say that it tastes like the sound of cicadas; but that is just another illustration of how difficult it is, to describe the tastes of things.

But why call it Shiraz? This grape – the Syrah – has nothing to do with the town of Shiraz, notwithstanding the legend, believed here and there on the banks of the Rhône, that the grape came to those parts with the returning Crusaders, and notwithstanding the fame of Shiraz as the birthplace of the great wino Hafiz. Syrah is the grape of Hermitage, a wine that matures over decades to produce the most delicate and perfumed of all the products of the Rhône. The name 'Shiraz' makes the wine sound wild and hairy, to be glugged from the screw-capped bottle with the manly stoicism of a recent convert from beer. And to force Syrah up to 14 per cent or more, tricking it into early maturation, so as to put the result on the market with all its liquorice flavours unsubdued, puffing out its dragon breath like an old lecher leaning sideways to put a hairy hand on your knee, is to slander a grape that, properly treated, as it is on the hill of Hermitage or on the Côte Rôtie, is the most slow and civilized of seducers.

Like it or not, however, there is more Shiraz produced in Australia than all other red varietals combined. And that brings me to my second point, which is that, with a few exceptions like Wirra Wirra, Australasian wines do not taste of places. Hence they have decided to taste of grapes. They virtually shout the word Sauvignon or Riesling as they leap fully armed from the bottle, slashing you about the head with their stainless steel aromas.

But then we must remember New Zealand, which is much cooler, much quieter, much less aggressive than Australia, and gives much less offence. My own scepticism was overcome by a Pinot Noir from Montana, New Zealand's largest producer. Against all my expectations the result was an astounding success, an aromatic wine that would have gone on improving for many years and which already had great charm and character after only three years in the bottle. Of course it didn't taste like Burgundy. But it resembled the best red Burgundy in one important respect – that I went on drinking it and felt constantly improved.

Like many English conservatives I am ambivalent about New Zealand. English manners, English customs and the old English gentleness still endure, by all accounts, in those endless meadows of a pure English green; the village post office, the Anglican church, the Methodist chapel, the country pub and the cricket field still occupy their wonted place in rural society, so far as I know hunting with hounds has not been banned and maybe there is honey still for tea. On the other hand, the NZ voice in all the things that matter – sex, marriage and reproduction; God, apes and angels – is decidedly postmodern. Reading the literature produced by NZ feminists, animal rights activists and multi-culturalists I long ago decided that I could have no place in the intellectual life of Whare Wananga, as Canterbury will no doubt soon be called. Then again, on visiting the website of Canterbury University I discover that the drama society is currently putting on the *Philoctetes* of Sophocles, that the philosophy department is maintaining the great Australasian tradition in the philosophy of science, that all the old subjects are still on offer and that there is as yet no department of women's studies.

Of course this does not persuade me to visit the place: travel narrows the mind, and the further you go the narrower it gets. There is only one way to visit a place with an open mind, and that is in the glass. But the last time I went there, with a glass of Eradus Pinot Noir 2004, I heard only the murmur of those endless disputes with which Antipodeans uselessly wrack their con-sciences over who really owns the landscape. And this returned me to one of the most important things that I have learned from wine, which is that the person who plants vines in a place that previously never had them has a title superior to any other, whatever the course of events. If there is one departure from old English orthodoxy for which the New Zealanders deserve unstinting praise, it is their decision not only to plant vines but to study how to make wine as it ought to be made – in other words, as it has been made in France. Their reputation among winos stems largely from their conscientious attempts to match the Sauvignons of the Loire; but they deserve far more praise for their attempts to match the Pinot Noirs of Burgundy.

The open pastures of New Zealand, which these wines call vividly to mind, are designed for hunting with hounds, whether or not this noble sport is still permitted there. And the topic of hunting takes me on another vinous journey. Hounds are a distinct branch of the canine species, and the only one, to my knowledge, to relate to human beings as a pack. Those who keep cats to control mice, or terriers to control rats, are familiar with the kind of cross-species companionship that is forged through hunting. But those criminals who keep hounds to control foxes know this relationship in a heightened and poignant form. Hounds are not house-trained; they live rough, eating the raw flesh of fallen stock and superannuated horses. Their day-to-day life is hardly distinguishable from the life of wild canines. The huntsman is leader of the pack, and his hounds are attached to him by a bond that is not utilitarian like the bond between cat and cupboard, but existential, like the bond between the world and God. A cat tracking a mouse will be deaf to your cries. But the horn sounds in the ears of the pack like the voice of conscience, and can call it away from the quarry at almost any moment before the kill. Hounds behave as we were brought up to behave: when 'yes' turns suddenly to 'no', you think of England.

There is a wine, one of my favourites, which always brings this unique relationship to mind, and that is the wine called Faithful Hound, a red wine from Stellenbosch in the Cape, named after a hound who, abandoned by his master, kept a three-year vigil outside an empty cottage on Mulderbosch Farm, before dying unrewarded for his loyalty. This is no ordinary South African red, with the familiar taste of blood, fire and yesterday's barbecue. It is as near an approximation to a Saint-Julien as you are likely to find outside the village itself, beautifully made from a mixture of Merlot and Cabernet Sauvignon with a little Malbec for depth. Dark violet in colour, with a dense concentration of fruit, it releases the most subtle rounded bouquet from the glass. The 1998, disguised by a decanter, caused the company to praise my generosity in serving Ch. Léoville Lascases, and who was I to tell them that it was no such potion, but a wine costing a quarter of the price?

Wine has become one of the most important products of the Southern hemisphere. Countries like South Africa, New Zealand and Chile which a century ago were importing wine in small quantities from Europe, are now drinking large quantities of the home-grown product, and exporting the surplus around the globe. The reason for this change is less economic than cultural. During the twentieth century these countries have increasingly understood themselves, not as exiles from Europe, but as historic settlements, with a right to the soil and an identity that is shaped by it. The most important way of expressing this sentiment is by planting vines, symbol of the divine right to be where you are and to enjoy the god's protection. That is how the vine is seen in the

Old Testament, in the legends of Dionysus, in the Homeric literature and in the literature of Rome. It is why, in the days of Augustus, Italy was called Oenotria – wine land – and why nobody has ever been able to persuade an Italian, however far from the homeland he may have wandered, that he belongs anywhere else than on the vine-clad hillside where his ancestors were born.

Italian culture celebrates family, city and region; village ceremonies and village saints; local virtues, local vices and the local dishes that produce them. The root assumption of this culture is that it is best to be where you are, and hurrying onwards is dangerous. Maybe it all began as a reaction to Roman imperialism. It was Horace who wrote that *caelum non animum mutant qui trans mare currunt*, which is another way of saying that travel narrows the mind. But the culture has been recently updated, and now has a distinctly trendy image. The Slow Food Movement began in Italy. The Slow Work Movement no longer has a serious competitor there. And the Slow Drink Movement can be witnessed in every Italian bar.

True, those mad Australians are planting their global varietals and showing the natives how to make wine that can sell anywhere to anyone and never be remarked upon. But Italian wines remain as varied as the soils, the saints and the seasons that produce them. Nearly 3,000 years of continuous viticulture have ensured that the Italian varietals have grown into the soil, and the soil into the grapes, as almost nowhere else on earth.

Travel south, from the serene, smooth, temperate hills of Piedmont to the baked volcanic ridges of Calabria, and you will encounter a new varietal, a new technique, a new flavour and very often a new shape of bottle with each successive township. The reason why Italy attracts so many tourists is that it is a place where most people aren't tourists, and where local customs are still honoured more highly than the strangers who come trampling all over them in their ghastly summer clothes. And the local grapes survive, as revered as the saints who guard the vineyards and the grannies who guard the saints: grapes like the Barbera, the Nebbiolo and the white Cortese of Piedmont, the white San Vincenzo of the Veneto, the dark Gaglioppo of Calabria, the Montepulciano of Abruzzo and the Nero d'Avala of Sicily. And then there is the remarkable Sangiovese grape, from which the wines of Chianti are made: a grape that is no sooner transported to a new village than it hybridizes, to become a local product, as rooted in the soil as the generations buried there. The Sangiovese of Montepulciano, from which the celebrated *Vino Nobile* is made, is quite different from that of Florence, while only 6 kilometres outside Florence, in a natural amphitheatre on a hillside, is a 6-hectare vineyard planted with a clone of the Sangiovese grape that grows only there, producing the local wine called Camposilio, a complex, tightly knit elixir, that is no more a Chianti than a donkey is a mule. Or consider the Marzemino which thrives in the basaltic soil of the Trentino region. The Marzemino of Isera, a village near to Rovereto, claims to be the wine cited both in the recorded notes to the Council of Trent and in the mad aria 'Fin' caldo vino', with which Mozart's Don Giovanni expresses his unassuageable lust for sensuous enjoyment. Yet all Tridentines agree that their Marzemino must not be confused with the Marzemino of Padua, which is an altogether inferior product.

One remarkable varietal is the Aglianico, planted in the Vulture region of Apulia since pre-Roman times. This intense red grape, grown on volcanic soil some 500 metres above sea level, in a climate of hot and cold extremes that few of the global varietals could tolerate, produces a dry wine of remarkable depth and complexity. Matured in barrels for 20 months, it is best kept for a few more years in bottle, when it clears from ruby red to Tiepolo garnet, with all the scents of the sun-baked hillside contained in its smooth embrace. It is a wine for celebrations, for those *noctes cenaeque deum* – nights and feasts divine – that Horace invokes in fragrant verses that share the charm of his native grape.

Horace would no doubt have stayed drinking the wine of Apulia, had his ancestral estates not been confiscated after he fought for Brutus against Anthony. The vineyards have suffered periods of neglect since Horace's day, but are now restored to glory, with the century-old firm of D'Angelo taking the lead in producing what must surely be one of the most seductive reds to come out of southern Italy. D'Angelo's Aglianico del Vulture is a full-bodied wine, beautifully balanced, with the tannins in the background and the fragrance emerging like incense before the long procession of fruit. It proved to be the perfect accompaniment to dinner with my teenage protégées in Edinburgh, where they were studying. I feared that my tutorials would have been obliterated by university, the purpose of which is to teach Facebook, The Prodigy and David Beckham. But no – when the bottle appeared and the glasses were filled, *Nunc est bibendum* they said in unison, which is as far as they ever got with Horace. My protégées are daughters of Romanian refugees, and their presence in my life is an all-but-inexplicable by-product of a period of intense revolt: revolt against communism and all those who excused it; revolt against the socialist establishment, the post-war consensus and the welfare culture – revolt, some would say, against human nature itself. I am not sure when I first awoke to the fact that British institutions of Higher Education had turned in the nihilistic direction that I deplored, and that scholarship in this country would henceforth have to be conducted outside the academy, if it were to honour truth rather than orthodoxy as its goal. But two episodes certainly had a profound impact on me. The first was a ceremony I happened to witness at Glasgow University, on a day when my own invited lecture had been subjected to a semi-official boycott, as part of a 'no platform for fascists' policy. A crowd of old farts in academic robes were conferring an honorary degree on Robert Mugabe. On the strength of what contribution to the life of the mind? I asked. Nobody could tell me. The second episode was the news of another honorary degree – that conferred on Mrs Ceauşescu by what was then the Polytechnic of Central London, in acknowledgement of her reputation as a chemist (a reputation denied by no Romanian chemist except a few oddballs who had been locked up for their own protection).

Not everybody went along with the arse-licking that our establishment lathered on the Ceauşescus. Jessica Douglas-Home led a band of intrepid dissidents, who visited those in need, awakened the world to the facts, and, at no little risk to themselves, defended the Romanian villages from Ceauşescu's mad design to raze them to the ground, as he had razed much of Bucharest. If the Romanian countryside still lives, it is in part thanks to Douglas-Home and the trust that she founded in those dark years – the Mihai Eminescu trust, named after Romania's national poet.

The Mihai Eminescu Trust is the one example that I know of effective Romanian patriotism – and why should it matter that it was founded by an English woman? Since the fall of Ceaușescu the Trust has taken on the task of reviving the Saxon villages of Transylvania. Visitors to the region will know its astonishing beauty, which provoked Ceaușescu in the way that Paradise provoked Satan. But they may not have discovered that there is a more than palatable wine produced there, and that this wine is available in Britain. True, the wine is produced by Germans, from a French grape, and matured in oak imported from Hungary. But if you are to subtract France, Germany and Hungary from Romania, precious little remains: certainly not Eminescu, Enescu or Ionescu or any other escu, except perhaps Ceaușescu or the fescue grass with which he hoped to cover the burial mounds of 20,000 villages.

La Cetate (which means Beside the Castle) is a fruity Merlot produced in Oprisor by the Carl Reh Winery. The 2000 has a vanilla finish that you can almost lick off the glass, and is deeper and fruitier than any wine that you are likely to encounter at a comparable price. Growing such wines is one part of Romania's attempt to reclaim its identity as a part of Europe, with historic ties to France and to its own Francophone culture.

Whether this is possible, now that the *pays réel* of France has disappeared beneath the *pays légal* of the European Union, is anyone's guess. But Romania is not the only country that depends for its identity and its spiritual formation on the moral life of France. There is also Spain, which was invented by Prosper Mérimée, and set to music by his countrymen, among whom Bizet (setting Mérimée's *Carmen*) was the first. Perhaps the greatest invocation of the country is Debussy's, in *La puerta del vino* from the second book of Preludes. Debussy went to the Iberian peninsula once, for a weekend, saw his mistake, and fled back to Paris.

Like Debussy, I know Spain intimately, having driven my rickety old scooter over the Pyrenees for a couple of days, when I failed to reach anywhere of note. Hence Spain is still unspoiled in my imagination, and to think of it – still more, to drink of it – is a source of unpolluted merriment. The villages and bodegas that I visit in my glass are whitewashed, flagstoned, perched on steep inclines, with the parched, mean, gritty, clay-bound soil falling from their tight perimeters like terracotta skirts.

Rioja too is a French invention. Although vines have grown in this apparently beautiful region from time immemorial, the idea of growing them properly took root only when the phylloxera epidemic wiped out the vineyards of Bordeaux, and the growers moved south. Since that time, Rioja has been scientifically made, and is now carefully controlled by law.

The Spanish bodega represents a business rather than a place, and is less a vineyard than a factory, often buying in grapes from all over the region. Hence you must go by the firm, rather than the *terroir*, and for all its merits, Rioja will never take you, as French wines take you, to a small, specific spot of named and hallowed earth. Red Rioja is made from the Tempranillo, mixed with smaller quantities of Garnacha (the French Grenache), Mazuelo and Graciano. It is matured in oak, usually American oak, which explains the vanilla flavour and the long finish. The wine is divided by the official classification into four types, distinguished by bottle age and cask age: plain Rioja, Rioja de Crianza, Reserva and Gran Reserva. Only in the best vintages can a Gran Reserva be made, and to drink such a wine at its best you should keep it for ten years. A glass of old Gran Reserva is like a vision into a candlelit crypt, where gaudy archbishops doze among vessels of gold.

Think of ordinary Spanish wine, however, and promptly there comes to mind the peculiar forward taste of the Tempranillo grape, blazing with life but coated with a creamy mask like the face of a flamenco dancer. The combination of oak and Tempranillo works in the uniquely favoured region of Rioja (favoured in particular by those winemakers from France); but it doesn't work in the Valdepeñas, where *gran reserva* may often connote an overdose of flakey make-up. Nor should we forget that there are Spanish wines – and some of the very best – that either blend the Tempranillo with more northern varietals, or avoid it entirely.

The most interesting of such wines, in my experience, is that of Bierzo, planted in ancient vineyards along the pilgrims' route to Santiago de Compostela and made from the indigenous Mencía grape. This is the wine that the French pilgrims would never drink, bringing with them instead their own supplies of Madiran from the other side of the Pyrenees. Recent intensive research has persuaded me that those French pilgrims were wrong. Bierzo is grown on chalky foothills so steep that they must be worked by donkey; and whenever I have offered a share of this wine to Sam the Horse he has turned quickly away, as though hearing the last neighs of the many equines who have crashed to their death for the sake of this bloodstained remnant of their labour. But Bierzo justifies, in human eyes, the labour of producing it. Thanks to the impoverished and sun-baked soil it is rich in minerals, with a blood-dark colour and brooding taste like a bitter-sweet love-song of Lorca.

There are those who say that Spain no longer exists. In 1921 José Ortega y Gasset published *España Invertebrada*, prophesying the decline of his country, as it lost the customs that had placed honour above pleasure in the Spanish heart. Ortega died in 1955, just as the barbarian invasions were beginning, and so had no opportunity to compare the effect of consumerism on Spaniards with its effect on the British who were raping and pillaging the length of the coast. Still, we must take Ortega's word for it, and assume that the Spaniards have declined to their present condition from a state of dignified dutifulness, and that the futile chivalry of Don Quixote once typified their national character.

However, I know people who have traipsed across Spain in search of those dried-olive characters that Ortega cherished, and I have listened credulously to their reports. For Spain abounds, so they say, in sequestered valleys, sheltered from the global locust storms, where sturdy old vines suck the rocky undersoil, and grapes fill with the taste of revenge. What changed everything, and undid the work of Mérimée, Bizet, Chabrier, Debussy and Ravel, was not the moral ailment diagnosed by Ortega, but the civil war to which it led. Of course civil wars are proof, in a way, of the nation and of people's love for it. Why should you fight, if you did not regard this soil, this landscape, this history, this community as *yours?* Hence the enduring division among patriotic Englishmen between roundheads and cavaliers. And hence American feeling over the 'war between the states', which – despite appalling casualties – is looked back on today with a shared mourning, the object of heartfelt threnodies from shore to shore. This conciliatory grief is, however, the legacy of an original forgiveness, made possible by the generous sentiments of Ulysses Grant and Robert E. Lee. And students of the American civil war will inevitably ask themselves whether any such gestures were made in Spain, and if so by whom? The spirit of revenge, which

Lorca portrays in *Blood Wedding*, and of which he himself was a victim, is present too in those who now seek to dig up the mass grave in which the poet is buried – not to achieve reconciliation, but to open the wounds. Judge Garzón, who has already disturbed the fragile equilibrium of Chile with his accusatory zeal, now seeks justice for the victims of the civil war – but only for the victims on one side. And as the American example illustrates, the wounds of civil war are not healed by justice, but by forgiveness, which is our long-stop moral resource. Such is the thought which hovers in the glass whenever I fill it with that Lorca-flavoured Bierzo.

The crimes of the twentieth century, now receding from human memory with the rapidity that guilt alone can generate, ought to have put the concept of forgiveness firmly on the syllabus of philosophy. And if they haven't done so (which I suppose they haven't) then we might at least hope (if hope is the word) that the daily spectacle of the Islamists punching the air, gnashing their teeth, and generally making the kind of fool of themselves that people make when they cannot look in a mirror and see the thing they hate (and not only because it hides behind a beard), would have reminded us that forgiveness was planted in the heart of our civilization and runs like a golden thread through all the rules and maxims by which our ancestors were instructed. Glass in hand, I feel well-disposed to all Spaniards, ready to forgive those on the Right who violently overthrew their legal government, and those on the Left who murdered priests and religious in such astonishing quantities, as they pulled down in a fury the icons of old Spain. But have the Spaniards forgiven each other? Something about their current behaviour leads me to doubt that they have. And I cannot help thinking that, had they understood the message of 'La puerta del vino', as Debussy crafted it, both sides would have put off the bloodletting to the morrow, and settled down to a long-drawn-out nirvana in *mañana*. It is a disquieting thought that a country like Spain should have entered a civil war yet more savage than the war between the States, even though, unlike the Americans, it had the instrument of reconciliation to hand, and had only to turn on the tap.

Part Two: Therefore I Am

5

Consciousness and Being

It would be an exaggeration to say that the three words that introduce the second part of this book contain the whole of philosophy. But it would not be far from the truth. Philosophy arises from reflecting upon reason, consciousness and being – the three ideas expressed in turn by 'therefore', 'I' and 'am'.

It is often the little words, the unobtrusive nuts and bolts of syntax, that conceal the deepest philosophical problems. Bertrand Russell set English-speaking philosophy on its modern path with an article devoted to 'the' – a word that does not have its equivalent in everyone's language, and which makes no sense, when standing alone, in ours. Russell's article expounded his celebrated 'theory of descriptions'; it was the beginning of 'analytical' philosophy, laid the foundations for logical atomism and logical positivism and was the first of many blows struck against the ancient practice of metaphysics by the iconoclasts of Cambridge.

Consider 'therefore'. What more useful word than this one, which makes connections without which we could not negotiate our days? But what does it mean? And does it have any single or settled meaning? Wine vividly reminds us that thoughts may be connected by association, even if not by logic. 'He is a man and therefore a human being' is logically impeccable, and shows 'therefore' on its best behaviour. 'He is a man, and therefore a house, an income, a protector' may very well enter the mind of the woman whose glass he has just filled; but it shows 'therefore' in less respectable guise. This is not logic, but speculation – to be criticized not logically but morally.

In all its normal uses, the word 'therefore' goes hand in hand with 'why?': it answers our need for a reasoned account of things, by showing that there is either a cause or a reason for their being as they are. Causes should be distinguished from reasons: causes explain, reasons justify. But both are expressed in terms of 'why?' and 'therefore'. Moreover, reasons are of many kinds: some logical, some practical; some compelling their conclusion, others only inviting it. Nevertheless, notwithstanding the deep differences, in normal discourse the word 'therefore' links things in consecutive ways, drawing on laws, conventions and expectations that are the common property of the speakers. It exerts a controlling force over what we say – implying that the things it connects are either joined by nature or linked by rational argument. And rational beings are, by definition, beings who understand and take advantage of connections made in that way.

Rational beings live in another world from the non-rational animals – a world of laws and times and plans and goals. They also live in another way – with intentions as well as desires, convictions as well as beliefs, values as well as needs, happiness as well as pleasure. Their emotions are not to be understood as animal emotions are understood, in terms of appetite and aversion, since they involve judgement, reflection and a concept of self and other. Rational beings experience remorse, guilt, and shame as well as hostility and fear. They find their fulfilment in love, duty, aesthetic contemplation and prayer. And all this is reflected in their appearance. Unlike animals they smile – and 'smiles from reason flow/ To brute denied, and are of love the food', as Milton expresses it. As I pointed out in discussing Greek wine and *eros*, rational beings do not merely look *at* things, they look *into* things, as lovers look into each other's eyes; they reveal their inner thoughts in frowns and blushes, and their gestures shine with the soul within. Their relations are informed by a conception of good and evil, right and duty, and they approach each other as unique individuals who demand recognition for their own sakes and not merely as instruments for some purpose that is not their own. All this and more is what we mean, or ought to mean, when we refer to them as persons.

Even in the sphere of thought rationality manifests itself in ways that defy the laws of reasoning. Our 'therefores' dance along imaginary roads like the followers of Bacchus, strewing flowers about them and linking ideas like pearls on a string. Here, however, a word of caution. The experience of one thing may lead us to think of another, in two quite different ways. Suppose I am looking at a landscape by Francesco Guardi, in which little houses with flaking yellow stucco nestle beside a dusty roadway in the light of a setting sun. And suppose this leads me to recall a walking holiday in Calabria, the old houses along the roadway, the flavour of the dusty air at sundown, the touch of my companion's hand when she stopped suddenly in the roadway and said that peculiar thing, and what I might have said to her, but didn't by way of a reply ... Here my looking at the pigment-spattered canvas leads me to two quite different collections of ideas. On the one hand I am led to imagine houses with flaking stucco by a dusty road, in Guardi's inimitable sunset style, so full of the sense of time's passing and the consolations of decay. On the other hand I am set off on a reverie of my own, for which Guardi can claim no special credit, and which leads me through memories of sights, smells and sensations, and through imagined episodes and things that I might have said but didn't. The first collection of thoughts refers to things that I *see in* the canvas – things which form part of the intentional object of my experience and which belong to it intrinsically. The second collection concerns *associations* with the picture – not things that I see *in* the picture, but things that I imagine by means of it.

The distinction here is of particular relevance to the understanding of wine. It is often said that, while the senses of sight and hearing admit of double intentionality – so that I can see or hear *in x* what *x* itself can neither contain nor be – the senses of taste and smell act only by the association of ideas. Thus when, in *Remembrance of Things Past*, Marcel finds that the taste of a madeleine brings back the memories and imaginings of a lifetime, these are merely associations of the taste, and not features of it. He does not taste the past *in* the madeleine, as I see the houses *in* the picture or hear the sadness *in* the song.

Whether that is exactly so, and whether wine operates on the imagination only in the way of Proust's madeleine, are questions to which I return in the next chapter. But already we see that there are two quite different phenomena here. Imagination may lead us along a path of dreams and associations, transforming our thoughts in response to some perception; or it may focus on the presented object, transforming our perception in response to our thoughts. Just where wine is situated between these two exercises of our imaginative powers is one of the deep questions that all winos must ask, if they are to understand their dear companion. Is wine like daydreams or like art? Does it point inwards to our subjective impressions and memories, or outwards to the world – bringing order as Tintoretto, Wordsworth or Mozart brought order, by reshaping the objects of our perception?

Ancient philosophy, Christian religion and Western art all see wine as a channel of communication between god and man, between the rational soul and the animal, between the animal and the vegetable kingdoms. Through wine the distilled essence of the soil seems to flow into the veins, awakening the body to its life. And having swamped the body wine invades the soul. Your thoughts race; your feelings break free; you plan the triumphant career, the immortal work of art, the world takeover, or the new kitchen. The Greek poet Bacchylides tells us that 'irresistible delight sweeps from the wine-bowls and warms the heart. Hope of love returned darts through the mind, imbued with the gift of Dionysus, winging the thoughts to heights supreme. Straightway it overthrows the battlements of cities and every man sees himself as a great monarch. With gold and ivory his palace gleams, and corn-laden argosies bring him from Egypt over the sun-bright sea wealth beyond count ...'[1] Yet tomorrow morning all will be forgotten. Hence wine symbolizes those radical changes, those soarings and plummetings from one existential plane to another, that characterize the life of the rational being. Perhaps this way of working on us is neither the way of daydreams nor the way of art, but something entirely *sui generis*.

No artist has seen this more clearly than Wagner. Isolde presents Tristan with what they both believe to be the drink of death, snatching the cup from his hands to be certain of her share. Then they fall into each other's arms. Even a glass of water would have done the trick, wrote Thomas Mann, since there is no reason now to pretend. But that is not the point. The love potion that Brangäne has substituted for the drink of death symbolizes what it also permits. It is a force working from within, from the body. This is how erotic love must be experienced if it is to be genuine –

[1] Fr. 16.

a conquest of the soul by the body, and of the body itself by that world of magic, of simples, of vegetable mystery and unconscious life, to which love joins us in an act of self-renewal.

Likewise, when Siegfried is presented with the drink of forgetting (*Götterdämmerung*, Act 1), and it slides down his body into his soul, you hear that vegetable invasion once again, obliterating memory, rubbing out the image of Brünnhilde, bringing down the once exalted Siegfried to the level of ordinary ambition, so that he will betray his love and deserve his death.

The experience of wine shows how to understand the great existential transformations that form the enduring theme of Western art. A few works have come from opium – 'Kubla Khan', *The Bride of Lammermoor*, De Quincey's *Confessions*; a few more have been kick-started by cannabis. But far more owe their life, their subject-matter and their symbolism to alcohol. For wine reminds the soul of its bodily origin, and the body of its spiritual meaning. It makes our incarnation seem both intelligible and right. This too is an exercise of the imagination, and maybe it is of quite another kind from the two that I discussed in relation to Guardi.

Those thoughts lead us on from 'therefore' to 'I'. Contained in this word are some of the most intransigeant problems of philosophy: the problems of consciousness, of the subjective viewpoint, of the relation between subject and object, of free-will and moral obligation – and each of those problems brings us back, as we explore it, to the concept contained in 'therefore', the concept of the rational being. Modern philosophy began with Descartes, and with his study in depth of the 'I' – a study which, precisely because of its depth, was entirely futile. 'I' does not denote, as Descartes thought, a 'substance' hidden from public perception; there is nothing to be discovered by looking inwards, and the relentless concentration on the first-person case, which Descartes initiated but which came to its apogee in our time with the phenomenological method of Edmund Husserl, has generated one of the greatest heaps of jargon-infested rubbish in the history of ideas. There are no deep truths about the self; but the shallow truths are all-important and hard to state. Thomas Nagel has a nice way of putting the point. Imagine, he counsels, a complete description of the world, according to the true theory (whatever it turns out to be) of physics. This description identifies the disposition of all the particles, forces and fields that compose reality, and gives spatio-temporal coordinates for everything that is. Not a thing has been overlooked; and yet there is a fact that the description does not mention, the fact which is more important than any other to me – namely, which of the things mentioned in the description is me? Where in the world of objects am I? And what exactly is implied in the statement that *this* thing is *me*?[2]

We tremble here on a vertiginous edge, and it is important not to fall, but to stay there tottering. That is one of the great gifts of wine, in my experience, that it enables you to hold the problem of the self before your mind, and not fall into the Cartesian abyss. The self is not a thing but a perspective; but, as Nagel reminds us, perspectives are not *in* the world but *on* the world, and being on but not in is a difficult balancing act that can be successfully accomplished only in a meditative posture of the kind induced by that smiling meniscus over which the I stays bowed while the it is nourished.

What I mean can perhaps best be explained in terms of the problem of consciousness. Consciousness is more familiar to us than any other feature of our world, since it is the route by which anything at all becomes familiar. But this is what makes consciousness so hard to pinpoint. Look for it wherever you like, you encounter only its objects – a face, a dream, a memory, a colour, a pain, a melody, a problem, a glass of wine, but nowhere the consciousness that shines on them. Trying to grasp it is like trying to observe your own observing, as though you were to look with your own eyes at your own eyes without using a mirror. Not surprisingly, therefore, the thought of consciousness gives rise to peculiar metaphysical anxieties, which we try to allay with images of the soul, the mind, the self, the 'subject of consciousness', the inner entity that thinks and sees and feels and which is the real me inside. But these traditional 'solutions' merely duplicate the problem. We cast no light on the consciousness of a human being simply by re-describing it as the consciousness of some inner homunculus – be it a soul, a mind or a self. On the contrary, by placing that homunculus in some private, inaccessible and possibly immaterial realm, we merely compound the mystery.

[2] Thomas Nagel, *The View from Nowhere*, Oxford 1986.

Putting the point in that way makes it clear that, in the first instance at least, the problem of consciousness is a philosophical, not a scientific problem. It cannot be solved by studying the empirical data, since consciousness (as normally understood) isn't one of them. We can observe brain processes, neurones, ganglions, synapses and all the other intricate matter of the brain, but we cannot observe consciousness, even though observation is itself a form of it. I can observe you observing; but what I observe is not that peculiar thing which you know from within and which is present, in some sense, only to you. So it would seem at least, and if this is some kind of mistake, it is a philosophical and not a scientific argument that will tell us so.

One source of the problem of consciousness is therefore the manifest asymmetry between the first-person and the third-person points of view. When you judge that I am in pain it is on the basis of my circumstances and behaviour, and you could be wrong. When I ascribe a pain to myself I don't use any such evidence. I don't find out that I am in pain by observation, nor can I be wrong. But that is not because there is some *other* fact about my pain, accessible only to me, which I consult in order to establish what I am feeling. For if there were this inner private quality I could misperceive it: I could get it wrong; and I would have to *find out* whether I am in pain. I would also have to invent a procedure for identifying my inner state without reference to publicly observable conditions – and that, Wittgenstein plausibly argued, is impossible.[3] The conclusion to draw is that I ascribe pain to myself not on the basis of some inner characteristic but on no basis at all.

Of course there is a difference between knowing what pain is and knowing what pain is *like*. But to know what it is like is not to know some additional inner *fact* about it, but simply to have felt it. We are dealing with familiarity rather than information. 'What it's like' is not proxy for a description, but a refusal to describe. We can spell it out, if at all, only in metaphors. Q: 'What's it like, darling, when I touch you there?' A: 'Like the taste of marmalade, harmonized by late Stravinsky.' And this intrusion

---

[3] This is not the place to expound Wittgenstein's 'private language argument'. But see Roger Scruton, *Modern Philosophy*, London 1993, Ch. 4.

of metaphor into the very heart of self-knowledge reminds us of our attempts to describe the taste and significance of wine. It is precisely because what we are describing is so *shallow* that we have recourse to these deep descriptions. And yet the descriptions, if they do their work, are metaphors, which take us on a tour through other vistas, before returning to their point of departure, in *this, here, now.* There are philosophers who have attempted to describe 'what it's like' in terms that are both *deep* and *literal*, purporting to give the internal structure of the first-person case. An example is Edmund Husserl, pioneer of 'phenomenology'. And if you want to know how philosophy should not be done, then read that philosopher's *Phenomenology of Internal Time Consciousness* – or at least, open the book, and alongside it a bottle of something better.

Similarly, we are not going to get very far in understanding consciousness if we concentrate on the idea of 'feeling' things. For there are conscious mental states that have nothing to do with feeling. We feel our sensations and emotions, certainly, just as we feel our desires. All of those mental states would once have been classified as passions, as opposed to the mental actions – thought, judgement, intention, deduction – which are not felt but done. I can deliberately think of Mary, judge a picture, make a decision or a calculation, even imagine a centaur, but not mentally create a pain in the finger, a fear of spiders or a desire for more cake. Even if I can have a pain by willing it, or overcome my desires by an act of will, this does not mean that pains and desires are actions, but only that they are passions which I can affect through mental discipline, in the way that a medium might move a wardrobe. Moreover, there are psychologists and philosophers who seem quite happy with the idea of 'unconscious feelings'. We may balk at the expression, but we know what they mean. Feeling is a mark of consciousness only if we interpret 'feeling' as 'awareness'. But what is it, to be aware of something? Well, to be conscious of it.

How do we fight ourselves free from this tangle of circular definitions and misleading pictures? Two ideas seem to me to be especially helpful in explaining our sense of consciousness as a realm apart. The first is that of supervenience. Mental states generally, and conscious states in particular, emerge from other states of organisms. A useful analogy is the face in a picture. When a painter applies paint to a canvas he creates a physical object by purely physical means. This object is composed of areas and lines of paint, arranged on a surface that we can regard, for the sake of argument, as two dimensional. When we look at the surface of the painting, we see those areas and lines of paint, and also the surface that contains them. But that is not all we see. We also see a face that looks out at us with smiling eyes. In one sense the face is a property of the canvas, over and above the blobs of paint; for you can observe the blobs and not see the face, and vice versa. And the face is really there: someone who does not see it is not seeing correctly. On the other hand, there is a sense in which the face is not an additional property of the canvas, over and above the lines and blobs. For as soon as the lines and blobs are there, so is the face. Nothing more needs to be added, in order to generate the face – and if nothing more needs to be added, the face is surely nothing more. Moreover, every process that produces just these blobs of paint, arranged in just this way, will produce just this face – even if the artist himself is unaware of the face. (Imagine how you would design a machine for producing *Mona Lisas*.)

One way of expressing that point, is to say that the face is *supervenient* upon the blobs in which we see it. Maybe consciousness is a supervenient property in that sense: not something over and above the life and behaviour in which we observe it, but not reducible to them either. I would be tempted to go further in this direction, and describe consciousness as an *emergent* property: a property with causal powers over and above the powers possessed by the life processes from which it is, in some sense, composed.

The second helpful thought is one first given prominence by Kant, and thereafter emphasized by Fichte, Hegel, Schopenhauer and a whole stream of thinkers down to Heidegger, Sartre and Thomas Nagel. This is to draw a distinction between the subject and the object of consciousness, and to recognize the peculiar metaphysical status of the subject. As a conscious subject I have a point of view on the world. The world *seems* a certain way to me, and this 'seeming' defines my unique perspective. Every conscious being has such a perspective, since that is what it means to be a subject, rather than a mere object. When I give a scientific account of the world, however, I am describing objects only. I am describing the way things are, and the causal laws that explain them. This description is given from no particular perspective. It does not contain words like 'here', 'now' and 'I'; and while it is meant to explain the way things seem, it does so by giving a theory of how they are. In short, the subject is in principle unobservable to science, not because it exists in another realm but because it is not part of the empirical world. It lies on the edge of things, like a horizon, and could never be grasped 'from the other side', the side of subjectivity itself. Is it a real part of the real world? The question begins to look as though it has been wrongly phrased. I refer to myself, but this does not mean that there is a self that I refer to. I act for the sake of my friend, but there is no such thing as a sake for which I am acting.

That fatal drink – the drink of atonement – which Isolde offers to Tristan reminds us of a remarkable property of wine – at least of wine that we can savour. At the very moment of heightened consciousness, in which the wine brings into focus the choices and concerns which we have been putting out of mind so as to wash them down in style, we are also aware of our predicament, as incarnate beings, whose conscious life erupts from forces that lie outside the reach of direct decision. We can choose, in that moment, to think of Anna, to recall a poem, to meditate on God and salvation, to review the household finances. But we cannot choose to be or not to be in that heightened state of mind that rose within us as the wine went down. The wine confronts us with the mystery of our freedom: it amplifies our power to say 'I' and with that word to roam freely in the world of thought, to take decisions, to commit ourselves to actions both now and in the future. And yet it operates on us through the causal network in which our body is ensnared.

Kant, who enjoyed wine and provided a pint bottle for each guest at his regular dinner parties, wrote more beautifully of this paradox than any other philosopher. The use of the word 'I', he suggested, distinguishes the rational being from all other objects in the natural world, and also defines his predicament as a creature both bound and free. Descartes had argued for the supreme reality of the self, as a unitary substance, whose nature is infallibly revealed to me by my introspective thoughts. That view, Kant argued, is profoundly flawed. For it tries to make the self, as subject, into the object of its own awareness. I know myself as *subject*, not as object. I stand at the edge of things, and while I can say of myself that I am this, here, now, those words contain no information about *what* I am in the world of objects.

Yet there are two things which I know about myself, and about which I cannot be mistaken, since any argument against them would presuppose their truth. The first is that I am a unified centre of consciousness. I know without observation that this thought, this sensation, this desire, and this will belong to one thing; and I know that this thing endures through time, and is subject to change. I am directly aware, as Kant put it, of the 'transcendental unity of apperception', and this defines the I as the single unified owner of all my mental states.

The second thing that I know with certainty is that I am free. This freedom is contained in the very ability to say 'I', which is the decision from which all other decisions follow: I *will* climb that hill, kiss that woman, storm that fortress. Saying such things I change my whole stance to the world, put myself in a condition of readiness, and do so by my own free choice. Every utterance, every train of thought, proceeds by these free gestures. And to that argument Kant added another, and for him far more powerful, consideration, namely that reason tells me not only to do certain things, but that I *ought* to do them. I ought to help that person in distress; and not doing so it is again *myself* that I blame. I focus on that very centre of being from which decisions flow the full force of moral condemnation. Our whole way of thinking about ourselves is built upon the 'moral law', and since 'ought implies can', we can engage in practical reasoning only on the assumption that we are free.

But this leads to a strange question: what kind of world must it be that contains a thing like me – a thing with freedom and self-knowledge? It must be a world of enduring objects, Kant argued, objects with identity through time. And I am such an object: the thing which, deciding this here now, will do that there then. A world of enduring things is a world bound by causal laws: so Kant set out to prove in the immensely difficult section of the *Critique of Pure Reason* entitled 'The Transcendental Deduction of the Categories'. Without the web of causality, nothing 'preserves itself in being' long enough to know or be known. So my world, the world of the free being, is a world ordered by causal laws. And causal laws, Kant thought, must be universal and necessary. They refer to connections in the very nature of things, connections which cannot be suspended on this or that occasion and merely for the convenience of people.

Building his argument in this way – by steps too many, too complex and too controversial to detain us here – Kant drew the following conclusion. Any being who can say 'I' and mean it is free; and any being who can say 'I' and mean it is situated in a world of universally binding causal laws. I am governed by a law of freedom, which compels my actions, and a law of nature, which binds me in the web of organic life. I am a free subject and a determined object: but I am not *two* things, a determined body with a free soul rattling inside. I am *one* thing, which can be seen in two ways. This is something that I know to be true, but which lies beyond understanding. I can never know *how* it is possible, only *that* it is possible.

That which cannot be grasped intellectually, however, can be made present in sensory form. This is the lesson of art, which has provided us down the centuries with sensory symbols of conceptions that lie beyond the reach of the understanding – symbols like the late quartets of Beethoven, which present the idea of a heart filled in solitude by a God who can be known in no other way; or like the landscapes of Van Gogh, which show the world burst open by its own self-knowledge. There is no way of explaining such works without using paradoxical language: for what they mean cannot be spelled out properly in words and arguments, but must be grasped in the immediate experience.

Wine too has a part to play in presenting what the intellect cannot encompass. That first sip of a fine wine stirs, as it makes its way downwards, the rooted sense of my incarnation. I know that I am flesh, the by-product of bodily processes which are being brought to a heightened life by the drink that settles within me. But this very drink radiates the sense of self: it is addressed to the soul, not the body, and poses questions that can be formulated only in the first-person case, and only in the language of freedom: 'what am I, how am I, where now do I go?' It invites me to take stock of my situation, to wrap up the day's events, and to take those decisions which were waiting on this moment of calm. In other words, it presents, in a single experience, the doubled-up nature of the person who drinks. He may not have the words to describe this experience: and anyway words will never suffice. Through wine we know, as through almost nothing else that we consume, that we are one thing, which is also two: subject and object, soul and body, free and bound.

This knowledge contained in wine is put vividly to use by the Christian Eucharist. Christ, holding the cup to his disciples, declares that 'this is my blood of the New Testament, shed for you and for the remission of sins'. The blood in question is not the physical stuff that goes by that name, but something intimately bound up with the 'I' of Christ. The bread just eaten at the altar – the body of Christ – is made conscious by the wine. Bread and wine stand to each other as body to soul, as object to subject, as the thing *in* the world to its reflection at the edge.

I do not wish to imply that only a Christian can understand the mystery of wine, any more than it is only a Christian who can understand the Eucharist. Different people and different communities renew themselves in different ways. But the Eucharist reminds us that this renewal is an *inward* thing – a repossession of freedom. And with freedom comes *agape*, the strange and transforming ability to give, 'the love to which we are commanded', as Kant put it, whose meaning dawned on me that day in war-torn Beirut. In the Christian view the Eucharist is described as 'these gifts', gifts which represent the original gift of himself that Christ made on the cross. And by conveying this idea through wine, the Christian Eucharist provides us with the sensory image of a thought beyond words. Before considering this mystery, however, we must examine the third word in our heading: 'am'.

Of all the little words that have troubled human thought, the verb 'to be' has been the most potent. It features in those deep questions which point us towards the metaphysical abyss: 'why is there anything?' 'Is being a property?' 'How can we think of what is not?' 'And how can non-beings have properties?' Some philosophers write of the 'question of being', though what that question is, and what might be its answer, are as controversial as anything in philosophy. Aristotle and Aquinas constantly refer to the idea of being when the going gets tough, just as I, in my weakness, refer to the idea of going when the *being* gets tough. However, while we all acknowledge that there is an idea of going, not everyone is persuaded that there an idea of being, or that there is anything more to being than the concept of truth. But what concept is that? And how can you explain what truth is if you do not refer to being? Round and round the argument goes, and after a while creates a compelling urge to duck out of it. What does it matter that there is or is not Being, in addition to the things that are? And why should we think that there is such a study as metaphysics, as Aristotle described it, as the study of being *qua* being? Why not *qua* being *qua*?

And would Aristotle have defined the science of metaphysics in that way if he had known what thinkers like Heidegger would have done with the result, spinning disastrous spider-webs of nonsense around 'the question of being', breaking up being into a thousand fragments like being-for-others, being-towards-death, ahead-of-itself-being, puffing up the copula with flatulent pseudo-thought, and all the while forgetting that there are languages in which the 'is' of predication isn't? Consider this, ostensibly part of a commentary on Aquinas:

> *the proposition stating the necessity of questioning to human existence includes in itself its own ontological proposition which says: man exists as the question about being. In order to be himself he necessarily asks about being in its totality. This question is the 'must' which he himself is and in which being as that which is questioned presents and offers itself, and at the same time, as that which necessarily remains in question, withdraws itself. In the being of the question, which man is (so that he needs to question) being as that which is questioned both reveals itself and at the same time conceals itself in its own questionableness.*

So there you are: the question about being is what your irritating aunt Mabel *is*; and don't worry that the question of being ends up, in that passage, as the being of the question – it will all come out fine and dandy in the end, when being conceals itself once more in its own questionableness. The author of the passage, the theologian Karl Rahner, is capable of sustaining prose like that for 500 pages, and the only writers that are reliably more obscure are those (and there are quite a few of them) who set out to explain what Rahner says. Don't go there, is my advice: life is too short, and we need to get to the end of this chapter before finishing the bottle.

As long as we keep a tight hold of grammar, and fight against what Wittgenstein described as the 'bewitchment of the intelligence by means of language', we find that, after all, being is not such a bad idea. As David Wiggins has shown, the 'is' of identity is one of the more fertile of the little words from which philosophy begins.[4] And being features in some of the most striking arguments that have been given for the existence of God. Some of these arguments continue to fascinate both theists and atheists with their air of profundity – which theists take at face value, and atheists as the outward sign of fallacy.

One is the argument from contingent being, due largely to Avicenna (Ibn Sina), a philosopher who flourished in the early eleventh century of our era in Isfahan, and who is ever to be esteemed by winos, for recommending that we drink as we work. 'At night I would return home,' he tells us in his autobiography, 'and occupy myself with reading and writing. Whenever I felt drowsy or weakening I would turn aside to drink a cup of wine to regain my strength, and then I would go back to my reading.' All praise to Avicenna for defying the Koranic injunction against wine, and for citing it as an example of sloppy reasoning. The sentence 'Wine intoxicates', he writes in the *Ishârât*, has no clear truth-value. 'We should take into account whether potentially or actually, and whether a little or a large amount'. But yet more praise for the argument from contingent being, which bypasses all the nonsense prattled out by Richard Dawkins, Christopher Hitchens and the likes, and goes straight to the core concept of any theology worth the name, which is that of contingency. Being, Avicenna argued, is caught in three predicaments: there are impossible beings (those whose definition involves a contradiction), contingent beings (those which might not have existed) and necessary beings.[5] The contingent being (*mumkin bi-dhatihi*)

---

[4]   See David Wiggins, *Sameness and Substance Renewed*, Cambridge 2001.

[5]   Avicenna's argument, contained in the *Najât*, is full of subtleties which I pass over, for the reader's sake. Those interested can find translations of the relevant passages in G. Hourani, 'Ibn Sina on necessary and possible existence', *Philosophical Forum*, IV (1972), 74–86. The argument is set out, together with the tradition of discussion that it initiated, in Herbert A. Davidson, *Proofs for Eternity, Creation, and the Existence of God in Medieval Islamic and Jewish Philosophy*, Oxford 1987, pp. 281–406.

has the potentiality both to be and not to be, without contra-diction. You and I are contingent beings in that sense, and even if I am granted a certain intuition of my own existence, that certainty is merely a personal possession and neither guarantees my survival, nor refutes the view that there are possible worlds in which I am not.

A necessary being is one that is 'true in itself' – i.e. whose existence follows from its nature – whereas a contingent being is 'false in itself' and owes its truth to other things – in other words, is contingent upon the thing that causes or sustains it. The necessary being has no essence (*mahiyya*, or 'whatness') other than existence itself. Hence it cannot be distinguished from others of its supposed kind, all of which are identical with it. The necessary being therefore is one (*wahid*): a point later taken up by Spinoza and used to argue that nothing exists *except* the one necessary being, but connected by Avicenna with that central concept in all Islamic thinking, the concept of *tawhîd*, which means recognizing, in heart and mind and soul, the essential and transcendent oneness of God. This oneness is also a unity, the necessary being having no parts or internal structure, even though it turns out to have the attributes traditionally accorded to God.

Avicenna argued that since all contingent beings are contingent upon some other thing to which their existence is owed, there must be a necessary being on which they all depend. Avicenna argued for this in one way, Maimonides, taking up the argument, in another. Suppose, Maimonides argues, that there is no necessary being, and that all beings might not have been. Since time, in which all contingencies occur, is infinite (there being, on the hypothesis, no being who can set limits to it) then it is true of any contingent being that there will be some time at which it is not; and therefore some time at which all contingent beings are not – a time of utter nothingness. But this null point of the universe must already have existed, since past time, like future time, is infinite. And since nothing can arise out of nothing, then there would, from that point, be forever nothing. But there is something – namely this thing, which is pondering the question of being. So the hypothesis must be false, which means that there *is*, after all, the necessary being on which all other things depend. And this thing is – to adapt Avicenna's language – *causa sui* (*wajib al-wujud bi-dhatihi*); it is dependent on itself, the sustainer of everything. And it is *one* thing, a unity, admitting, in the words of the Koran, 'no partners'.

One of the many insights that are contained in this argument, and all the subtle (if at times tedious) metaphysics that flowed from it in the medieval schools, is the implication that the world of contingent beings, to which we belong, is governed by its own laws, the laws of generation and passing away. We discover those laws through scientific investigation, and they are the laws of nature which bind us all. They include those laws of genetics which, in the view of Dawkins, provide a final refutation of the belief in God. But, according to Avicenna, there is another relation of dependence than the one explored by science: the relation of the contingent to the necessary, of the world to its 'sustainer' (*rabb*, to use the Koranic term), and this is not a relation subject to empirical enquiry, nor one that can be known or refuted by scientific advance.

And that sends us straight back, as it sent Avicenna in one of his midnight meditations, to those other two words from the heading to this part: 'therefore' and 'I'. The relation of dependence which binds the world to God gives the reason why things are as they are. But this reason is not a cause: causes are the subject-matter of science and are spelled out by the universal laws that we discover through experiment and observation. The causal relation is a relation in time, which binds temporal (and therefore contingent) entities. In referring to the ultimate reason of things we are dealing here with another kind of answer to the question 'why?', and another meaning of *therefore*. And this is what gives sense to the life of prayer. We do not suppose that God can be summoned to our aid at every instance, or that He is waiting in the wings of nature, dealing out the cards. If we take the ideas behind Avicenna's argument seriously then we move towards another idea of God than that which informs the superstitious mind. God's freedom is revealed in the laws which bind us, and by which He too is bound, since it would be a loss of God's freedom, and not a gain, were He to defy the laws through which we understand Him. But this does not mean that God is beyond our reach. He is in and around us, and our prayers shape our personal relation with Him. We address Him, as we address those we love, not with the 'why?' of explanation, but with the 'why?'

of reason. We want to know the end, rather than the cause, and to school ourselves in the discipline of acceptance.

Why should we do this, and how? We do this because we, like God, exist on the very edge of things, with one foot, or rather one vista, in the transcendental. We, like Him, are in the world but not of the world, and although Avicenna did not put it in the way that I have put it, he was schooled by wine into the exploration of the inner life. Imagine yourself, he writes, suspended in the air, free from all sensations, and all contact with bodies, your own included. It is obvious that this thought-experiment is possible, and indeed for the true wino it occurs every day. Yet, in imagining yourself thus, as a 'floating man', you do not imagine away that core of being, the self (*nafs*), the 'I' which is the very subjectivity on which the experiment depends. I don't go along with the conclusion that Avicenna then drew, which is the conclusion later drawn by Descartes, that the I is a substance, a primary being *in* the world. Indeed I draw the conclusion that I have attributed to Kant, namely that the subject is not in the world at all, but stands always at the edge of it, in relation to the other persons whom he can address I to I, one of whom and the greatest of whom is God.

As Kant brilliantly showed, the person who is acquainted with the self, who refers to himself as 'I', is inescapably trapped into freedom. He rises above the wind of contingency that blows through the natural world, held aloft by Reason's necessary laws. The 'I' defines the starting point of all practical reasoning, and contains an intimation of the freedom that distinguishes people from the rest of nature. There is a sense in which animals too are free: they make choices, do things both freely and by constraint. But animals are not accountable for what they do. They are not called upon to justify their conduct, nor are they persuaded or dissuaded by dialogue with others. All those goals, like justice, community and love, which make human life into a thing of intrinsic value, have their origin in the mutual accountability of persons, who respond to each other 'I' to 'I'. Not surprisingly, therefore, people are satisfied that they understand the world and know its meaning, when they can see it as the outward form of another 'I' – the 'I' of God, in which we all stand judged, and from which love and freedom flow.

That thought may be poured out in verse, as in the *Veni*

Creator Spiritus of the Catholic Church, in the rhapsodic words of Krishna in the *Bhagavad Gita*, in the great Psalms that are the glory of the Hebrew Bible. But for most people it is simply there, a dense nugget of meaning in the centre of their lives, which weighs heavily when they find no way to express it in communal forms. People continue to look for the places where they can stand, as it were, at the window of our empirical world and gaze out towards the transcendental – the places from which breezes from that other sphere waft over them.

If we are to follow this way of thinking – which is something I propose to do in the remainder of this book, since it is a way of drinking too – we should take seriously the status of the word 'I'. This is an 'indexical', a word that *points*, like 'this' and 'here' and 'now'. And if we say that it points to *something* we should be careful to insist that this something is also a nothing, a place on the edge of things which has no identity in the world of objects. This is, in fact, contained in that Arabic word for soul – *nafs* – which is nothing more than the reflexive pronoun. And if there is a question of Being, it seems to me, it concerns this something which is also nothing, this point of view which vanishes when we turn to hold it in our grasp.

It is not only Arabic that has connected the soul with the reflexive pronoun. In Sanskrit the pronoun is *atman*, and the great Upanishads which the Hindu sages have bequeathed to mankind contain what is perhaps the most profound attempt to get *inside* Being, and to know it as it is in itself, and as it is *for* itself: as *atman*. Observing contingent beings, the Upanishads argue, we are confronted only with appearances that come and go, and not with the being that sustains them. Wherever we look, whether outwards to objects, or inwards to our own thoughts and desires, we encounter only properties, transitory states and vacillating sensations – the veil of Maya, and not the being that it hides from us. How do we approach being itself, therefore, so as to know it as it is? The question, phrased using the reflexive pronoun, answers itself. We need to enter the self, the *atman* of being. Having done so we will discover the universal self of the world, which the Hindu sages call Brahman. The path to this discovery is a path of renunciation, a path of selfless action in which we discard all attachment to success, profit, pleasure and reward, and do each thing that we do for its own sake. In this way we leave behind our own self, which is an illusory self, and attain to that other Self, which is the divine *atman*.

That makes it look as though the Upanishads are repeating the fallacy of Descartes and Avicenna, making the self – the *atman* which is the truth of the world – into an object, depriving it of its subjectivity, its nature as an I. Not so, however, and this is the subtle part of Hinduism that winos, I believe, are better placed to appreciate than most other mortals. Suppose we set out to remove from our consciousness all that is fleeting, all that is contingent, all that is desired. What then remains? Not physical objects, not space or time, not causality and the web of natural laws. All these things belong to the veil of Maya, and come before us as *distractions* from the central spiritual task. Remove these things, however, and we remove all the ways in which one thing can be distinguished from another. We remove what Leibniz called the *principium individuationis*, so that what we confront at the end of the path of renunciation is not an individual, nor something that contains individuals. Individual things have been *left behind*. Brahman is not an object, not even an object of thought; it is *only* a subject – an eternal thinking of itself, which is also identical with itself, the point of view outside things which is a point of view on them. This Brahman is Eternal, because time has been left behind; it is One, because number has been left behind. And it is Self, because that is all that we have retained in the journey towards it. Arriving at our destination we discard the dross of individual existence, and become one with the One, putting ourselves beyond all harm. It is thus that the King of Death describes Brahman to the seeker Nachiketa in the *Katha Upanishad*:

> *When a man is free from desire, his mind and senses purified, he beholds the glory of the Self and is without sorrow. Though seated, he travels far; though at rest, he moves all things. Who but the purest of the pure can realize this Effulgent Being, who is joy and who is beyond joy. Formless is he, though inhabiting form. In the midst of the fleeting, he abides forever. All-pervading and supreme is the Self.*

The Upanishad adds that the wise man, knowing *atman* in his true nature, transcends all grief. This encounter with the subjectivity of the world frees us from the attachments that are the source of grief, and offers redemption in the form of a supreme tranquility, the tranquility of the eternally contemplating I. Now the Hindus do not believe that it is easy to reach this condition; indeed it may need many lives before a person is finally on the path of the Hindu saint, leaving behind his empirical self for the sake of the transcendental. But I take heart from the Vedas, which tell us that Soma, the god of wine, is a fitting object of our worship, and from the Hindu scholars, who tell us that Soma is an avatar of Brahman, wine symbolizing the divine bliss that we feel when we reach the fount of Being. And I would go further and say that we idle and sensual creatures, whose attempts at sainthood begin each morning and have fizzled out by late afternoon, can nevertheless gain some apprehension of the *atman* by taking a glass of wine in the evening, and so perceiving a path to the inwardness of things. To *take* that path requires sacrifice and renunciation; and you certainly cannot achieve the goal of philosophy merely by swallowing a drug, whatever people might have thought in those early enthusiasms for mescalin and LSD.

However, wine shines a light along that path, and the beam it casts reaches far into the inner darkness, highlighting the puzzling forms of things with a glow of subjectivity. Wine, properly drunk, transfigures the world at which you look, illuminating that which is precisely most mysterious in the contingent beings surrounding you, which is the fact that they *are* – and also that they *might not have been*. The contingency of each thing glows in its aspect, and for a moment you are aware that individuality and identity are the outward forms taken by a single inner fire, and that this fire is also you.

It is the *first* glass of wine that gives its real taste, wrote Schopenhauer, just as it is the first encounter with another's features that reveals what he truly is. And among Western philosophers it is Schopenhauer who has taken the Upanishads most seriously, rephrasing in Kantian language the thesis that the ultimate reality is One and Eternal and that individuality is a mere appearance. For Schopenhauer, however, the ultimate reality is Will, not Self, and his philosophy promises not peace but an eternal restlessness. I have often wondered why he took this unsatisfactory path, and am inclined now to put it down to his fondness for beer. Schopenhauer was not in the habit of steadying before his face each evening the glass in which the I confronts its own reflection. There is a knowledge contained in wine, a knowledge that you yourself bring to it: in your close encounter with the aroma you sense that all is ultimately at rest in its being, each thing curled like an embryo within its own appearance. And with that first sip each evening, you return to a world of amniotic tranquillity.

How is this so? What is it about wine, that enables it to carry such a message?

6

The Meaning of Wine

It is appropriate to begin from the feature of wine that has been most abused: its ability to intoxicate. What exactly is intoxication? Is there a single phenomenon that is denoted by this word? Is the intoxication induced by wine an instance of the same general condition as the intoxication induced by whisky, say, or that induced by cannabis? And is 'induced' the right word in any or all of the familiar cases? Why all this fuss about *wine*? Is there something about wine that removes it altogether from the class of drugs, as Chesterton once suggested, when he wrote that 'the dipsomaniac and the abstainer are not only both mistaken, but they both make the same mistake. They regard wine as a drug and not a drink'? It would be strange if Chesterton, who was right about most things, were wrong about wine.

There is a deft philosophical move which can put some order into those questions, which is to ask whether intoxication is a natural kind – in other words, a condition whose nature is to be determined by science, rather than philosophy. The question 'what is water?' is not a philosophical question, since philosophy cannot, by reflecting on the sense of the term 'water', tell us anything about the stuff to which that term refers, except that it is *this* kind of stuff, pointing to some example. Now we can point to a case of intoxication – a drunken man say – and explain intoxication as *this* kind of state, thereupon leaving the rest to science. Science would explore the temporary abnormalities of the case, and their normal or typical causes. And no doubt the science could be linked to a general theory, which would connect the behavioural and mental abnormalities of the drunk with those of the spaced-out cannabis user, and those of the high-flying junkie. That theory would be a general theory of intoxication as a natural kind. And it would leave the philosopher with nothing to say about its subject-matter. However, we can quickly see that the question that concerns us cannot be so easily ducked. The drunk is intoxicated, in that his nervous system has been systematically disrupted by an intoxicant (in other words, by an agent with just this effect). This intoxication causes predictable effects on his visual, intellectual and sensory-motor pathways. When my heart and soul lit up with the first sip of Château Trotanoy 1945, however, the experience *itself* was intoxicating, and it is as though I tasted the intoxication as a quality of the wine. We may compare this quality with the intoxicating quality of a landscape or a line of poetry. It is fairly obvious from the comparison and from the grammar of the description that we are not referring to anything like drunkenness. There are natural kinds to which the experience of drinking wine and that of hearing a line of poetry both belong: for one thing they are both experiences. But the impulse to classify the experiences together is not to be understood as the first step in a scientific theory. It is the record of a perceived similarity – one that lies on the surface, and which may correspond to no underlying neuro-physiological resemblance. When we ask what we understand this intoxication to be, therefore, we are asking a philosophical rather than a scientific question. For that, to my way of thinking, is the central task of philosophy: to give a comprehensive theory of *how things seem to us* rational beings. (And to do so, I would add, while avoiding the inspissated jargon and futile theory-mongering of Husserlian phenomenology.)

Furthermore, there is a real question about the relation between the intoxication that we experience through wine, and the state of drunkenness. The first is a state of consciousness, whereas the second is a state of unconsciousness – or which tends towards unconsciousness. Although the one leads in time to the other, the connection between them is no more transparent than the connection between the first kiss and the final divorce. Just as the erotic kiss is neither a tame version nor a premonition of the bitter parting to which it finally leads, so is the intoxicating taste of the wine neither a tame version nor a premonition of drunkenness: they are simply not the 'same kind of thing', even if at some level of scientific theory they are discovered to have the same kind of cause.

It is also questionable to speak of the intoxication that we experience through wine as 'induced by' the wine. For this implies a separation between the object tasted and the intoxication felt, of the kind that exists between drowsiness and the sleeping pill that causes it. When we speak of an intoxicating line of poetry, we are not referring to an effect in the person who reads or remembers it, comparable to the effect of an energy pill. We are referring to a quality in the line itself. The intoxication of Mallarmé's *abolit bibelot d'inanité sonore* lies there on the page, not here in my nervous system. Are the two cases of intoxicatingness – wine and poetry – sufficiently alike to enable us to use the one to cast light on the other? Yes and no.

Non-rational animals sniff for information, and are therefore interested in smells. They also discriminate between the edible and the inedible on grounds of taste. But they relish neither the smell nor the taste of the things that they consume. For relishing is a reflective state of mind, in which an experience is held up for critical inspection. Only rational beings can relish tastes and smells, since only they can take an interest in *the experience itself*, rather than in the information conveyed by it. The temptation is therefore to assimilate relishing to the interest we have in colour and pattern, in the sound of music and in works of literary and visual art. Like aesthetic interest relishing is tied to sensory experience, and like aesthetic experience it involves holding our normal practical and information-gathering interests in abeyance. Why not say, therefore, that wine appeals to us in something like the way that poetry, painting or music appeal to us, by presenting an object of experience that is meaningful in itself? Why not say that the intoxicating quality is in the wine, in just the way that the intoxicating quality lies in the line of poetry? Our question about wine will then reduce to a special case of the general question, concerning the nature of aesthetic qualities.[1]

---

[1] This general question has been defined for all subsequent discussion by F. N. Sibley, in 'Aesthetic and Non-Aesthetic' and 'Aesthetic Concepts', both reprinted in J. Benson, B. Redfern and J. Roxbee Cox (eds), *Approach to Aesthetics: Collected Papers in Philosophical Aesthetics*, Oxford 2001. I take Sibley to task at length in *Art and Imagination*, London 1974.

The Sensory and the Aesthetic

Philosophers have tended to regard gustatory pleasures as purely sensory, without the intellectual intimations that are the hallmark of aesthetic interest. Sensory pleasure is available whatever the state of your education; aesthetic pleasure depends upon knowledge, comparison and culture. The senses of taste and smell, it is argued, are lower down the intellectual ladder, providing pleasures that are more sensory than those provided by sight and hearing. Unlike the senses of sight and hearing, they do not represent a world independent of themselves, and therefore provide nothing, other than themselves, to contemplate. This point was argued by Plato, and emphasized by Plotinus. It was important for Aquinas, who distinguished the more cognitive senses of sight and hearing from the less cognitive senses of taste and smell, arguing that only the first could provide the perception of beauty.[2] Hegel too, in the Introduction to his *Lectures on Aesthetics*, emphasizes the distinction between the pleasures of the palate and aesthetic experience, which is 'the sensuous embodiment of the Idea'.

Frank Sibley has argued that this philosophical tradition is founded on nothing more than prejudice, and that the relishing of tastes and smells is as much an aesthetic experience as the relishing of sights and sounds.[3] All those features commonly thought to characterize aesthetic experience attach also to our experience of tastes and smells. A smell or taste can be enjoyed 'for its own sake'; it can possess aesthetic qualities, such as finesse, beauty, harmony, delicacy; it can bear an emotional significance or tell a story, like the taste of the madeleine in Proust; it can be moving, exciting, depressing, intoxicating and so on. And there is good and bad taste in smells and tastes just as there is good and bad taste in music, art and poetry. All attempts to drive a wedge between merely sensory and truly aesthetic pleasures end up, Sibley thinks, by begging the

---

[2] See Plotinus, *Enneads*, 1, 6, 1; Aquinas, *Summa Theologiae*, I, II, 27, 1; Roger Scruton, *Art and Imagination*, op. cit., p. 156; Hegel, Introduction to *Aesthetics: Lectures on Fine Art*, vol. 1, tr. Knox, Oxford 1981.

[3] See F. N. Sibley, 'Tastes, Smells and Aesthetics', in *Approach to Aesthetics*, op. cit.

question. We should not be surprised, therefore, if there are art forms based on smell and taste, just as there are art forms based on sight and sound: the Japanese incense game, for example, or the somewhat extravagant but by no means impossible keyboard of olfactory harmonies envisaged by Huysmans in *À rebours*. Perhaps *haute cuisine* is such an art form; and maybe wine too is an aesthetic artefact, comparable to those products like carpentry that bridge the old and no longer very helpful division between the 'fine' and the 'useful' arts.

Sibley's argument is challenging, but not, it seems to me, successful. Consider smells: the object of the sense of smell is not the thing that smells but the smell emitted by it. We speak of smelling a cushion, but the smell is not a quality of the cushion. It is a thing emitted by the cushion, that could exist without the cushion, and indeed does exist in a space where the cushion is not – the space around the cushion. Hence smells linger in the places from which their causes have departed. The visual appearance of the cushion is not a thing emitted by the cushion, nor does it exist elsewhere than the cushion, or linger in a place after the cushion has left it. (After-images are not appearances, but mental images, which are only accidentally connected with the way things look.) Moreover, to identify the visual appearance we must refer to visual properties of the cushion. The object of my visual perception when I see the cushion is the cushion – not some other thing, a 'sight' or image, which the cushion 'emits'. To put it another way: visual experience reaches through the 'look' of a thing to the thing that looks. I don't 'sniff through' the smell to the thing that smells, for the thing is not represented in its smell in the way that it is represented in its visual appearance. Crucial features of visual appearances are therefore not replicated in the world of smells. For example, we can see an ambiguous figure now as a duck now as a rabbit; we can see one thing in another, as when we see a face in a picture. There seems to be no clear parallel case of 'smelling as' or 'smelling in', as opposed to the construction of rival hypotheses as to the cause of a smell. Hence there is a great difficulty – a near impossibility – of making, for smells, the kind of distinction that I made in the last chapter in relation to the picture of Guardi: the distinction between meaning and association, between what we experience *in* the object and what the object merely calls to mind.

One conclusion to draw from that is that smells are ontologically like sounds – not qualities of the objects that emit them but independent objects. I call them 'secondary objects', on the analogy with secondary qualities, in order to draw attention to their ontological dependence on the way the world is experienced.[4] Smells exist *for* us, just as sounds do, and must be identified through the experiences of those who observe them. However, smells cannot be organized as sounds are organized: put them together and they mingle, losing their character. Nor can they be arranged along a dimension, as sounds are arranged by pitch, so as to exemplify the order of between-ness.[5] They remain free-floating and unrelated, unable to generate expectation, tension, harmony, suspension or release. You could concede that smells might nevertheless be objects of aesthetic interest, but only by putting them on the margin of the aesthetic – the margin occupied by the sound of fountains, where beauty is a matter of association rather than expression, and of context rather than content. But it would be more illuminating to insist on the radical distinction that exists, between these objects of sensory enjoyment which acquire meaning only by the association of ideas, and the objects of sight and hearing, whose meaning can be directly seen and heard.

If asked to choose, therefore, I would say, for philosophical reasons, that the intoxication that we experience in wine is a sensory but not an aesthetic experience, whereas the intoxication of poetry is aesthetic through and through. To say as much is to imply that the aesthetic is not reducible to the sensory, and that aesthetic enjoyments have a cognitive and exploratory character that distinguishes them from purely physical pleasures. But it does

---

[4]   On the theory of secondary objects see Roger Scruton, *The Aesthetics of Music*, Oxford 1997, Ch. 1; 'Sounds as Secondary Objects and Pure Events', in Casey O'Callaghan and Matthew Nudds (eds.), *Sounds and Perception*, Oxford 2009.

[5]   As David Hilbert noticed long ago (*Foundations of Geometry*, 1899), between-ness is one of the foundational concepts of geometry, permitting the axiomatization of distance and direction. Hence there is a geometry of sound, but not of smells, and in music the root experience is one of musical objects situated in, and moving through, a shared musical space.

not matter very much whether you agree or disagree with the distinction, or whether you are or are not disposed to describe the enjoyment of wine as 'aesthetic'. What matters is the cognitive status of wine – its status as an object of thought and a vehicle of reflection.

The Cognitive Status of Wine

My excitement at a football match is not a physiological condition that could have been produced by a drug. It is directed towards the game: it is excitement *at* the spectacle and not just excitement *caused by* the spectacle; it is an effect directed at its cause, which is also a way in which that cause is *understood*. Something like this is true of the wine. The intoxication that I feel is not just an effect caused by the wine: it feeds back into my experience of the wine, so as to become part of its taste. It is a way of relishing the wine. The intoxicating quality and the relishing are internally related, in that the second cannot be properly described without reference to the first. The wine lives in my intoxication, as the game lives in the excitement of the fan: I have not swallowed the wine as I would a tasteless drug; I have taken it into myself, so that its flavour and my mood are inextricably bound together.

To put the point in another way: there are two kinds of intoxication, that which is experienced as a quality of its cause – like the intoxicating character of wine – and that which occurs merely *as a result* of its cause, without changing the way the cause is experienced. The first clue to understanding wine is, then, this: that the intoxication induced by wine is also directed at the wine, in something like the way the excitement produced by a football game is directed at the game. The cases are not entirely alike, however. It is without strain that we say that we were excited at the game, as well as by it; only with a certain strain can we say that we were intoxicated at the wine, rather than by it. And this connects with the second question mentioned at the start of this chapter: the question of knowledge. Is there something that we learn from, and in, the taste of wine, as we learn things from, and in, our visual images?

In describing my visual experience I am describing a visual world, in terms of concepts that are in some sense *applied in* the experience and not deduced from it. Another way of putting this is to say that visual experience is a *representation* of reality. As already noted, taste and smell are not like that. I might say of the ice-cream in my hand that it tastes *of* chocolate or that it tastes *like* chocolate, but not that I taste it *as* chocolate, as though taste were in itself a form of judgement. The distinction here is reflected in the difference between the cogent accounts of paintings given by critics, and the far-fetched and whimsical descriptions of wines from the pens of wine writers. Winespeak is in some way ungrounded, for it is not describing the way the wine is, but merely the way it tastes. And tastes are not representations of the objects that possess them.[6]

In *Brideshead Revisited* Evelyn Waugh describes Charles and Sebastian, alone together at Brideshead, sampling the Earl's collection:

> '... *It is a little, shy wine, like a gazelle.*'
> '*Like a leprechaun.*'
> '*Dappled, in a tapestry meadow.*'
> '*Like a flute by still water.*'
> '... *And this a wise old man.*'
> '*A prophet in a cave.*'
> '... *And this is a necklace of pearls on a white neck.*'

---

[6] This is a controversial claim, as is what I say concerning the status of winespeak. Some have likened wine criticism to criticism in the arts, in which descriptions aim to be accepted in experience, rather than to be truthful to qualities that could have been identified in some other way. See Kent Bach, 'Knowledge, Wine and Taste: What Good is Knowledge (in Enjoying Wine)?', in Barry C. Smith (ed.), *Questions of Taste: The Philosophy of Wine*, Oxford 2007, and the rejoinder by Keith and Adrienne Lehrer, 'Winespeak or Critical Communication?' in Fritz Allhoff (ed.), *Wine and Philosophy: A Symposium on Thinking and Drinking*, Oxford 2008. John W. Bender, writing in the same volume, in an article entitled 'What the Wine Critics Tell Us', tries to give a systematic parallel between the descriptions of wine and the descriptions of artworks, identifying both as part of a process of reasoning in which judgement and discrimination are the goals. The problem, however, is that, while art critics describe *works of art*, wine critics describe tastes, and wines are not represented in their tastes as artworks are represented in the way they look or sound.

'*Like a swan.*'
'*Like the last unicorn.*'

The dialogue expresses the callow love between two adolescents, as they explore each other's imaginative powers. But does it describe the wines that they are drinking? Not in the way that I describe a painting, by detailing what I perceive in it. A prophet in a cave is not something that you can taste in a wine as you can see St Jerome in Titian's painting. Nor does this description of a wine bear much resemblance to the descriptions that we give of music, when describing its expressive power – like the 'anguished' (*beklemmt*) that Beethoven wrote on the score of the Cavatina of the B flat late quartet. Wine is not a representational medium; but it is not an expressive medium either: we cannot read emotions into the savours that rise from the glass as we read them into music, for these savours, though intentionally produced, are not *marked* by intention as the notes in music are. Somehow the descriptions that we offer, however appropriate they might seem, never migrate from their origin in the mental life of the speaker, to their goal, in the wine that brings them to mind.

This does not mean that we cannot describe the taste of a wine, or break it down into its sensory components. If I say of a wine that it has a flowery nose, lingers on the palate, with ripe berry flavours and a hint of chocolate and roasted almonds, then what I say conveys real information, from which someone might be able to construct a sensory image of the wine's taste.[7] But I have described the taste in terms of other *tastes*, and not attempted to attach a meaning, a content, or any kind of reference to it. The description I gave does not imply that the wine evokes, means, symbolizes or presents the idea of chocolate; and somebody who didn't hit on this word as a description of the wine's flavour would not show that he had missed the meaning of what he drank or indeed missed anything important at all.

Our experience of wine is bound up with its nature as a drink – a liquid which slides smoothly into the body, lighting the flesh as it journeys down. As I suggested in the last chapter, this endows

---

[7] Hence the (limited) use of 'aroma wheels' in identifying tastes and scents, and in grouping them as sensory kinds. See that given by A. C. Noble at www.winearomawheel.com.

wine with a peculiar inwardness, an intimacy with the body of a kind that is seldom achieved by solid food, since food must be chewed and therefore denatured before it enters the gullet. Nor is it achieved by any smell, since smell makes no contact with the body at all, but merely enchants without touching, like the beautiful girl at the other end of the party.

The symbolic use of wine in religious cults is reflected in art and literature, in which magic drinks are conceived as mind-changing and even identity-changing potions. We find this symbolism easy to understand, since it draws on the way in which intoxicating drinks, and wine pre-eminently, are 'taken into oneself', in a way that tempts one almost to a literal interpretation of that phrase. It is as though the wine enters the very self of the person who drinks it. Of course there is a great difference in this connection between good wine and bad, and the self learns in time to welcome the one as it fights against the other. But it is precisely because the self is so actively engaged that this battle has to be fought and won, just as the battles between good and evil and virtue and vice must be fought and won. There is more at stake when it comes to taste in wine than mere taste, and the adage that *de gustibus non est disputandum* is as false here as it is in aesthetics. We are not disputing about a physical sensation, but about choices in which we are fully engaged as rational agents.

The symbolism of the drink, and its soul-transforming effect, reflects the underlying truth that it is only rational beings who can appreciate things like wine. Even if taste is a less cognitive sense, therefore, it has an aspect which is closed to non-rational creatures, and that aspect includes the one we are considering, which is the aspect of intoxication. Animals can be drunk; they can be high on drugs and fuggy with cannabis; but they cannot experience the kind of directed intoxication that we experience through wine, since this is a condition in which only rational beings can find themselves, depending as it does upon thoughts and acts of attention that lie outside the repertoire of a horse or a dog. Relishing is something that only a rational being can exhibit, and which therefore only a rational being can do. Hence when, in my duties as a wine critic, I try out a bottle on Sam the Horse, stirring a glass-full into his oats and studying his reaction, I can make no distinction between his relishing the wine and his merely enjoying it. The taste is a source of pleasure to him, but not an *object* of pleasure. He does not focus his thinking on the *taste* of the wine – indeed he has no such concept, and no ideas that could be captured by a phrase like 'me tasting this'. Still less does he experience the intoxicating quality of the wine as a quality of *it*. It is, for him, no part of the flavour, even if it is part of what he feels in absorbing it.

Types of Stimulant

In saying that, however, I imply that not all forms of intoxication, even for rational beings, are species of a single genus. It is therefore necessary to make some distinctions among the substances that we take in search of stimulation, intoxication or relief from the *lacrymae rerum*. In particular we should distinguish between four basic kinds of stimulant: those that please us, but do not alter the mind in any fundamental way, even if they have mental effects; those that alter the mind, but which impart no pleasure in their consumption; those that both alter the mind and also please us as we consume them; and finally those that alter the mind and do so, at least in part, *by* and *in the act of* pleasing us. There are intermediate cases, but those broad categories offer a map, I think, of this hitherto uncharted territory. So I shall deal with each in turn.

1   Those that please, and which have mental effects, but which do not alter the mind. Tobacco is probably the most familiar example of this. It has mental effects, leading to a reduction in nervous tension and a heightening in concentration and control, but it does not fundamentally alter the mind, so as to cause the world to appear different, so as to interfere with perceptual and motor pathways, or so as to hamper or redirect the emotional and intellectual life. The pleasure involved is intimately connected with the mental effect, and although the case is not exactly like that of wine, there is a definite sense in which the taste of a good cigar, say, is relaxing, in the way that the taste of a good wine is intoxicating – i.e. the mental effect forms *part* of the gustatory quality. This is an odd phenomenon, which has its parallel in aesthetics. It arises when there is a distinct experience of *savouring* whatever it is

you consume: something that, as I said above, no non-rational animal can do, and which we can do only when the mental effect of a substance can be read back, so to speak, into the way it tastes. Some sense of what this involves can be gained from considering the second kind of stimulant, which is not savoured at all:

2 Stimulants that have mind-altering effects, but which do not bring any pleasure in the consumption of them. The most obvious examples of this are drugs that you swallow whole like Ecstasy, or drugs that you inject like heroin. Here there is no pleasure in the taking of the drug, but radical mental effects as a result of it – effects which are wanted for their own sake and regardless of how they were caused. There is no question of savouring a dose of heroin, and the mind which is disengaged in the ingestion of the stuff remains in a certain sense disengaged thereafter. The mental effects of the drug are not directed towards the drug or towards the experience of using it: they are directed towards objects of everyday perception and concern, towards ideas, people, images and so on. You take no pleasure in the drug itself, even if there are other pleasures that result from using it. It should be obvious that this is quite unlike either the first case, or the third case that I now consider:

3 Stimulants that have mind-altering effects but which give pleasure in the act of consuming them. The two most interesting cases are cannabis and alcohol. I refer to alcohol in general and not just to wine. The psychic transformation that occurs through the consumption of pot is, the experts tell us, quite far-reaching, and outlasts the moment of pleasure by hours or days. Nevertheless, the moment of pleasure definitely exists, and is not dissimilar to that provided by tobacco: though it involves a loss rather than a gain in mental concentration. Likewise alcohol also has a mind-altering effect, heightening emotions, muddling thoughts, and interfering with nervous pathways; and this mind-altering effect outlasts the moment of pleasure, and is in part unconnected with it. It is precisely because the mental transformation outlasts the pleasure, indeed, that we are driven to contrast the case of the alcoholic, who has become addicted to the effect of drink and more or less indifferent to its taste, from that of the wine-

lover, for whom the mental transformation *is* the taste, so to speak, and outlasts it only in the way that the pleasure of seeing an old friend survives after his visit is over. Hence the need to distinguish a fourth kind of case, the one that really interests me:

4 Stimulants that have mind-altering effects which are in some way internally related to the experience of consuming them. The example, of course, is wine, and that is what I meant earlier in referring to the intoxicating quality of the taste. It is in the act of drinking that the mind is altered, and the alteration is in some way bound up with the taste: the taste is imbued with the altered consciousness, just as the altered consciousness is directed at the taste. This again is near to the aesthetic experience. We all know that you cannot listen to a Beethoven quartet with understanding unless your whole psyche is taken up and transformed by it: but the transformation of consciousness is read back into the sound that produces it, which is the sound of that transformation, so to speak. Hence the well-known problem of musical content: we want to say that such music has a meaning, but we also want to deny that the meaning is detachable from the way the music sounds.

While I have compared cannabis and alcohol, it is very important to be aware of the differences between them. Obviously there are significant medical and physiological differences. Alcohol is rapidly expelled from the system and is addictive only in large doses – at least to those like us whose genetic make-up has been influenced by the millennia of winemaking. The Inuit of the Arctic Circle, and others whose ancestors never cultivated the grape, are unable to process alcohol harmlessly and become quickly addicted to it; but for the purpose of what follows I refer only to you and me. And of you and me it can safely be said that cannabis is vividly to be contrasted with wine from the physiological viewpoint. The effects of cannabis remain for days, and it is both more addictive and more radical, leading not just to temporary alterations of the mind but to permanent or semi-permanent transformations of the personality, and in particular a widely observed loss of the moral sense. This loss of the moral sense can be observed too in alcoholics, but it is not to be explained merely by addiction. Addiction to tobacco, whether smoked or chewed, seems to lead to no demoralization of the victim, and while people commit crimes under the influence of drugs and cause accidents under the influence of alcohol they do neither under the influence of smoking. The temporary nature of the physiological effects of wine is of great importance in describing its emotional aura. The effect of wine is understood, by the observer as much as the consumer, as a temporary possession, a passing alteration, which is not, however, an alteration that changes the character of the one in whom it occurs. Hence you can go away and sleep it off; and the ancient characterizations of Silenus (the tutor and companion of Dionysus) are of a creature alternating drink and sleep, with a crescendo of drunkenness between them. Moreover, and more importantly, alcohol in general, and wine in particular, has a unique social function, increasing the garrulousness, the social confidence and the goodwill of those who drink together, provided they drink in moderation. Many of the ways that we have developed of drinking socially are designed to impose a strict regime of moderation. Buying drinks by round in the pub, for example, has an important role in permitting people to rehearse sentiments of reciprocal generosity and to cohere as a group, without relying on any specific intimacies.

Cannabis also has a social function, and is associated in the Middle East with a hookah-smoking ritual that produces a mutual befuddlement, briefly confused with peace, a commodity rarely to be found in the region. Each intoxicant both reflects and reinforces a particular form of social interaction, and it is important to understand, therefore, that the qualities that interest us in wine reflect the social order of which wine is a part.

Wine is not simply a shot of alcohol, or a mixed drink. It is a transformation of the grape. The transformation of the soul under its influence is merely the continuation of another transformation that began maybe fifty years earlier when the grape was first plucked from the vine. (That is one reason why the Greeks described fermentation as the work of a god. Dionysus enters the grape and transforms it; and this process of transformation is then transferred to us as we drink.) Although we know that human skill is involved in this transformation, it is skill of quite another kind from that of the cocktail mixer, being a skill of husbandry, and in a certain measure the result is a tribute not just to the skill of the grower and the winemaker, but to the whole ethological process that turned us from hunter-gatherers to farmers. (Maybe there is some echo of this in the story of the drunkenness of Noah.)

The Effect of Wine

When we raise a glass of wine to our lips, therefore, we are savouring an ongoing process: the wine is a living thing, the last result of other living things, and the progenitor of life in us. It is almost as though it were another human presence in any social gathering, as much a focus of interest and in the same way as the other people there. This experience is enhanced by the aroma, taste and the simultaneous impact on nose and mouth, which – while not unique to wine – have, as I have argued, an intimate connection to the immediate intoxicating effect, so as to be themselves perceived as intoxicating. The whole being of the drinker rushes to the mouth and the olfactory organs to meet the tempting meniscus, just as the whole being of the lover rises to the lips in a kiss. It would be an exaggeration to make too much of the comparison, ancient though it is, between the erotic kiss and the sipping of wine. Nevertheless, it is not an exaggeration, but merely a metaphor, to describe the contact between the mouth and the glass as a *face-to-face* encounter between you and the wine. And it is a useful metaphor. Whisky may be *in* your face, but it is not exactly *face-to*-face as wine is. The shot of alcohol as it courses through the body is like something that has *escaped from* the flavour, that is working in an underhand way. The alcoholic content of the wine, by contrast, remains part of the flavour, in something like the way that the character of an honest person is revealed in his face. Spirits are comparable in this respect to cordials and medicinal drinks: the flavour detaches itself readily from the effect, just as the face and gestures of a shallow person detach themselves from his long-term intentions. The companionship of wine resides in the fact that its effect is not underhand or concealed but present and revealed in the very flavour. This feature is then transmitted to those who drink wine together, and who adapt themselves to its way of honest dealing.

The ancient proverb tells us that there is truth in wine. The truth lies not in what the drinker perceives but in what, with loosened tongue and easier manners, he reveals. It is 'truth for others', not 'truth for self'. This accounts for both the social virtues of wine and its epistemological innocence. Wine does not deceive you, as cannabis deceives you, with the idea that you enter another and higher realm. Hence it is quite unlike even the mildest of the mind-altering drugs, all of which convey some vestige, however vulgarized, of the experience associated with mescalin and LSD, and recorded by Aldous Huxley in *The Doors of Perception*. These drugs – cannabis not exempted – are epistemologically culpable. They tell lies about another world, a transcendental reality beside which the world of ordinary phenomena pales into insignificance or at any rate into less significance than it has. Wine, by contrast, paints the world before us as the true one, and reminds us that if we have failed previously to know it then this is because we have failed in truth to belong to it, a defect that it is the singular virtue of wine to overcome.

It is true, as I have suggested, that wine shines a certain light into the inwardness, the *atman*, of contingent things, and it points towards – without providing – another way in which being might be known. But it does this without eclipsing the light that shines on our world, and without deceiving us into thinking that we have entered another and less illusory alternative. It respects our illusions, and even amplifies the more benign among them. But it does not provide an escape route from reality.

For this reason we should, I believe, elaborate our description of the characteristic effect of wine, which is not simply an effect of intoxication. The characteristic effect of wine, when drunk in company, includes an opening out of the self to the other, a conscious step towards asking and offering forgiveness: forgiveness not for acts or omissions, but for the impertinence of existing. Although the use of wine in the Christian Eucharist has authority in the Last Supper, as recorded in the New Testament, there is another reason for the centrality of wine in the Communion ceremony, which is that it both illustrates and in a small measure enacts the moral posture that distinguishes Christianity from its early rivals, and which is summarized in the prayer to 'forgive us our trespasses, as we forgive them that trespass against us'. That remarkable prayer, which tells Christians that they can obtain forgiveness only if they offer it, is one that we all understand in our cups, and this understanding of the critical role of forgiveness in forming durable human societies intrudes too into the world of Islam, in the poetry of Hafiz, Rumi and Omar Khayyam, winos to a man. In *surah* xvi verse 7 of the Koran wine is unreservedly praised as one of God's gifts. As the prophet, burdened by the trials of his Medina exile, became more tetchy, so did his attitude to wine begin to sour, as in *surah* v verses 90–91. Muslims believe that the later revelations cancel the earlier, whenever there is a conflict between them.[8] I suspect, however, that God moves in a more mysterious way.

Taste and Cognition

The Communion wine returns me to a point that I emphasized earlier: that the pronounced mental effects of wine are, so to speak, read back into their cause, so that the wine itself recalls them in its taste. Just as you savour the intoxicating flavour of the wine, so do you savour its reconciling power: it presents you with the taste of forgiveness. That is one way of understanding the Christian doctrine of transubstantiation, itself a survival of the Greek belief that Dionysus is actually *in* the wine and not just the cause of it. Although most attempts to describe the experience of wine are either literal comparisons of taste with taste, or else whimsical rhapsodies of the kind I discussed earlier in connection with Charles and Sebastian at Brideshead, there are these intense cases in which the boundary between association and meaning becomes blurred: the mental effects of wine become so intense as to invade the taste, so that we have an experience which is not wholly unlike that of seeing emotion in a painting or hearing it in music. Exactly what conclusions we should draw from this I do not know. But it should not lead us to ignore the fundamental difference between tastes and other qualities, and it is worth summarizing what these are.

First, tastes are not qualities in the way that colours are. Every patch of blue is a blue something, if only a patch. But not every

[8]   The later revelations come earlier in the canonical ordering of the text – a fatal mistake, in my view, given the manifest inspiration of the Meccan *surahs* and the inflexible anger of so much that is attributed to the years in Medina.

strawberry taste is a strawberry-tasting something. The taste can be there without the substance, as when I have a taste in the mouth, but have swallowed nothing. The taste is in the mouth in something like the way the smell is in the air or the sound is in the room. Tastes belong with smells and sounds in the ontological category of secondary objects. Hence the taste of a wine can linger long after the wine has been swallowed.[9] Tastes can detach themselves from their causes, as sounds do in music, and lead an emotional life of their own. Since they are associated with, rather than inherent in, their objects, they have a facility to launch trains of association, linking object to object, and place to place, in a continuous narrative such as was elaborated by Proust.

Connected with that feature of tastes is the well-known difficulty we experience in describing them. Colours belong to a spectrum, and vary along recognized phenomenal dimensions, such as brightness and saturation. Our descriptions of colours also order them, so that we know where they stand in relation to one another, and how they pass over into each other. Tastes exhibit order in certain dimensions – for example the sweet–bitter, bland–spicy continua. But most of their peculiarities show no intrinsic ordering and no clear transitions. We describe them, as a rule, in terms of their characteristic causes: nutty, fruity, meaty, cheesy and so on. Hence the process of discriminating and comparing tastes begins with an effort of association, whereby we learn to identify the characteristic cause. We learn to place tastes in a gustatory field, so to speak, whose landmarks are the familiar things that we eat and drink, and the places and processes that produce them.

This last point returns me to the earlier one concerning the epistemological innocence of wine. The 'this worldly' nature of the heightened consciousness that comes to us through wine means that, in attempting to describe the knowledge that it imparts, we look for features of our actual world, features that might be, as it were, epitomized, commemorated and celebrated in its flavours. Hence the traditional perception of fine wine as the

---

9   The quality of 'lingering' on the palate, like the related quality of 'finish', is delivered by retronasal olfaction – the secondary application of the sense of smell to that which has already been captured by the mouth.

taste of a *terroir* – where that means not merely the soil, but the customs and ceremonies that sanctified it and put it, so to speak, in communion with the drinker. The use of theological language here is, I believe, no accident. Although wine tells no lies about a transcendental realm, it sanctifies the immanent reality, acquainting us with its hidden subjectivity, presenting it under the aspect of Brahman. That is why it is so effective a symbol of the incarnation. In savouring it we are knowing – by acquaintance, as it were – the history, geography and customs of a community.

Since ancient times, therefore, wines have been associated with definite places, and been accepted not so much as the taste of those places, as the flavour imparted to them by the enterprise of settlement. Wine of Byblos was one of the principal exports of the Phoenicians, and old Falernian was made legendary by Horace. Those who conjure with the magical names of Burgundy, Bordeaux and the Rhine and Moselle are not just showing off: they are deploying the best and most reliable description of a cherished taste, which is inseparable from the idea and the history of the settlement that produced it. The Ancient Egyptians, incidentally, while they often labelled wines with the place of their production, and would trade with all the best suppliers around the Mediterranean, would classify wines by their social function. Archaeologists have recovered amphorae labelled as 'wine for first-class celebrations', 'wine for tax collection day', 'wine for dancing' and so on.[10] It is doubtful, however, that these descriptions can function as a guide to taste. It is easy to imagine a tasting in which the punter holds the glass to his nose, takes a sip and then says 'Burgundy'; rather more difficult to imagine him saying 'tax collection'. Why is that?

Here we should again return to the religious meaning of wine. At the risk of drastically oversimplifying, I suggest that there are two quite distinct strands that compose the religious consciousness, and that our understanding of religion has suffered from too great an emphasis on one of them. The first strand, which we overemphasize, is that of belief. The second strand, which is often overlooked by modern thought (though not by those pioneering

---

[10] See the informative account by Patrick McGovern, *Wine in the Ancient World*, London 2004.

sociologists of religion like Émile Durkheim and Max Weber), is the strand that might be summarized in the term 'membership', by which I mean all the customs, ceremonies and practices whereby the sacred is renewed, so as to be a real presence among us, and a living endorsement of the human community. The pagan religions of Greece and Rome were strong on membership but weak on belief. Hence they centred on the cult, as the primary religious phenomenon. It was through the cult, not the creed, that the adept proved his religious orthodoxy and his oneness with his fellows. Western civilization has tended in recent centuries to emphasize belief – in particular the belief in a transcendental realm and an omnipotent king who presides over it. This theological emphasis, by representing religion as a matter of theological doctrine, exposes it to refutation. And that means that the real religious need of people – a need planted in us, according to some, by evolution and according to others by God (though why not by both?) – seeks other channels for its expression: usually forms of idolatry that do not achieve the refreshing humanity of the cult.

Far from supposing the cult to be a secondary phenomenon, derived from the theological beliefs that justify it, I take the opposite view, and believe that I have modern anthropology, and its true founder, Richard Wagner, on my side.[11] Theological

[11] Claude Lévi-Strauss, in the 'overture' to *Le cru et le cuit*, Paris 1964, credits Wagner as the founder of structural anthropology. It is true that a discipline called anthropology existed before Wagner's day, Kant being the first to introduce it as a university course of study in his *Anthropologie in pragmatischer Hinsicht*, put together from lecture notes in 1798. The recognition of religion as a deep need of the human psyche, which would always express itself in symbolic form, is conveyed by Wagner's transformation of Feuerbach in *Die Religion und die Kunst*, in *Gesammelte Schriften und Dichtungen*, vol. x, Leipzig 1911. The study of ancient myth and religion as giving form to universal psychic realities was, indeed, already common in German culture, not least because of Hegel. The true origin of the approach was probably Georg F. Creuzer's *Symbolik und Mythologie der alten Völker*, Leipzig, Darmstadt, 1810–12, a work which caused much controversy in its day. It was not until Wagner, however, that an example was offered of a fabricated religion, in which the gods were deduced from the need and not the need from the gods. This was surely the first attempt at a comprehensive anthropology of religion.

beliefs are rationalizations of the cult, and the function of the cult is membership. It is through establishing a cult that people learn to pool their resources. Hence every act of settling and of turning the earth to the common needs of a community, involves the building of a temple and the setting aside of days and hours for festivity and sacrificial offering. When people have, in this way, prepared a home for them, the gods come quietly in to inhabit it, maybe not noticed at first, and only subsequently clothed in the transcendental garments of theology.

Now it seems to me that the act of settling, which is the origin of civilization, involves both a radical transition in our relation to the earth – the transition known in other terms as that from hunter-gatherer to farmer – and also a new sense of belonging. Settled people do not belong only to each other: they belong to a place, and out of that sense of shared roots there grow the farm, the village and the city. Vegetation cults are the oldest and most deeply rooted in the unconscious, since they are the cults that drive out the totemism of the hunter-gatherer, and celebrate the earth itself, as the willing accomplice in our bid to stay put. The new farming economy, and the city that grows from it, generated a sense of the holiness of the planted crop, and in particular of the staple food – which is grass, usually in the form of corn or rice – and the vine that wraps the trees above it. Such, surely, is the prehistory of the bread and wine of the Eucharist. Moreover, the fruit of the vine can be fermented and so stored in a sterilized form. It provides a place and the things that grow there with a memory, so becoming a symbol of a settled community and its will to endure.

At some level, I venture to suggest, the experience of wine is a recuperation of that original cult whereby the land was settled and the city built. And what we taste in the wine is not just the fruit and its ferment, but also the peculiar flavour of a landscape to which the gods have been invited and where they have found a home. Nothing else that we eat or drink comes to us with such a halo of significance, and by refusing to drink it people send an important message – the message that they do not belong on this earth.

7

The Meaning of Whine

In the nineteenth century the banner of temperance was raised not by politicians but by private citizens, many of them animated by a ferocity that is seldom witnessed, now that social problems are bequeathed to Nanny State. What disturbed the do-gooders of Victorian England was not only the sight of ruined alcoholics on the city pavements but also the knowledge of the far greater number of drinkers who were sitting at home, happily raising their glasses, their vice invisible to the public eye. H. L. Mencken defined puritanism as 'the haunting fear that someone, somewhere, may be happy'. When we read of the rallies and pledges of the temperance groupies, and of their busy-body policing which respected neither the privacy nor the social relationships of their victims, we are apt to breathe a sigh of relief that then was then and now is now.

Let it be said in favour of puritanism, however, that not all pleasures are innocent. Every society – ours included – divides sexual pleasures into the innocent and the guilty. The temperance movements arose from the tendency to transfer that natural moral reaction to a realm where it has no clear meaning. It is not excess that makes for sexual guilt but the wrong choice of object, while all drinking is innocent unless it is overdone. At the same time, as Mencken reminds us, it is the anxiety over 'what others are up to' that animates puritanism in all its forms.

If there is a sin attached to wine, it resides, I would suggest, not in drinking, but in the divorce that can occur between pleasure and virtue. Every culture thrives by permitting some pleasures, and forbidding others. And those pleasures that underpin the culture must be governed by good habits. In our

Abrahamic inheritance, good habits are those that express the
spirit of charity. The virtuous drinker is the one for whom 'the
ferment of love possesses the wine', as the Sufi poet Rumi puts
it.

The puritan legacy can be seen in many aspects of British and
American society. And what is most interesting to the anthro-
pologist is the ease with which puritan outrage can be displaced
from one topic to another, and the equal ease with which the
thing formerly disapproved of can be overnight exonerated from
all taint of sin. This has been particularly evident in the case of
sex. Our parents and grandparents were concerned that young
people should look on sex as a temptation to be resisted.
However, they did not see chastity as a preparation for sexual
enjoyment: in their eyes it was precisely the enjoyment that was
wrong. As a result they made no real distinction between virtuous
and vicious desire. The whole subject was taboo, and the only
answer to the question of sexual urges was 'don't!' The old idea
of chastity as a form of temperance eluded them. Yet what
Aristotle said about anger (by way of elucidating the virtue of
praotes or 'gentleness') applies equally to sex. For Aristotle it is
not right to avoid anger absolutely. It is necessary rather to
acquire the right habit – in other words to school oneself into
feeling the right amount of anger towards the right person, on the
right occasion and for the right length of time.

In just such a way we should define sexual temperance, not as
the avoidance of desire, but as the habit of feeling the right desire
towards the right object and on the right occasion. The Sufi
philosopher al-Ghazâlî, influenced in this matter by Aristotle,
describes the virtue of chastity, in the *Mizân al-'Amal*, as serving
'to ensure the self's subordination to its rational component, so
that enjoyment and restraint conform to the intellect. It is a mean
between licentiousness and lack of desire'. That is what true
chastity consists in, and it provides one of the deep arguments in
favour of marriage that it rescues sex from the realm of appetite,
and situates it in the realm of virtue. It does this by allying sex to
character, so that desire and love go hand in hand, each
amplifying and controlling the other. All this is brilliantly worked
out and illustrated in the novels of Jane Austen, and it is the real
cause of the insatiable appetite of Janeites for those works, that
every sentence is gently propelled by desire, but a desire

inseparable from the judgement of its object, and from the sense of what is really at stake, when a woman gives way to her seducer. Puritans lack this sense of measured and personalized desire. When sexual taboos were lifted, therefore, they found no further reason to refrain from indulgence. Since no virtue was at risk in our sexual transgressions, these ceased overnight to be transgressions. Thereafter no proof of the damage done to children by premature experiment, no proof of the moral and medical chaos of uninhibited sexuality, could be heard. Puritanism turned an absolute no into an absolute yes. And it looked around for other pleasures that it could forbid, not because God was offended by them but because someone was profiting from them. Hence you can portray young people on the screen as engaging in sexual orgies, swearing and exhibiting every kind of nastiness. But you must never show a young person with a cigarette in his mouth, since that will be condoning sin – not the sin of the smoker, but the sin of those who profit from his vice. Portraits of famous smokers like Brunel, Churchill and Sartre have been doctored by the Ministry of Truth in order to remove the offending item from between their fingers, and side by side with the poster on the school notice board that advises twelve year olds on safe sex and free abortion, is the absolutist edict saying that thou shalt not smoke.

Puritans have had as much reason to target drinking as to target smoking, now that drinks are big business in the hands of a few large corporations like Diageo. And here it is somewhat easier to sympathize with them. For drunkenness does not merely harm the individual; it can destroy his capacity for human relations, and turn his world into a sea of bitterness. It is therefore vital, if we are to save one of the greatest of human goods from the Inquisition, that we find another and more humane way to approach the problem of alcohol than the way of interdiction. And that is why we should take a lesson from Aristotle, and see the question not in terms of thou shalt and thou shalt not, but in terms of the right and the wrong way to drink.

St Paul tells us 'be not drunk with wine, wherein is excess; but be filled with the Spirit'. The point of this passage is not to urge spirits in the place of wine, but to warn us against excess. The Spirit is not hostile to wine – after all, it is present in the wine at

Communion, according to Christian doctrine, and it was Paul's advice to his dearest companion to 'take not only water, Timothy, but also a little wine' (1 Tim. 5.23). Indeed Christianity is one of those Mediterranean religions that has made the drinking of wine into an obligation. It is another aspect of the puritan legacy that it makes no distinction between drunkenness and mild intoxication, or between the different drinks that produce either state. It is not surprising, therefore, that the reaction against puritanism is equally undiscerning in the drinks that it recommends and in the way of drinking them.

The American reaction is typified by a striking new journal, called *The Modern Drunkard*, a copy of which was recently thrust into my hand in a Washington bar by a gentleman so large that his voice sounded from some unseen region beyond his stomach. The journal relates how a party of innocent rednecks, all dressed as Santa Claus, was broken up one recent Christmas by truncheon-wielding traffic policemen, even though none of the drunks was remotely capable of driving home. It contains an inspiring interview with the Emperor of the Hobos, 'Soup Bone' Balmett, who has puked his way from jail to jail across the continent in pursuit of his constitutional rights. And it offers useful advice on the forgotten art of staggering, in an article that makes it abundantly clear that drunkenness is understood by American beer-drinkers as the last remaining way of letting the masculine – or at any rate the male – hang out. But nowhere does it address the real question of drink, which is what to drink, how, when and with whom. Its focus is on beer and grain spirits, and its main concern is to advise its readers how to drink enough of them, and still be capable of absorbing more.

I am reminded of George Crabbe's lines on 'Inebriety':

> *Lo! The poor toper, whose untutored sense*
> *Sees bliss in ale, and can with wine dispense;*
> *Whose head proud fancy never taught to steer*
> *Beyond the muddy ecstasies of beer.*

I think we should take a lesson from Crabbe and *The Modern Drunkard*, and try to understand the distinction between virtuous and vicious drinking by reflecting on the drink that has been, in our civilization, both the vehicle of the real presence of God, and the symbol of our ways of reaching him. In order to present a cogent answer to the whiners and whingers who hope to govern us, we should study the ways in which wine can be incorporated into the moral life of rational beings, so as to enhance rather than diminish their fulfilment. What I say will apply, however, to other alcoholic drinks, to the extent that they can be incorporated, like wine, into social rituals that bring happiness and understanding, and which collectively banish despair.

In the normal case, we endeavour to remain true to ourselves in our cups, and to display nothing when under the influence that we would wish to hide when not. Many of the ways that we have developed of drinking socially are designed to impose a strict regime of moderation. Buying drinks by round in the pub, for example, has an important role in both permitting people to practise affordable hospitality, and controlling the rate of intake and the balance between the inflow of drink and the outflow of words.

I earlier referred to that great exponent of the old Anglican virtues, the Rev George Crabbe. It is an unfortunate blemish in the libretto that Montagu Slater derived from Crabbe's poem of *Peter Grimes* that the villagers are so unkindlily portrayed in their cups. Their words, which are meant to outline the closed and suspicious society from which Peter is excluded, also convey Slater's snobbish attitude towards the public house culture:

> *We live, and let live, and look –*
> *We keep our hands to ourselves.*
> *We sit and drink the evening through*
> *Not deigning to devote a*
> *Thought to the daily cud we chew*
> *But buying drinks by rota!*

In fact the practice of buying rounds in the pub is one of the great cultural achievements of the English. It enables people with little money of their own to make generous gestures, without the risk of being ruined by them. It enables each person to distinguish himself from his neighbours and to portray his individuality in his choice of drink, and it causes affection progressively to mount in the circle of drinkers, by giving each in turn the character of a warm and hospitable friend. In a way it is a moral improvement on the Greek symposium, where the host alone appeared in the character of the giver, and also on the common room and the country house. The round of drinks enables even the speechless and the downtrodden briefly to receive the thanks, the appreciation and the honour of their neighbours. It is a paradigm case of 'social inclusion', to use the jargon of our rulers, and it is hardly surprising that everything is now being done to ensure that the practice dies out.

The blemish in Slater's libretto is more than overcome by Britten's music, which ties the drinkers together in a warm unison melody over syncopated chords, and shows that, if Grimes is excluded, it is because there really is a society-forming power in communal drinking. And it is not only Grimes who stands apart from the intimacy of Auntie's tap-room. The pub contains another outsider – Mrs Sedley – appalled to find herself in beer-fumed company, forced into society by her need for laudanum, and with a drug-addict's inability to see others as anything but the means to satisfy her craving. Britten shows us the social virtue of communal drinking, and the unhappy fate of those who find their stimulus from things swallowed without taste, and consumed without courtesy.

A fermented drink like beer or wine is not simply a shot of alcohol, and must never be confused in its effect with spirits or even with cocktails. In the last chapter I suggested that the transformation of the soul under the influence of wine is the continuation of another transformation that began maybe fifty years earlier when the grape was first plucked from the vine. When we raise a glass of wine to our lips, therefore, we are savouring a living thing. It is as though the wine were another human presence in any social gathering, as much a focus of interest as the other people there.

This understanding of the social function of fermented drinks has been incorporated in a thousand ways into Western societies. Its most evident manifestation is in the practice of 'toasting'. People raise their glasses in celebration, to signify their goodwill towards others and their projects, and to give proof of their readiness to take this benevolent feeling *into* themselves, as a kind of renewal of the heart. The acknowledgement of the social virtues of wine appears too in the world of Islam, in the poetry of Hafiz, Rumi and Omar Khayyam. It is a sign of the puritanical extremism of the versions of Islam that seem so threatening today, that they emphasize the Koranic interdiction of wine, and forget that many of the rivers of paradise, according to the Holy Book, are actually made of the stuff (see, for example, *surah* 47 verse 15).

And here it is right to register a protest against the worst of the whiners – the humourless mullahs who have infested our cities, corrupting the youth with their ego-flattering edicts, and inviting the lonely children of immigrants to join their cause, which is the cause of not joining. Their attempts to reintroduce religious censorship to the nation states of Europe have yet to be endorsed with any precise legal enactment. But they collectively exemplify what, to me, is the real tragedy of Islam, which is that it has entered the modern world shorn of its culture.

The vital role played by the Muslim philosophers of the Middle Ages in the transmission of classical thought is a familiar theme of intellectual history. In my own academic specialism, which is the philosophy of music, I am sensible that there is only one great philosopher who has written a book devoted entirely to the subject, and that is al-Fârâbî, who was himself a distinguished musician, and whose work is a formidable attempt to reconcile the neo-Platonist theory of cosmic harmony with the modes of early Arab music. Nor – to take another of my interests – is there a Western classic dealing with the moral status of animals that remotely compares with *The Case of the Animals versus Man before the King of the Jinn*, compiled by the 'Ikhwan as-Saffa' – a brotherhood of philosophers who lived in the fertile crescent in the tenth and eleventh centuries of our era. The idea of courtly love (from which flowed so much of our medieval literature) entered Europe from Muslim Andalusia, and found its first theological underpinning in the writings of Avicenna, while the dispute between al-Ghazâlî and Averroës over the nature and limits of philosophical knowledge is as relevant today as when it was first set down.

But what has happened to that great and disputatious culture? Where, for example, will you find printed copies of the philosophers? In American university libraries, certainly. But not in the bookshops of Damascus or Baghdad. And this puts the current conflict with Islam in a certain perspective. To call it a 'clash of civilizations', as Samuel Huntington famously did, is to assume that two civilizations exist.[1] But one of the contenders has never turned up on the battlefield. The clash that we witness is between Western secularism and a religion which, because it has lost its self-conscious part, can no longer relate in any stable way to those who disagree with it.

Close on thirty years ago Edward Said published his seminal book *Orientalism*, in which he castigated the Western scholars who had studied and commented upon the society, art and literature of the Middle East. He coined the term 'orientalism' to denote the denigrating and patronizing attitude towards Eastern civilizations that he discerned in all Western attempts to portray them. Under Western eyes the East has appeared, according to Said, as a world of wan indolence and vaporous dreaming, without the energy or industry enshrined in Western values, and therefore cut off from the sources of material and intellectual success. It has been portrayed as the 'Other', the opaque reflecting glass in which the Western colonial intruder can see nothing save his own shining face.

Said defended his thesis with high-spirited and brilliant prose, but also with highly selective quotations, concerning a very narrow range of East–West encounters. And while pouring scorn on Western portrayals of the Orient, he did not trouble himself to examine any Eastern portrayals of the Occident, or to make any comparative judgements whatsoever, when it came to assessing who had been unfair to whom. Had he done so he would have been forced to describe a literature in Arabic which is either entirely Westernized in the manner of Cairo's Naguib Mahfouz (who narrowly escaped death at the hands of a knife-wielding Islamist in 1994, and by the time of his death in 2006 was increasingly censored), or which, having turned its back on Western culture, retreats into 'the shade of the Koran', as recommended by the Muslim Brotherhood leader, Sayyid Qutb.[2] It is cool and quiet in the place to which Qutb invites his readers. But it is also dark. And although Qutb has not been censored by the Egyptian authorities, it is relevant to point out that he was hanged.

[1]	Samuel P. Huntington, *The Clash of Civilisations and the Remaking of World Order*, New York 1996.

[2]	Sayyid Qutb, *Fi zilâl al-Qu'rân*, 1954–64.

Said was attacking a tradition of scholarship which can fairly claim to be one of the real moral achievements of Western civilization. The orientalist scholars of the Enlightenment created or inspired works that have entered the Western patrimony, from Galland's seminal translation of the *Thousand and One Nights* of 1717, through Goethe's *West-Östlicher Divan* and FitzGerald's *Rubaiyat of Omar Khayyam*, to Szymanowski's Hafiz settings, Mahler's *Das Lied von der Erde*, the Hindu invocations of T. S. Eliot and Pound's translations of the Confucian Odes. Of course this tradition was also an appropriation – a remaking of Eastern material from a Western perspective. But why not acknowledge this as a tribute, rather than a snub? You cannot appropriate the work of others, if you regard them as fundamentally 'Other'.

In fact Eastern cultures owe a debt to their Western students. At the moment in the eighteenth century when 'Abd al-Wahhab was founding his particularly obnoxious form of Islam in the Arabian peninsula, burning the books and cutting off the heads which contained thoughts that disagreed with him, Sir William Jones was collecting and translating all that he could find of Persian and Arabic poetry, and preparing to sail to Calcutta, where he was to serve as a judge and to pioneer the study of Indian languages and culture. Wahhabism arrived in India at the same time as Sir William, and began at once to radicalize the Muslims, preaching the cultural suicide that the good judge was doing his best to prevent.

If the orientalists had a fault, it was not their patronizing or colonialist attitudes but on the contrary, their lamentable tendency to 'go native' in the manner of Sir Richard Burton and T. E. Lawrence, allowing their love of Islamic culture to displace their perception of the people, to the point where they failed, like Lawrence, to recognize that the people and the culture no longer had much in common. Nevertheless, their work remains a striking tribute to the universalism of Western civilization, and has now been vindicated by Robert Irwin, in a book which shows Said's *Orientalism* to be a tissue of half-truths.[3] Irwin exposes the mistakes, oversights and downright lies

[3] Robert Irwin, *The Lust for Knowing: The Orientalists and their Enemies*, London 2006.

contained in Said's book and, if it was not obvious before, it is certainly obvious now, that the principal reason for Said's popularity in our universities is that he provided ammunition against the West.

This is, however, a depressing conclusion to draw. For it seems in general to be true that many of those appointed as the guardians of Western culture will seize on any argument, however flawed, and any scholarship, however phony, in order to denigrate their cultural inheritance. Which makes it seem as though we too are now entering a period of cultural suicide, learning first to despise, and eventually to forget, the outlook that led those noble orientalists to undertake a task that only someone steeped in Western culture would dream of – the task of rescuing a culture other than their own. Indeed this is, in my view, the true meaning of binge drinking: it is an attempt by people who have lost their culture, to fill their minds with a bottled substitute.

In the light of this we have no choice, it seems to me, than to assume 'the white man's burden', and to follow those orientalists into the breach. It is our duty not merely to instruct young people in the culture that they are losing, but also to help our Muslim neighbours to step back into *their* culture, to understand that there are ways of reading the Koran that adjust its commandments to the changing world of social interaction. How is this to be done?

A version of this question is familiar to all people whose faith rests in a holy book. What guarantee do we have that the book is a revelation granted by the Almighty? There is only one possible answer: because God himself tells us so, in the course of the revelation. The circularity of this is apparent to a child. Yet circularity is inescapable. Revelations from God are all that we can hope for, and in the nature of the case there can be no independent proof of them – no proof, that is, compatible with the belief in God's transcendence. This means that there are three ways of reading a sacred text like the Koran. The first way says that it is a human product, presented through the most pretentious of pseudonyms – that there is nothing to it, save the thoughts of the one who first assembled the words. The second way says that it is the voice of God himself, every word of which issues from the Almighty. The third way (the way of hermeneutics) says that it is, indeed, the record of a revelation, but a revelation which, because it has passed, as it must, through a merely human medium, and one embroiled in the contingencies of a situation that has long since disappeared, must always be reinterpreted, in order to glean its real meaning, which is the meaning for us, here, now.

In our current circumstances the first of those ways of reading the Koran is dangerous: a provocation which entirely ignores the hold that a sacred text acquires over those who live within its shadow. But the second way is equally dangerous. To attribute these tense and stuttering verses to God, and to assume that this cry in the Arabian wilderness fourteen centuries ago is an unrevisable imperative binding in its every word, is to be in conflict with reality, launched on a path that can only end in the murder of God's 'enemies'. Only the third reading is safe, and it is the one that Jews and Christians have long practised in relation to the Bible. Yes, they have told themselves, we see in this the hand and the voice of God – but passed through what fallible witnesses, what awestruck and bewildered secretaries to the nameless I Am!

Something of this approach was adopted by the early Muslim jurists, in recognizing that we can add to, extend and adapt the *shari'ah*. This we do by individual effort or *ijtihad*. We should therefore reject the long-standing tradition which tells us that 'the gate of *ijtihad*' is closed. We should make a decisive move against the pseudo-scholarship of the Wahhabists, and encourage Islam to move forward in the direction that it was taking in the days of Averroës, the direction which will reconcile God and man, and enable Muslims once again to unwind. We should insist that the edicts of which Muhammad was the mouthpiece are in need of interpretation, and that a practice that seemed good to Avicenna, Hafiz, Rumi and Omar Khayyam cannot be as bad as the mullahs declare. The Koran inveighs against wine as 'a Satanic device' (e.g. 5.19), while insisting that the wine-filled rivers of paradise are 'a delight to those who drink'. I would reconcile these statements by the following piece of *ijtihad*. Wine is not an entitlement, but a reward. To drink wine without deserving it is therefore a sin; but once the question of merit has been settled in your favour, you can join the symposium of the righteous. Sure, for the pious, this question is settled only after death. But it is only the most venial of sins to anticipate that event, and to help oneself to a cup or two now. And this, note, is the attitude taken in the *Thousand and One Nights*, in which the Koranic ruling against wine is respected as an ideal to which mortals cannot easily attain, and the transgression of which would surely be forgiven by a loving God. And some delightful forms of *ijtihad* are offered, by way of reconciling the life of piety with the occasional need for a drink.[4]

Goethe described Spinoza as a 'god-intoxicated man', because he believed himself and everything in the world to be a 'mode' of the one divine substance. The description would be more aptly applied to Muhammad, who recited his verses in the grip of a spirit so strong and unbrookable that he felt himself to be taken hold of and shaken to his core by God. The crammed syntax and stuttering rhythms of the *surahs* testify to the Prophet's intoxicated state, and is it surprising if, returning shaken to his congregation, he should be distressed to find that they too were intoxicated, not with God, but with one of God's creatures? The Christian solution to this problem – which is to identify the two intoxicants, so as to swallow God and wine in a single gulp – seems not to have occurred to the Prophet. And so, impetuously, and to the great grief of mankind, he ended by forbidding the one source of reconciliation for which the Muslim world has forever after hungered, namely:

> *The grape that can with logic absolute*
> *The two-and-seventy jarring sects confute*

as Omar Khayyam put it. And those two and seventy sects are still at it, tearing the Muslim world to shreds, as their victims pant for the forbidden drink that will bring understanding and forgiveness in the place of dictatorial rage.

But the Koran is right in one respect: Satan can make use of wine, as he makes use of every good thing. Occasional intoxication may be forgivable; but alcohol can become an addiction – and the Arabs have long been familiar with this addiction, which is one reason why we use their word for the pure substance – *al-kuhul* – which causes it. And if we are to understand the particular application of 'virtue ethics' that I wish

---

[4] See, for example, the reasoning offered to the pious Sheikh Ibrahim in Night 36.

in this chapter to put across, we should see that addiction is part of the problem.

Aristotle's celebrated theory of virtue as the mean between extremes should not be taken too literally. Nevertheless, very many virtues can be understood through the contrast between opposing vices – in this case the soul-destroying need of the alkie and the equally destructive whining of the mullahs. Looking at our city streets, in which ignorant drunks punch and puke, while haughty Muslims hurry past with murder in their hearts, we see the beginnings of a future civil war, in which the two vices turn to confront each other and 'ignorant armies clash by night'. To avert this dire event we must not only teach Muslims to drink, but also teach ourselves to drink better – and that means teaching ourselves to incorporate drink into a life properly lived, and lived for the sake of others.

Aristotle's theory of virtue was also a theory of moral education. It is possible, he believed, to learn to be good; and we do this by acquiring good habits. We may not at first wish to acquire these habits, and it may be that we have to be trained into them by rewards and punishments that have nothing to do with their true utility. But if we do not acquire them when young it becomes increasingly difficult to rectify the deficiency, as other habits grow in their place. The good habits are hard to acquire, since they involve *overcoming* our natural inclinations, disciplining our appetites, making the space in our motives that can be occupied, in due course, by rational choice. The bad habits are easy to acquire, since they stem from appetite, and from allowing immediate gratification to determine our choices. The good habits are the virtues, the bad habits vices. And the important feature of both is that they determine not just what a person will do on the particular occasion, but also the motive from which he acts. The courageous person does not merely confront danger resolutely: he acts from the motive of honour. It would be shameful to him to act otherwise, and this sense of shame has been built into the habit that governs his behaviour. The cowardly person gives way to fear, and runs away because of his self-centred passion.

All that was carefully spelled out by Aristotle. And it is hard to deny either its truth in general or its relevance to our situation today, when children often develop at random, with no one troubling to curtail their appetites or to guide them along the path of virtue. This deficiency is particularly evident in the matter of temperance. Binge drinking is simply a special case: as we know, there is also binge eating, binge television, binge internet, binge sex. In all these matters temperance involves being responsive to the true social significance of the activity which the binger abuses. Temperate eating, for example, means eating at specific times, in company, while politeness, manners and amiable conversation push natural appetite into the background. The absence of this discipline is in part responsible for the so-called 'obesity' epidemic. Temperance, as much as courage and prudence, involves the motive of shame. Temperate people are ashamed to give way to appetite in circumstances where reason forbids this: they refrain from eating or drinking when this would display them as the pawns of their animal desires; they are alert to the social significance of eating, drinking and sexual interest, and ashamed to behave as though their appetite for these things could eclipse all respect for their companions.

Hence temperance involves acquiring the motive that the Greeks called *aidōs*, by which they understood a kind of respect towards the other and a readiness to be ashamed before him. This motive is not timidity or shyness but, on the contrary, a kind of openness to the other, a valuing of his judgement, and a search for full mutuality. The Greeks regarded *aidōs* as the principal guard against wrongdoing and did not see wine as an impediment to its exercise. On the contrary, the symposium culture had *aidōs* as one of its goals. Plato makes the point several times in *The Laws*, describing wine as a medicine for the production of *aidōs* in the soul (672d., 5–9). Pindar had the same idea in mind when he wrote, in the ninth Nemean Ode, that

> *Peace loves the Symposium, as*
> *The new-living glory of triumph grows with soft song:*
> *The voice becomes bold beside the mixing bowl.*
> *Let someone mix it, sweet prophet of the revel,*
> *And pass round in silver cups*
> *The mighty child of the vine.*

This reverence towards the other is, as Pindar says, an instrument of peace, a conscious step towards asking and offering forgiveness. Hence wine, properly drunk, can form part of an education in temperance, and it is for this reason that adolescents should be judiciously exposed to it and not, as in America, forbidden to taste it until they have learned how to binge on everything else.

When Aristotle made the idea of virtue central to moral philosophy, it was in the context of a particular theory of practical reasoning. The major premise of the 'practical syllogism', he held, is not a belief but a desire. Desires derive from habits, and good habits are those that express themselves in the right desires – desires the satisfaction of which brings happiness or *eudaimonia*. The virtues are dispositions to want what truly fulfils us. Virtuous drinking is an aspect of temperance – but temperance understood in the Greek sense (*sōphrosune*), as the moderate exercise of an appetite, rather than the absolute refusal to indulge it. To understand what moderation consists in, we should study the circumstances in which we are improved by drink, and fulfilled in consuming it. These are, primarily, social circumstances, when the barriers to communication are steadily eroded by the flow. But not any way of drinking, even in company, is virtuous. The virtuous drinker is the one who incorporates drink into the project of *agape* or neighbour-love. The vicious drinker is the one whose drinking is a threat to his neighbour and a derogation from his other-directed duties. If you drink as I recommend, and as the old wine culture encourages, you too can join the ranks of the virtuous drinkers. Properly used, alcohol is a stimulus to conversation, a solvent of awkwardness and a reminder that life is a blessing, and other people too. There is a thin line between this benevolent and insightful state of mind and the phony sentimentality to which incautious drinking so easily leads. And the ancient adage that *in vino veritas* is as false of drunkenness as it is true of those first moves towards it. Drunken declarations of passion, whether of love, anger, forgiveness or grief, are all infected by a dangerous falsehood, and are the spiritual fruit of vice.

Aristotle was of the view that crimes committed when drunk should be more severely punished than those committed when sober, since they exhibit not one fault but two: the offence against the other, and the additional offence against the self, that comes from destroying the power for rational judgement. However, occasional drunkenness should be distinguished from the drunken habit. Someone who on some isolated occasion takes a drop too much does not show, in his subsequent misdemeanours, a vicious character. Moreover, the effect of his loss of judgement cannot be known in advance, and so forms no part of his initial intention in drinking. Shakespeare has a nice illustration of this in the tragedy of *Othello*. Iago poisons Cassio with wine, as a result of which Cassio loses his judgement and begins drunkenly brawling. The consequences are enormous, Cassio becoming the unwitting accomplice in Iago's satanic plot. Immediately afterwards Iago poisons Othello with a *thought*. And here the intentionality lies in the poison itself. In both cases a person's soul is filled with falsehood: Cassio's briefly; Othello's permanently. And this falsehood shows itself in gross behaviour, a loss of judgement, and an inability to see things in proportion which, in Othello's case, turns love to hate and marriage to murder. But the poison in Cassio is quickly expelled, and has not become a habit, precisely because judgement can reassume its sovereignty. The poison in Othello cannot be expelled, since it is a poison of judgement itself. And the question raised by the play is whether Othello himself is to blame for this.

Two curt maxims were inscribed above the gate of Apollo's temple in Delphi: 'Know Yourself', and 'Nothing to Excess'. The maxims are connected. To know yourself you must control yourself, and to control yourself you must keep the mean. If you want to be happy, Aristotle argued, you must cultivate virtue, and to be virtuous is to avoid extremes. This does not mean that you should be timorous, ascetic or puritanical, since those too are extremes. It means that you should match your passions to their objects, feeling anger when it is right to be angry and joy when what is called for is joy. Such is the golden mean – the *aurea mediocritas* of Horace: not the absence of passion, but the balance among passions that leaves the self in charge.

That ancient wisdom was applied to the moral life, to manners and to the arts. Vice meant the eclipse of reason by desire. Bad manners meant the disregard for others that comes about, when appetite takes over. Bad taste meant vulgarity, coarseness and emotional disarray, a lack of *aidōs*. To achieve happiness and equilibrium we must discard all such excesses and put other-directed moderation in their place.

This ancient plea for moderation is a reminder that virtue should be cast in human form if it is to be humanly achievable. Saints, monks and dervishes may practise total abstinence; but to believe that abstinence is the only way to virtue is to condemn the rest of mankind. Better to propose the way of moderation, and live thereby on friendly terms with your species. So it seemed to Montaigne, at least, and so it seems to me. Moderation is the life-choice over which we can all agree. It is the Tao, the true path of Confucius, the road to Enlightenment. Even Kant, the stern advocate of Reason against Passion, recognized that it is better to put passion to Reason's use than to deny it entirely. The Golden Mean is achieved through balance rather than denial, and is as foreign to the puritans and the mad mullahs as it is to the bingers.

The balanced acrobat is the one who allows none of his movements to outweigh the others, who remains aloof from the conflicting impulses of his limbs in pursuit of a harmony of the whole body. The balanced painting is one in which all the lines of force within a picture are resolved in the ensemble. The balanced judgement is the one that listens to all sides and strives to choose reasonably between them, rising above the contest of opinions in pursuit of knowledge. In every area, it seems, balance requires two things: contrast and resolution. The contrast might be one of opinions, of feelings, of movements, of appetites. But the resolution comes about when we rise to another level, so as to exert some kind of rational discrimination or control. We achieve balance when we refuse to be immediately led by any one opinion, any one desire, any one appetite or movement, and work at one remove from all of them, in the interests of truth and harmony.

When we speak of excess, therefore, we don't mean to refer to the strength or urgency of our appetites. It is not the strength of sexual desire that makes a rapist or a porn addict; it is not the strength of bodily appetite that leads to obesity or binge drinking. In every case excess means lack of control, and lack of control means a failure to give due weight to all the many reasons that tell against your impulse. What makes a soldier courageous, Aristotle argues, is not the lack of fear: that would be mere stupidity. Nor is it rage against the enemy: that would be rashness, which is as much a vice as cowardice. Courage is the ability, in the midst of both fear and rage, to stay at one remove from both of them, doing what honour requires. Virtue does not mean suppressing our passions, but rising above them, to the point where reason can prevail. The courageous person is the one who overcomes fear, not the one who doesn't feel it.

Excess is by its nature addictive. The coward starts by running away, and soon acquires the habit. Likewise with the porn addict, the binge drinker and the bully: each does something that makes it more likely that he will do it again. When you give way to an impulse, and allow no countervailing consideration to stand in its way, you weaken your capacity to resist it. Hence excess leads to excess, and bad habits get worse.

Moreover, human interest depends on contrast. Pleasure achieved through contest and variety never repeats itself and is always new. Pleasure achieved by giving way to an impulse is on the path to repetition; hence it is quickly jaded, and must be constantly reinforced. We see this in the case of violent and pornographic movies, where audiences advance quickly from the softer to the harder versions as their pleasure palls. Only constant shocks to the system can maintain an appetite that derives from shocks to the system. That was why censorship existed, in the days when there was still a system to shock: for once we are embarked on this path, there is no stopping before the end, which is one of total degradation.

The wine promised in Paradise will be drunk by virtuous souls, from whom all excesses have been refined away. Here below, however, excess lies in wait for us, setting up those addictive patterns which we see all around us. Addiction to rage is as difficult to cure as addictions to sensual pleasure, and maybe the 12-step method advocated by Alcoholics Anonymous is the best we can do for the mullahs. But nobody should doubt that the destruction wrought by the alcoholic is wrought equally by the divinewrathaholic: the same posture of unassuageable need; the same inability to turn aside from the cup that burns him; the same cancelling of realities by sentimental dreams. For there is a sentimentality of anger and violence, every bit as destructive as the sentimentality of love. In both cases the root thought is 'look at me, feeling this – how righteous I am, and how justified I sit in the circle of my own emotions'. For the sentimentalist there is no other, but only self, and the object of emotion, be it of love or of hatred, is built to satisfy a need. His condition illustrates the fundamental feature of vice in all its forms, which is narcissism – the short-circuited love of self which refuses to acknowledge the reality of others.

Perhaps there is no finer portrait of what addiction does to the soul than that given by Dostoevsky, in the character of Marmeladov, at the beginning of *Crime and Punishment*. Dostoevsky knew the problem well, and went on to wreck himself and his family through his addiction to gambling. The drunken Marmeladov accurately accuses himself, lays bare the reality of his vice to the astonished Raskolnikov, and laments in perceptive words the sufferings of his wife and daughter. And yet his psychological penetration is entirely functionless. This is not *self*-knowledge that he utters, since it makes no connection with the will, the decision-making part of him, the 'I'. And that is what the two Delphic inscriptions mean: self-knowledge comes with moderation, and is eclipsed by excess. In describing his vice and its effects Marmeladov uses the word 'I' as others might use the word 'he': accurately recording the behaviour of an object, while he, as a subject, withdraws into the comforts of the bottle. That is how we should understand sentimentality: a self-centredness that is actually a loss of self. It involves an inability to take responsibility for the world as it is, or to see the demands of others as demands on *me*. I, the addict, stand apart from the world, alone with the need that comforts and destroys me.

I was reminded of Marmeladov when a Muslim friend recounted to me her conversation with a neighbour, whose daughter was to be sent back to Pakistan for an arranged marriage. The man had come around especially to indulge his sentimental grief over his daughter, knowing that he would have a warm-hearted audience in my friend. He dwelt in mournful detail on the girl's distress, on her listless despair and threats of suicide, on her broken heart over an English boyfriend, over her dread of the man whom her relatives had chosen as her destiny. The tears ran down his cheeks as he described his daughter's sufferings, just like the tears with which Marmeladov described the sufferings of the daughter whom he had condemned to prostitution. But when my friend protested at the man's criminal attitude, he abruptly ceased to weep and reached for his bottle – a toxic draught of pure religion, with which he cursed England and the English, and left in a fury, saying that his daughter will do as she is told.

All this has a great bearing on the appreciation of wine. There is virtue and vice in the wine that we drink, just as there is in our way of drinking it. And here too virtue resides in balance, meaning the resolution and transcendence of contrasting tastes.

My career as a wino took an enormous step forward when Desmond offered me that fairly ordinary Puligny-Montrachet from Nicolas. I say 'fairly ordinary' now, but the first thing that struck me then was that this was no ordinary wine at all. Something more than grapes and sunlight had gone into the making of it, and this something more, I realized, involved knowledge, skill, patience, culture and history. If I was asked now to say what it is that distinguishes a properly made white Burgundy from all other versions of the Chardonnay, I would without hesitation say 'balance'. This is a wine in which no one quality eclipses the others, but all seem to work together and resolve into an inclusive whole. That is why the pleasure is always new, as one or other of the many layers shines through to the surface and momentarily steals the light.

Now it is possible, with a little thought, to diagnose contributory flavours in a great wine: the lactic acids in the Puligny, for example, which impart their distinctive buttery flavour; the hint of vanilla from the oak; the malic acids that laugh on the tongue; the mineral resonance of marl and limestone; the length of the taste, both in the mouth and afterwards, which makes each sip into an unfolding sequence of flavours. You can pull the taste apart – up to a point at least – and take an interest in some disaggregated strand of it. And you will discover that some strands can be imitated and amplified, so as to become strident contenders for immediate and exclusive attention.

Thus by amplifying the oak in a Chardonnay you can brand the wine through its taste rather than through its geography or history (both of which are eclipsed by such modern excesses). Soon you have created a popular taste which, because it depends upon loud-mouthed self-assertion, leads quickly to the extinction of all contrasting flavours. Oakey Chardonnay can be produced as well in New Zealand as in Sicily, as well in South Africa as in California. Some producers even dispense with the oak casks and put oak shavings into the steel vats – which is rather like making Retsina by adding turpentine.

The case perfectly illustrates the path from balance to excess. Balance is hard to achieve, requires training to appreciate, and transports you to a realm of harmony, serenity and discrimination. Emphasize one feature, one appetite, one clamorous impulse, however, and you will no longer have to trouble yourself with balance. You will create a taste based not in restraining something but in letting it rip. You will have launched a new form of excess. And because excess breeds excess you will find yourself more and more driven to emphasizing the feature that distinguishes your product, be it oak, resin, high alcohol, the intense forward fruit flavours that can be squeezed out of Shiraz, or the gooseberry mouth-spray of fast-fermented Sauvignon.

I sense a connection between the excesses of the new branded wines and the excesses of the culture to which they minister. Take the case of Germany, where the Riesling grape has been trained over centuries to produce slow-maturing wines of immense subtlety. These wines, which come to us in beautiful bottles bearing the names of historic villages of the Rhine and its tributaries, owe their aromatic complexity and their seemingly immortal freshness to an alcohol content so low that maturation is only just achieved. The new culture of excess has as little time for such wines as for the music of Mozart, which they resemble. Hence the Germans have begun to manufacture Riesling forced up to 13 per cent and sold under brand names, advertising the product with posters in which English yobbos egg on their fellows to get drunk on it. In the old German wines you could taste all the virtues that distinguished the German people: their industry, restraint, precision, scholarship and *Heimatsgefühl*. In the new wines you taste only the vices that they share with us.

To the same culture of excess belongs the screw cap. To the naïve observer the cork is there to keep the wine in the bottle and the air out of it, with the result that a small – actually very small – proportion of vintage wines are 'corked', meaning spoiled by a defective stopper. To such an observer, the screw cap is the answer. I would respectfully retort that the risk of corking is essential to the ritual. Drinking precious wine is preceded by an elaborate process of preparation, which has much in common with the ablutions that preceded ancient religious sacrifices. The bottle is retrieved from some secret place where the gods have guarded it; it is brought reverentially to the table, dusted off and uncorked with a slow and graceful movement while the guests watch in awed silence. The sudden 'pop' that then occurs is like a sacramental bell, marking a great division in the scheme of things, between a still life with bottle, and the same still life with wine. The wine must then be swirled, sniffed and commented upon, and only when all this is duly accomplished can it be poured with ceremonial priestcraft into the glasses.

Wine properly served slows everything down, establishing a rhythm of gentle sips rather than gluttonous swiggings. The ceremony of the cork reminds us that good wine is not an ordinary thing, however often you drink it, but a visitor from a more exalted region and a catalyst of friendly ties. In short, thanks to the cork, wine stands aloof from the world of getting and spending, a moral resource that we conjure from the transcendental with a pop.

The screw cap has quite another meaning. It gives way at once, allowing no ritual of presentation and no sacramental sound effects. It deforms the bottle with metallic shards: imagine a still life with opened screw cap – impossible. It encourages the quick fix, the hasty glug, the purely self-centred grab for a slug of alcohol. It reduces wine to an alcopop and shapes it according to the needs of the drunkard. It reminds us of what we should lose, were the rituals of social drinking to be replaced by the mass loneliness of the binge-drinking wanderers.

The burden of my argument in this chapter is that we can defend the drinking of wine, only if we see that it is part of a culture, and that this culture has a social, outward-going, other-regarding meaning. The new uses of wine point towards excess and addiction: they are moving away from the old way of drinking, in which wine was *relished* and *savoured*, to the form of drinking typified by Marmeladov, who clutches his bottle in a condition of need.

When people sit down together in a public place – a place where none of them is sovereign but each of them at home – and when those people pass the evening together, sipping drinks in which the spirit of place is stored and amplified, maybe smoking or taking snuff and in any case willingly exchanging the dubious benefits of longevity for the certain joys of friendship, they rehearse in their souls the original act of settlement, the act that set our species on the path of civilization, and which endowed us with the order of neighbourhood and the rule of law. When, however, people swig drinks without interest in their neighbours, except as equal members of the wild host of hunter-gatherers, when their sole concern is the intoxicating effect and when the drink itself is neither savoured nor understood, then are they rehearsing that time before civilization, in which life was solitary, poor, nasty, brutish and (the only good part of it) short. Understandably, the first and natural effect of this way of drinking is an implacable belligerence towards the surrounding signs of settlement – an urge to smash and destroy, to replace the ordered world of house and street and public buildings, with a ruined wasteland where only the drunk is at home. Binge drinking may look like a communal act; in fact it is an act of collective solitude, in which not Bacchus but Narcissus reigns supreme.

Here I should temper my remarks, however, remembering that the quality of drunkenness also depends on the quality of the consciousness that is dissolved in it. The traditional morality which abhors drunkenness as a soul-destroying vice is undeniably on the right lines. And yet, if we remember the light which has peeped into the human tent from the little corners where the real drunks have rolled from it, we might be reluctant to be absolute in our condemnation. Think of Turner, alone with his bottle of port and his candle, staring into the flame until those glorious sunscapes took shape in it. Think of Baudelaire, taking glass after glass until his sonnet-shaped desolation turned to a kind of joy. Think especially of the famously drunk composers, whose long-haul visions rolled over bottles to their final chord. Only a real drunk could have got inside the skin of old Russia as Musorgsky did in *Boris Godunov*. And it is to the grain spirits of Finland that we owe the inspiration of Sibelius, who was carried home night after night, his body poisoned and his mind withdrawn.

The experts tell us that alcohol burns off the brain cells, cramping thought and reducing its scope and vivacity. The symphonies of Sibelius cast some doubt on this idea. Although, it is true, they became more terse, more spare, more intensely inward as the composer pickled his brain, their musical scope becomes larger, with a more thought-through development and a harder logic. The easy-going lyricism of the first and second, in which repetition and ostinato are the main architectonic devices, gradually gives way to the brilliant elaboration of poetic ideas – as in the fifth and sixth – and thence to the musical argument of the seventh, whose relentless logic has all the necessity of a Bach contrapunctus.

It is true that, at a certain point, the brain seems to have shut down. But it was not because it was destroyed – the wonderful recovery of inspiration towards the end of Sibelius's life is proof of that. It is rather that, in the brain of the real drunk, life itself is pickled, its flavour reduced to a spicy essence like a cucumber shrunk to a gherkin. Real life outside the bottle loses its flavour; becomes bland and insipid when compared with the pickled life within. And the drunk sits in his corner, savouring his inner visions, not bothering now to transcribe them into notes, words or brush-strokes, indifferent to the flow of ordinary conversation or to the empty gestures of politeness. Officious people might carry him home; but it hardly matters where they dump him, since his home is the bottle, in which the creatures of his dreams lie curled and shrivelled in their essential natures.

I have witnessed this sublime condition only in others. And while it may add glamour to drunkenness, it does not really excuse it, and certainly can provide no argument for drunkenness in people without culture or brains. So let us return to the *real* justification of wine, which is the practice of virtuous drinking. Here is one way to do it. First surround yourself with friends. Then serve something that is intrinsically interesting: a wine with roots in a *terroir*, that reaches out to you from some favoured place, which invites discussion and exploration, and which takes attention away from your own sensations and bestows it instead on the world. Into the aroma that rises from the glass, conjure as best you can the spirit of absent things. Share each memory, each image and each idea with the company; strive for a sincere and relaxed affection; most of all, think of the topic and forget yourself.

Such occasions need to be worked on, and rarely have I had the time or the peace of mind required to organize them. For a few years, however, *nel mezzo del camin' di nostra vita*, I lived alone in London and, feeling the need for views and experiences different from my own, and a circle of friends who might agree to differ, I established a regular symposium at my flat. Those attending included the art critic Peter Fuller, the philosopher Anthony O'Hear, the political scientist Norman Barry, the composer David Matthews, the novelist Ian McEwan, the psychoanalyst Juliet Mitchell, and the philosopher Sebastian Gardiner. Our discussions were among the most fruitful that I have known, partly because of the underlying differences of world view and the deep tensions which, in other circumstances, might have spurred distrust. And what made those discussions possible, and created the unique atmosphere in which people who disagreed nevertheless learned from their disagreements, was the presence of wine. No drink could have brought us together, as wine brought us together, so that we could swallow each other's opinions, and know them from within as things compatible with the human system, however surprising their taste. I kept a record of our meetings, and I sometimes return to it, since it is the record of real friendship, a rare commodity in our world of transient distractions. And one of those friends was wine – which is not to deny what Aquinas means, when he writes (discussing friendship) that it is 'nonsense to speak of friendship with wine or a horse'.

After moving to the country, however, there was a period in which I lived alone with a horse, and tried my best to achieve the other friendship which Aquinas believed to be impossible. This was not, indeed, my first experience of solitude. On the contrary, throughout my life I have been dogged by a kind of metaphysical loneliness – a falling out of the flow of things, so as to be alone with my thoughts and able only with difficulty to connect to other people. Eventually (though no thanks to Morgan Forster) I learned the art of connecting. Looking back, however, most of what I have learned from wine I have learned in solitude. My drinking has not as a rule been virtuous, although I have tried from time to time to make it so. But it has not been vicious either, since it has been entirely integrated into my attempts – a great many of them more solitary than I would have wished – to know and love the world of contingent beings.

And I take heart from the great Chinese poet Li Po (701–62):

A cup of wine, under the flowering trees;
I drink alone, for no friend is near.
Raising my cup I beckon the bright moon,
For he, with my shadow, will make three men.

The moon shines now through my darkened window, and I raise a glass of Mâcon-Solutré – which has the starched white simplicity of the moonlight itself – to my shadow on the floor. He raises his glass in friendly greeting.

8

Being and Bingeing

The misuse of drink in our society is one aspect of the general misuse of pleasure. The rule of *agape*, which tells us that others come first, that we exist not to claim good things but to give them, and that pleasure is not an end in itself but a good to be harvested from the love that we sow – this rule is laughed at by our modern educators, and has no place on the screen that babbles in the background of modern life. Even if the meditative wino can escape from the ambient madness into some convenient asylum where thought is permitted, virtue encouraged, and friendship enjoyed, he comes up against two redoubtable opponents: *jouissance* and *ressentiment*. One was singled out by Bataille and Barthes as the true goal of culture;[1] the other by Nietzsche as culture's unintended fruit. One makes a god of pleasure, the other an enemy of love. In the intellectual sphere the first is typified by the facetious hedonism of the French intellectual, the second by the philosophy of 'social justice' propounded by the grey gurus of the Anglo-American academy.

The philosophy of *jouissance*, which has dominated literary studies in the West since the events of 1968, allows every form of transgression as a challenge to the 'structures' of bourgeois power, and makes pleasure into the end of life. Such, as I read it, is the message of Michel Foucault's history of sexuality, and of Jacques Derrida's 'deconstruction'. And it is a message which has been echoed through French culture since Georges Bataille first raised *l'érotisme* to the place in our social sentiments once

---

[1] Georges Bataille, *L'érotisme*, Paris 1957; Roland Barthes, *Le plaisir du texte*, Paris 1973.

occupied by love. To pursue pleasure as a goal, to defy the traditions and institutions that stand in the way of it, to arrive in the circle of one's self-willed delights and there to contemplate their emptiness – such, it seems to me, is what we are taught by the nihilists who have shaped the new curriculum in the humanities. And their message is protected from criticism by the intimidating gobbledygook with which it has been armoured.

Equally pernicious, to my way of thinking, has been the philosophy of 'social justice', as expounded by Rawls and his followers – a philosophy devoted to remaking justice not as a feature of human actions and motives, but as a condition of society, regardless of how that condition comes about.[2] This way of thinking encourages people to believe that all inequalities are also abuses, that we are 'entitled' to whatever goods might rectify our adverse circumstances, and that justice is not a matter of respecting others and their freedom, but a matter of imposing a regimented equality on everyone, regardless of their energies, talents, agreements or aims.

On this view there is no need in the 'just society' for sacrifice, service or gift. If the remedy for poverty is an 'entitlement', then the remedy cannot be a gift offered to the sufferer, since it is already his by right. Nor should the sufferer feel gratitude, for that would be tantamount to denying his own entitlements. In a recent work, purporting to take the Rawlsian theory to the next 'frontiers of justice', Martha Nussbaum tells us that a theory of justice must confront the 'injustices' suffered by those with birth defects and other handicaps, and must be extended to confer rights on the animals.[3] In seeing all suffering in this way – as an 'injustice' that must be rectified – Nussbaum is assuming that we can rectify the contingency of being, that we can subdue the accidents of fate to a supreme and necessary equation. And inevitably that will mean creating an all-powerful state, able to take charge of everything, and to drive the goddess Fortuna to the twilit fringes of the human world. This machine-state will impose an order that has no relation to what we want, intend, agree or strive for, an order committed to upholding and perpetrating

---

[2]   John Rawls, *A Theory of Justice*, Oxford 1971.
[3]   Martha Nussbaum, *Frontiers of Justice*, Cambridge 1996.

injustice: and have we not seen this happening? Worse, Nussbaum is advocating a world in which *agape* will no longer be understood.

Suppose we follow her suggestion, and see those rejects that the Sisters of Charity had garnered from the war-torn streets of West Beirut as victims of 'injustice'. And suppose we work to establish the political system that would rectify their fate, by providing as best it can for the various 'capabilities' which govern human well-being. What then of the precious gift that they had received in that place of refuge – the gift of a love which they can reciprocate, and into which they can grow? Surely it would no longer be on offer. In place of love they would receive only the routine salves of a state that could never compensate for their great misfortune. In place of giving they would learn taking, and in place of gratitude they would learn resentment. That the meaning of life is to be found in service and sacrifice would be an idea foreign to their self-understanding, for they would never be confronted with the occasion for those practices, or with the person who would show what they humanly mean.

Avicenna's abstract question – how can there be contingent beings? – admits of a concrete answer. Case by case we can find our way to the subjectivity of objects, so as to understand each being from within, as a manifestation of the *atman*, the 'self of the world'. And its aspect is then changed for us. That which had appeared arbitrary is referred, instead, to the necessary being upon which all depends. Being then makes sense to us, not as mere being, nor as 'being there', but as 'being given'. This is the message of religion: and we come to understand it by encountering the spirit of gift within ourselves.

Mephistopheles describes himself to Faust as *der Geist der stets verneint*, the spirit that always negates. Just so is *agape* the opposite – the spirit that always creates, by following the path of gift and sacrifice. Through *agape* we overcome the guilt of our own existence; we recognize that contingency brings suffering, and that it is not for us to remake the world, but rather to give to those whose contingency renders them vulnerable as we are. This spiritual transformation, whereby we come to accept both suffering and sacrifice, and find in them the moral order that makes sense of our lives, is rightly described as a 'redemption'. Although it is hard to reach a sense of what this means by the way of abstract argument, art and religion can take us there through symbols. And wine both shines its light along the way and also, in its ritual use, places us in the centre of the mystery.

Wagner's *Parsifal* opens with a theme in A flat major, remaining off the beat for seven notes, ascending through a dissonant arpeggio and resolving, rhythmically, harmonically and melodically, with a downbeat in C minor. This theme develops through the Prelude, and later appears as the gifts of bread and wine are offered at the altar by the wounded Amfortas, and offered in turn to him. The theme dominates the Prelude for a reason: that it is in the music, not in the words or the action, that the meaning of the Eucharist is contained. The music *imports* into the drama an emotion nurtured outside it, in the long symphonic meditation of the Prelude.

Wagner had already made use of this technique in *Tristan und Isolde*, whose Prelude generates an emotion that listeners know from within long before they can put it into words, or understand the situation to which it is attached. In *Parsifal* the extra-dramatic presentation of emotion is yet more important: for there is nothing *in* the drama to which the feeling generated in the Prelude can fully attach itself. The Eucharist is, in Eliot's words, a 'point of intersection of the timeless with time', a glimpse from the edge into the heart of being. The emotion that we bring to it does not have a human object, nor is it tied in to some merely human drama. It stems from a primordial yearning that is contained within being itself, and which, according to the Christian vision, was brought to fruition in Christ's sacrifice. This yearning cannot easily be put into words, though it is immediately recognizable in the music, and recognizable not as an association of ideas, but as the very meaning of what we hear, developing through the melodic line, demanding the subsequent harmonization, and leading by logical steps to the marvellous answering phrase and the grieving, consoling, remorse- and joy-filled lapse towards the Prelude's end. And there it disappears into a great castle in the air, built from the dominant seventh of the key, not resolving but dissolving, like the stars at dawn.

The Eucharist presented at the end of Act 1 therefore comes before us as something that we have already lived through, not once only, but in that moment outside time captured in the Prelude. This moment is one of recognition, and also meditation.

We experience, as an immediate but wordless intuition, the emotional logic which leads from wrongdoing, through suffering and sacrifice, to forgiveness. Such is the gift of the Redeemer, that he brings forgiveness and therefore freedom – freedom from resentment, and from the instrumental view of each other that comes from the pursuit of our own advantage. By his example he purifies the community, showing that it is possible to *give*, even to those who hate you, and even in the extremes of suffering. And his hanging from that Cross, asking forgiveness for his tormentors, is in one sense of less significance than the story that he did so – the story that makes sense of the ritual that we see before us on the stage, by removing its contingency. This ritual is not a chance event, but the constant re-enactment of a necessary law. Here, performed each day, is the miracle of salvation: the renewal of a community, as it washes away its resentments in the blood of the sacrificial lamb.

Why is this ritual important, and why should wine be a part of it? The Christian 'thanksgiving' or Eucharist (a word used by the earliest Christian communities) grew out of the Jewish tradition of the festive meal, at which wine is obligatory as a sign of the joy given to mankind by a loving God. Such a meal begins with the Qiddush, in which first the cup is held up and God blessed as 'king of the universe, who creates the fruit of the vine', and afterwards the bread is broken and distributed to the company. This beautiful ritual, given an added significance by Christ's use of it to foretell and to ritualize his own passion, had its equivalent in the ancient mystery cults, and the gifts of bread and wine belong also to rituals associated with Ceres, Proserpine and Dionysus. This is no explanation of the Eucharist, but merely an addition to the things to be explained. But it points to another way of seeing things. The festive meal is a sacrifice, and one in which the company is drawn together by the experience of gift, and also – in the Christian way of seeing things – by the memory of the supreme gift, which is that of God himself, offered as sacrificial victim to redeem the sins of mankind. From this remembered sacrifice, and from the act of 'Communion' in which it is commemorated, Christians derive a mysterious comfort, a sense of renewal through love, mystically conveyed by George Herbert in lines that speak, but do not explain:

Love is that liquor sweet and most divine,
Which my God feels as blood, but I, as wine.

Wagner's music likewise speaks without explaining. And perhaps
we should leave the matter there, entrusting it to the hands of two
great artists, one a Christian priest, the other an agnostic man of
the world.

Nevertheless, the attempt at an explanation has been made –
by René Girard in a series of important studies, by his dissident
follower Eric Gans, and by a variety of other critics and
theologians.[4] The idea is this. We human beings, who live side
by side in a state of rivalry, are full of wrath – a wrath that derives
from the very *ressentiment* on which Nietzsche remarked, in other
words from the humiliation, anger, and desire to destroy which
are the natural outcome of competition and the spectacle of
another's triumph. History shows what happens when some
damn fool of a charismatic leader takes the lid off these
resents. People then hunger for a victim, and it is a feature
of the human condition, and indeed proof of original sin, that, if a
victim is needed, a victim will be found.

Deep down, however, we know that expressing our resentments does not free us from them, and that a violent assault on
the Jews, the kulaks, the bourgeoisie, or whoever, will not cleanse
the poison in our hearts but merely add to its venom. Only one
thing can cleanse us, namely offering and receiving forgiveness,
which is a redemption from hatred and not a countervailing force
which limits it. And we are raised to the level of this existential
change by an example whom we have placed before ourselves,
imposing on him the full burden of our aggression, and
nevertheless receiving his acquiescent love.

Our sin lies in the order of things: it is constantly with us, and
the real redemption must therefore occur outside time, an
endlessly renewed absolution. The Redeemer is the one whom
we have chosen as our example, who is also a sacrificial victim,
but who, to our astonishment, forgives his tormentors and

---

4   René Girard, *La violence et le sacré*, Paris 1972; *Le bouc émissaire*,
Paris 1982; Eric Gans, *The End of Culture: Towards a Generative
Anthropology*, Berkeley, California 1985; *Originary Thinking:
Elements of a Generative Anthropology*, Stanford, California 1997.

thereby points the way for us to forgive each other. However, his sacrifice must be re-enacted, and we ourselves must become part of it. Such events, which touch on the very mystery of our being in the world, are not understood merely through some theological doctrine or psychological analysis. They are understood in another way, through ritual and meditation. We rehearse in ourselves the sacrifice of the Redeemer, become one with him, and so rise to the existential level – the level above and beyond resentment – where he resides.

As I argued in Chapter 5, wine has an important part to play here. It enacts for us the primal unity of soul and body – the heart-warming liquid stirs us to meditation, seeming to bring with it messages that are addressed to the soul. But it does this through changes in the body, and we feel as an intuition what we can never really explain as a truth – the absolute identity of the free subject with the determined object: of this soul that I am with this body that is mine. In the Eucharist that intuition is put to dramatic use. The cup is not merely a symbol but an enactment. The Redeemer's sufferings, like his forgiveness, are offered to me, and made part of my being in the world. In this way I restore my position in the scheme of things, repossess myself of my freedom, and look on my fellows as free subjects, whom I can greet again in a spirit of love.

The argument of Chapter 7 reminds us that, in the path of all our social projects, including those of friendship and love, lie the addictions that defeat them, which replace the upward path to happiness with the downward slope to joyless pleasure. For the alcoholic the next drink takes precedence over all relationships. Sex addiction is similar, though here it is the other himself (or at any rate, his representation in images) who becomes the object of appetite, and the provider of narcissistic kicks. The addict becomes dominated by his craving, and loses the capacity to give himself, I to I. And it is for that reason, rather than from any concern for the ascending *eros* of which Plato writes, that we should beware of the traps that are laid by lust.

Parsifal has an interesting subplot, in which the central character is the schizophrenic Kundry. The theme of this subplot is lust, conceived as a 'fall' from the realm of freely given love into that of appetite. Kundry did not understand the gift that the Redeemer made, and mocked both him and the sacrificial love that he offered her. In punishment she was condemned to sexual slavery, and to the self-hatred that comes from treating herself as the object of lust. So great is her self-hatred that she has divided herself in two, one part – the part that longs for salvation – unaware of the other part – the part that is imprisoned in the flesh.

Klingsor, her enslaver, was himself too enslaved, though enslaved by lust, from which he sought to free himself by self-mutilation. But there is no freedom to be achieved in that way: the lustful approach to others cannot be extirpated by self-hatred but only overcome by love. Hence Klingsor remains locked in the short circuit of addiction, pressing in maddened frenzy on the button from which pleasure no longer comes. In the harrowing Prelude to Act 2 of *Parsifal* we encounter the soul of Klingsor, and we are shown *what it is like* to have become an object for oneself, immersed in resentment, incapable of love or gift or sacrifice and knowing no joy save joy in others' downfall. And in the Good Friday music of Act 3 we encounter the pure breeze of Redemption, in which all wrongdoing is cancelled by the gift of forgiveness, and each person awakens to his neighbour, to live once again in freedom. Between those two episodes is the story of Kundry's redemption.

In addiction we encounter a systematic loss of reality, and its replacement by a world of illusion. The alcoholic, the drug addict and the divinewrathaholic live in worlds of their own devising, which block out realities and mislead the soul into nightmares and dreams. Such, indeed, is the castle of Klingsor, which vanishes, with all its residents, just as soon as Parsifal takes hold of the spear – in other words, just as soon as the antidote to addiction has been wrested from its own deep extremes. Henceforth Kundry is no longer a divided self, since the part of her that had been imprisoned in illusion has vanished. Now at last she can be healed, and in the music that leads to her baptism in Act 3 we hear an extraordinary working over of the hitherto untended garden of her soul – a wrenching, almost atonal, chromaticism, which begins in the Schoenbergian Prelude and slowly takes on sense and direction, to resolve at last in the serene B major of the Good Friday music.

When we meditate on the being of things, I suggested, we are endeavouring to see them *from their own perspective*, as though each object were also a subject, with a reason for its being and not just a cause. This is the posture that the Upanishads recommend, and it is a posture from which the contingency of contingent beings becomes intelligible to us, as a form of dependency. But what exactly are we meditating upon, when we search in this way for the *atman* of the world? The Christian would say that we are meditating upon the Eucharist. But the same point can be made in Hindu terms. We are seeing the world as a gift, secured by the sacrificial attitude that puts others and their freedom before me and my needs. The world of contingent being is often described as what is *given*, the *data*. But it is only in a meditative posture that we can know what this truly means. The given-ness of the world is revealed to us only when our hearts are cleansed. That is the work of redemption, and we accomplish it through ritual, through meditation, and through the forgiveness that comes from both.

The idea of being as a gift, expressing the divine love from which the world proceeds, is common to the great religions: we find it spelled out in the *Book of the Divine Names* by Dionysus the Areopagite and, following him, by al-Ghazâlî, in the *Incoherence of the Philosophers*, by Maimonides in the *Guide to the Perplexed* and by Aquinas in the *Summa*. But it is an idea that remains for many of us occluded in our daily lives – a vision to be won, rather than a day-to-day reality. Rare are those moments, such as the one I encountered in Beirut, when the reality and sufficiency of gift-love (as C. S. Lewis called it[5]) is brought home to us. And that is why we must rehearse, through ritual and meditation, those brief encounters, and give them what standing we can provide in our daily lives. That is what *Parsifal* tells us, in its extended parable of the Eucharist. And that has been the theme of this book. Taken in the right frame of mind, wine shows us the meaning of that parable, and the value of a life in which gift-love has a central place.

[5] C. S. Lewis, *The Four Loves*, London 1960.

Appendix
What to Drink with What

What not to drink with anything. The world is awash with advice about what not to drink. All kinds of virtuous products, in which honest labour and the love of life have been distilled for your benefit – unpasteurized milk, for example – have been forbidden by the health fanatics. Not a week passes without a newspaper article rehearsing the damage done to the human constitution by spirits, carbonated drinks, coffee or cola, and it seems to me that the time has come to draw a line under all this nonsense and to lay down a few simple principles. The first is that you should drink what you like, in the quantities that you like. It may hasten your death, but this small cost will be offset by the benefits to everyone around you.

The second principle is that you should not, through your drinking, inflict pain on others: drink as much as you like, but put away the bottle before gaiety gives way to gloom. Drinks which have a depressive effect – water, for example – should be taken in small doses, for medicinal reasons only.

The third principle is that your drinking should inflict no lasting damage on the earth. By hastening your death, a drink does no real environmental damage – after all, you are biodegradable, and that may be the best thing to be said about you. But this is not, in general, true of the containers in which drinks are sold. In the virtuous England in which I grew up, drinks came in glass bottles, for which you paid an additional twopence, refundable on return of the bottle to the shop. This exemplary system was followed for many years, until driven out by the arrival of the plastic bottle, the greatest environmental disaster since the discovery of fossil fuels.

People who live in cities are less aware of this disaster than we country dwellers, since city streets, from time to time, are cleaned. Walk along any country lane, however, and you will encounter, every yard or so, a plastic bottle, flung from the window of a passing vehicle, to lie forever on the verge. Each year the accumulation increases, with particular products – Lucozade and Coca-Cola, for instance – adding insulting colours to the environmental injury.

I blame the drinks, as much as the people who jettison their containers. There is something about those fizzy sugar-solutions, with their childish flavours and logo-branded bottles, that elicits the 'me' response in otherwise grown-up people. The quick-fix at the plastic udder, the exhilaration of bubbles in the throat, and the burp of satisfaction as the liquid settles, all serve to narrow the drinker's perspective, and to obliterate the thought of a world beyond me and mine. And the self-satisfied gesture as the bottle is tossed from the window of the car – the gesture which says, I am king of the space through which this body travels, and f— the rest of you – is exactly what we must expect, when childish appetites are indulged in private at every moment of the day.

So here is my fourth principle: don't drink anything that comes in plastic bottles. Declare war on them and on the firms that use them. Withdraw your custom from every supermarket that sells its milk in plastic, refuse soft drinks on principle and drink water, if you must, only from the tap.

One last observation: I have found beer cans, water bottles, whisky halves and soda cartons along our verge, but never once have I found a wine bottle. Just as we should blame the bestial potion for the bestial character, therefore, so should we see, in the considerate behaviour of our winos, the moral virtue of the stuff they drink.

Plato. There is a dialogue of Plato to suit every wine. A fine claret will take you at a leisurely pace through *The Republic*, while with the *Phaedrus* a light rosé would be more appropriate, and only a bone-dry Manzanilla would do justice to the *Philebus*. *The Laws* would benefit from a robust Burgundy, giving courage and permission to the inevitable desire to skip. When it comes to the sublime *Symposium*, by contrast, something light and semi-sweet will help you to capture some of the gaiety of the company, and to drink to each of the participants as they rise to speak.

In Homer wine is always sweet, though maybe the poet was comparing wine to kisses and kind words rather than to ripened pomegranates. Whatever Homer's taste, modern habits demand that sweet wines be concentrated, syrupy, with a rich honeyed nose and a long slow treacly slide down the soothed oesophagus. Semi-sweet wines, of the kind that appealed to my suburban aunts, are looked on as semi-serious, and almost no one has a use for them, either on their own or with a meal.

One victim of this prejudice is Vouvray, a wine produced north of the Loire, on 5,000 acres of the wide valley of the River Brenne. Long-standing custom allows the wines to emerge dry, sweet or demi-sec depending on the year. The principal grape used is the Chenin Blanc, sometimes supported by Arbois or Sauvignon, and the result, when fully sweet, will mature over many years, acquiring rich complexities of flavour – especially if the grapes have been selected for noble rot, and treated like the Sémillon grapes of Sauternes. The sugar in a refined Vouvray is fully integrated into the structure, like the ornaments into a classical façade. Its fluted mineral columns, with their flower-filled capitals, call out for a firm base of argument, of the kind that Plato hoped always to provide: questions that we understand, and answers that surprise us. For this Plato should always be esteemed – not because his conclusions are the right ones, but because he attempted to prove the others wrong.

Aristotle. Readers of the *Metaphysics* will understand when I say that plain water is the only conceivable accompaniment. To swallow the driest book ever written you need plenty of liquid, and an attitude of Spartan detachment as you fight down the words. Before moving on to the *Prior Analytics* a ginger biscuit might be suitable. Only with the *Nicomachean Ethics* do things lighten up a bit, and here, because the argument is absolutely vital to the concept of virtuous drinking as I have been advancing it, I would recommend a celebratory glass or two. My best experience of the *Ethics* came, in fact, with a bottle of Sauvignon Blanc from the Beringer Estate in California – one of those original Californian wineries that have been a by-word for craftsmanship both before and after Prohibition.

Cicero. Not exactly a philosopher, though a jolly good bloke, who had much to say about the life of virtue, and whose creative ability to make himself hated ought to serve as an example to us all. His careful sentences, with their burden of dignified thought, are prime claret material, and should be approached after dinner, with a glass or two of Pauillac, where the poet Ausonius once had a villa. The great Ch. Lynch-Bages 1959 could not be better used, by anyone fortunate enough to have a bottle remaining. But while on the subject of Ausonius, how about the equally great 1959 from Ch. Ausone?

St Augustine. There are two St Augustines – the self-doubting soul revealed in *The Confessions*, and the humble servant of God, weighed down by certainties, who wrote the *De Trinitate* and the *City of God*. With the first a glass of the local Carthaginian would be appropriate, but since it is no longer exported you could do worse than to replace it with a Moroccan Cabernet Sauvignon. There is an excellent one grown in Meknès, bottled in France, and sold under the Bonassia label by Oddbins. The *City of God* requires many sittings, and I regard it as one of the rare occasions when a drinking person might have legitimate recourse to a cool glass of lager, putting the book to one side just as soon as the glass is finished.

Boethius. Once the most widely read philosopher in Christendom, now suffering an eclipse, the author of *The Consolation of Philosophy* surely deserves a libation or two from the meditative drinker. The suffering inflicted on Boethius surpassed the dose normally accorded to thinking people by morons; but he got his own back, when the *Consolation* persuaded princes, bishops and poets throughout Christendom that the unexamined life is after all not worth living. In respect for this great and beautiful work I suggest that you drink it down with a glass of aromatic Meursault.

Incidentally the great white-wine villages of Burgundy also produce reds, which are often comparable to, and far cheaper than, those produced in nearby villages planted with the Pinot Noir. Red Meursault, red Chassagne Montrachet and red St Aubin are all excellent. During a grim period of my life someone gave me a case of red St Aubin, from the beautifully named vineyard '*sur le sentier du clou*'. That *sentier* led to sanity, and, should you ever stumble across it, you should follow it too. It may not lead to consolation, but drink it with Boethius, Marcus Aurelius and a few readings from the Psalms and you will be a step or two nearer to that goal.

Avicenna. As one of the heroes celebrated in this book, Avicenna deserves special treatment, which will honour his stature as a great physician and lover of mankind (and of womankind too, he being the only philosopher of whom it is recorded that he shagged himself to death). The lands where he spent his days now groan under the rule of bearded bigots, and how to gather from the soil beneath their blaspheming feet sufficient grapes to provide a gust of laughter is a problem to which there is as yet no agreed solution. Meanwhile there is a wine produced on the edge of Avicenna's world in Anatolia, namely the red Kavaklıdere, made under Turkish government supervision, but not bad as a night-time refreshment of the kind that the philosopher ordained.

Averroës. Ibn Rushd, to give him his proper name, was another of those philosophers to whom the whiners gave a hard time. His offence was to try to vindicate the simple way of life, by showing that you can attain to the palace of truth by the path of credulity. Indeed, he suggested, it is wrong to introduce ordinary people to the philosophical reasons for beliefs that they acquired without philosophical reasons. To do so is to introduce doubt into minds that have no means to overcome it. He is right, but it is only philosophers who will know that. Averroës wished to go even further, suggesting that it is possible to spend your life watching TV, playing mindless games like soccer and wandering around with a DJ-playing iPod in your ears and nevertheless end up on good terms with God – so long as you perform the *salat* five times a day, and that kind of thing. I don't go along with him this far, but it was a nice try and deserves a glass or two of Hock in recognition.

Aquinas. Many times have I begun the *Summa Theologiae* of St Thomas, only to give up after a hundred or so of the questions. The great problem with this book is that its real contribution – the study of virtue and character, and the account of the good life for man – is reserved for the second part of the second part, and few people win through to this *Secunda secundae*, and none of them without the help of a good few bottles of Scotch. Scotch is as good as anything, to get you through that crazy stuff about angels and species. But when you have emerged onto the serene path of the virtues it is fitting to raise a glass of Sangiovese in honour of the saint. And it seems to me that, for this purpose, the best of the many sub-varietals of Sangiovese is that of Montepulciano. In his poem of 1685 – *Bacco in Toscana*, dedicated to the wines of Tuscany – Francesco Redi wrote that *Montepulciano d'ogni vino è re* – a judgement repeated by the locals at every opportunity. It was not until the twentieth century, however, that their wine was called *Vino nobile* by the Poliziani. (The townspeople take this name from Poliziano, the Renaissance philosopher who was born in Montepulciano, and who adopted the Roman name of his birthplace.) The *Vino nobile* is a rich ruby colour, with an alluring fragrance of ripe peaches above sun-drenched stones. It will march beside you over the long pilgrim's path of the *Secunda secundae*, and remind you that there are more good things on earth than are dreamed of in the Thomist philosophy.

Maimonides. Like Averroës, Maimonides wished to be the servant of mankind and as a result, like Averroës, he spent much of his life in exile. On the entirely reasonable 'Jews first' principle he devoted his energies to the great *Mishnah Torah*, collecting and commenting all the legal rulings contained or implied in the holy scriptures and traditions. But his *Guide to the Perplexed* is addressed to all of us, and is one of the truly consoling works of philosophy, the equal of Plato's *Apology* or Boethius's *Consolation*, and a work which I first read in Poland in 1979. In the days of communism, visits to Poland required moral fibre of the highest order. Every once in a while a kiosk announcing beer would take down its shutters and declare itself open, at which a queue three hundred yards long would instantly form in front of it. Here and there, in a random and unpredictable way, a few cases of Bulgarian plonk would find their way into the concrete bunkers which pretended to supply the proletariat with food. If you had Western currency, you could join the queue at the Tuzex shops, where the *nomenklatura* could cash in their privileges: and there, for a price, you could obtain whisky or even the occasional bottle of cheap Spanish wine. For the most part, however, and especially when travelling in country districts, you would have to survive on the state-produced vodka. There was little hope of finding any vermouth to drown its medicinal taste, and it was usually served lukewarm in quantities calculated to silence all complaint. The general strategy of the 'authorities', as they ironically called themselves, was to produce a collective hangover so leaden and immovable that all the lesser headaches of daily life would disappear beneath it. After four days travelling in the Polish countryside in those conditions, a day with Maimonides, in the park outside the walls of Kraków, was a great blessing. And as luck would have it the restaurant to which I repaired that evening, and where I intended to finish the book, had a supply of Yugoslav Cabernet Sauvignon. It was no better than an improvised reminder of wine. But it helped me to see that the *via negativa* which Maimonides advocated, as the only path to the knowledge of God, and which reaches that supreme goal by casting off all the predicates of our language, one by one showing that they do not and cannot apply to the Supreme Being, who is not even a being, but only not a non-being – that this *via negativa* must begin somewhere, and why not at the bottom of a wine glass, where an infinity of predicates congregate like fruit flies, all waiting to be applied? Even so, the supply of predicates soon ran out, and the glass required constant replenishment before the proof was accomplished and I glimpsed through the deepening haze the not-not-being of God.

Bacon. The author of *The Advancement of Learning* and the *Novum Organum* was the opposite of Maimonides in every way: a worldly politician, brilliant essayist, wide-eyed observer of the human condition, and intellectual iconoclast, who single-handedly destroyed the grip of Aristotelian science on the Western mind, and taught us to gain knowledge by applying positive predicates and by harvesting predicates with our eyes and ears. Any discussion of his insights should, I think, proceed by the comparative method. I suggest opening six bottles of a single varietal – say Cabernet Franc – one from the Loire, one from California, one from Moravia, one from Hungary, and if you can find two other places where it is grown successfully you will already have given some proof of the inductive method – and then pretending to compare and contrast, taking notes in winespeak, while downing the lot. Then one of the company should read

Bacon's essay on 'Death', after which a long silence would be appropriate.

Descartes. As the thinker who came nearest, prior to Monty Python, to stumbling on the title of this book, Descartes deserves a little recognition. This doesn't alter the fact that, through no fault of his own – for he was a secret kind of person – he has ended up as the most overrated philosopher in history, famous for arguments that begin from nothing and go nowhere, and deserving credit, if at all, for having made the 'thought experiment' central to philosophical method. I would suggest a deep dark Rhône wine, maybe a Châteauneuf-du-Pape from old vines, with the smooth velvet finish and liquorice and thyme aromas of the Provençal hillsides. Such a wine will compensate for the thinness of the *Meditations* and give you rather more to talk about.

Spinoza. Starting from the conclusions that Descartes failed to justify – namely that the constituents of the world are all either substances, attributes or modes – Spinoza set out to prove, first that there is at least one substance, and secondly that there is at most one, everything else being a 'mode' of that substance, conceived under one or other of the attributes of mind and body (thought and extension). This theory is not what got him into trouble with the Dutch Calvinist authorities, however, who were more disturbed by his attempt to give an account of politics in which the freedom of the individual is the ultimate aim of government. In honour of this gentle and frugal personality it would be right to drink a Burgundy from the lower price range. Indeed the last time that I understood what Spinoza meant by an attribute it was with a glass of red Mercurey, Les Nauges 1999. Unfortunately, I took another glass before writing down my thoughts and have never been able to retrieve them.

Leibniz. He may well have been right that this is the best of all possible worlds; at any rate, I have never doubted the trivial nature of Voltaire's attempt (in *Candide*) to show the opposite. It is impossible to delve into Leibniz without being immediately struck by the far-reaching nature of his thought, in which a conception of the entire universe is contained in every axiom, just as we all of us contain, according to Leibniz, a complete picture of the world from our own point of view. I would recommend a Crianza or Reserva Rioja, which should be opened an hour or two before the symposium to allow its archepiscopal flavours to breathe.

Locke. Locke's vision of philosophy as the handmaiden of science has since been adopted by mainstream Anglo-American philosophers, who have thereby cut their subject off from the humanities, from poetry, music and religion, from the attempt to comprehend the world in symbols and to see into the subjectivity of being. So beware of Locke's *Essay on the Human Understanding*, and begin with his *Second Treatise on Government*, which is where modern politics also begins. It is best taken with a glass of Chablis; indeed, in justice to Locke's genius, it would be appropriate to open one of those *grands crus* Chablis with muddy peasant names like Bougros, Grenouilles or Les Preuses.

Berkeley. If you must consume Berkeley, then wash him down with a glass of tar water and be done with it.

Hume. The extraordinary fact about Hume is that he drew such profound and far-reaching conclusions – about causality, about identity, about morality, justice and aesthetic judgement – from a naïve and blatantly false conception of the human mind. There is a leisurely wisdom in his prose that always warms the heart, and he is best taken, I think, by the fireside, with a glass of sweet white wine, maybe a Château Coutet or, if you are looking for a true bargain, the Château Septy from Monbazillac, the 2000 of which has all the E major sonority of a golden Sauternes, at half the price.

Kant. Although Descartes suggested (via Monty Python) the title of this book, it was Kant who set it in motion. A friend asked me what on earth it could mean, to suggest that there is a 'glass in itself', a noumenal entity which cannot be grasped through the senses, and which was revealed only in the 'view from nowhere', the 'intellectual intuition', which is available to no one save God. I filled the glass with white Hermitage 'Chante Alouette' from Charpoutier – the excellent 1977 vintage whose disappearance I deeply regret. And we tried an experiment: first holding the wine to the light, sniffing it, touching its cold surface with our fingers – and then drinking it, so as to 'know it in another way'. It was as though we had burst through the rough defences of a castle, and found ourselves in a brightly lit hall, where people in gorgeous robes made us welcome. That is what Kant is trying to convey. The noumenon and the transcendental perspective go together, and although this perspective is not available to us, we have intimations of what it would be like to achieve it. The exhilaration of the wine as it descends is like the revelation of its inwardness. And its inwardness is the inwardness in me, which always flits out of reach of my grasp – the transcendental self and its inexplicable freedom. I often repeat this experiment, and find it helpful to look at the argument of the Transcendental Deduction of the Categories as I do so. But I would not recommend white Hermitage, which is far too expensive, and in any case somewhat overfull in flavour, with the honey and walnut allure that requires a dish of octopus to subdue it. I would recommend, in fact, a bottle of Argentine Malbec; and it is never a bad idea to combine Kant's *Critique of Pure Reason* with the stories of Borges, which are full of Kantian paradoxes, and which remind us that there is no need to travel to Argentina.

Not all Kantian texts are so easy to accompany as the first *Critique*. Nothing seems to complement the second *Critique* or the other works on ethics. And when it comes to the *Critique of Judgement*, with its passing reference to 'Canary wine', I find myself trying out, first East India Sherry, then Tawny Port and finally Madeira, without getting any closer to Kant's proof that the judgement of beauty is universal but subjective, or his derivation of the 'antinomy of taste' – surely one of his most profound and troubling paradoxes, and one that must yield to the argument contained in wine if it yields to anything.

Fichte. It is to Fichte that we owe the philosophy of *Selbstbestimmung*, one version of which has occupied me in this book. But his philosophical prose is abominable beyond belief, and it is not surprising if the great drama of subject and object makes sense to us only because it was taken up by the far more vigorous intellect of Hegel. One work of Fichte's, however, has a certain rhetorical merit, and this is his *Speeches to the German Nation*, in which he makes his own passionate call for a pan-German nationalism, the need for which, he believed, had been demonstrated by the collapse of the German princedoms before the Napoleonic armies. It was thus that Fichte – or rather, to do

Fichte justice, it was thus that Napoleon – launched Germany on the path that was to lead twice over to the destruction of Europe. German guilt over these events is understandable; less understandable is their desire to discard all traditions, and to make even their wine taste of Euro-nothing. Typical of the newly packaged wines from the Rhineland is one labelled, in English, 'Fire Mountain'. It comes in a green Chianti bottle, is made by someone with the all-purpose Euro-name of Thierry Fontannaz and has only one German word on the label: Riesling. Pushed up to 12.5 per cent it tastes through and through of Australia. A more compelling symbol of the German flight from the past can hardly be imagined. But I would not insult Fichte by washing him down with such stuff. The best accompaniment to this rash, ill-tempered but ultimately well-meaning thinker is one of those fine old Rhineland wines, which stand as testimony to the local patriotism – the patriotism of village and vineyard, rather than that of *Volk und Kultur* – which he wished to discard. I would suggest a sweet *beerenauslese*, such as that from the Grafenstück at Bockenheim, a wine that just makes 8 per cent, and which therefore sells for next to nothing in a market aimed at British dipsos.

Hegel. Say what you like about his pretensions, his faulty logic, his love of abstractions, his determination to remake the world in his own image – the fact is that Hegel understood the modern world as no one before or since. It is to Hegel that we owe the theories of alienation, recognition, mutuality, struggle and right that have shaped our world; it is through the great parable told in *The Phenomenology of Spirit*, and in the lectures on aesthetics, politics and the philosophy of religion, that we can come to understand both the secret yearnings of the left-wing mind, and the incontrovertible right-wing response to them. *Bref*, Hegel is my particular hero among philosophers, and I can never think of his great justification of private property as the coming to consciousness of the free and individual self without visiting the wine cellar and finding instant confirmation of what he means. And I usually return with something good. With the passage about the master and slave I recently drank a Chianti Classico from the famous estate of Vignamaggio, where Leonardo's Mona Lisa was born, and where the clay soil and Sangiovese grape combine to produce a rich, black-cherry essence which may very well be the wine that was first called 'Chianti', back in 1404. It perfectly complemented that argument in the form of a drama, and made the conclusion – in which domination is transcended into the serene mutuality of the moral law – seem entirely natural, if not quite logically compelled.

There is another reason for drinking Tuscan wine with Hegel. There is a pernicious side to his philosophy that deserves to be refuted, the side which tells us that history is a continuous drama, with Act following Act towards some grand finale, that we are creatures of the *Zeitgeist*, condemned to be 'of our time'; that, because modernism is finished, we must now belong to postmodernism, because tonality is exhausted, we must now accept atonality; and so on. The refutation of this nonsense is Florence. No town of its size, save Athens, has ever achieved the greatness of Florence. But since the seventeenth century history has passed it by. A few revivals, an operatic premier or two, and the occasional spurt of local nationalism – the rest entirely the work of tourists like Henry James, E. M. Forster, Bernard Berenson and the EU, with its University Institute devoted to the ideas of the immediate past. Florence has remained as it was when the Medici family had finally murdered its way to extinction. Thereafter its treasures were subject to nothing worse than the sterilizing gaze of American scholars, the occasional flood from the Arno, and the more constant flood of voyeurs arriving and departing in coachloads. This tiny place, which over three hundred years produced artists, poets and thinkers at a rate that has never been equalled, is now dormant. It is not a modern city, nor a postmodern city, but a fragment of the past, and proof that you don't have to belong to the *Zeitgeist* or to have anything very much to do with it. And such is the flavour of its wine.

Schopenhauer. What can one say about the great pessimist except that he saw things as they are, and thereby showed that it is a mistake to see things as they are? From which it follows that things are not really as he saw them. Put it another way: 'how things are' is the name of another kind of illusion, and one which flatters the ego of the person who is 'seeing through' the pretence. Seeing through pretences is the great pretence. I picture Schopenhauer alone with his violin, not weeping over the world

– for that would be to acknowledge its value and the grief of its falling short – but playing a tune between himself and himself, summoning the oceanic Will behind the world of representations, and wanting to put his toe in it, if only to see how it feels. Such an image requires a good glass of New Zealand Chardonnay, maybe the mineral rich and buttery concoction called Muddy Water, in order to remind us that others have crossed that ocean, have retained both faith and hope and, landing in ridiculous places, have turned faith and hope to charity by planting vines.

Kierkegaard. *Fear and Trembling, The Concept of Dread, The Sickness unto Death* – what kind of a guy writes books with titles like that, and doesn't ever sign them with his own name? It is hardly surprising if the shadows that the Great Dane created are frequented by ghouls and vampires, eagerly looking for his corpse. In fact Kierkegaard wrote two great works about the subject of erotic love – *The Diary of a Seducer*, and *The Immediate Stages of the Erotic*, both contained in the first part of *Either/Or*. The second of them, a study of Mozart's *Don Giovanni*, is probably the only great work of music criticism written by a philosopher, and it should be washed down with the wine mentioned in the Don's mad aria in praise of wine and life (or at least, his kind of life), the Marzemino of Trentino.

I recently drank this wine in one of the regional restaurants set up in the great exhibition hall at Rimini, in order to cater for the Meeting of the Peoples which takes place there each year. I watched with amazement as my Irish companions shielded their glasses with their hands. To be seated at table with two fearsomely educated Irish people, and to be the only one drinking, is a rare experience – certainly a first for me. Mind you, one of them was reading the poems of Patrick Kavanagh while the other, a beautiful girl with dark eyes that matched the purple nectar in the glass, was playing melancholy Celtic airs on the violin. Their excuse was simple: this was their act, and they were rehearsing. It was my duty to drink the entire bottle.

The melancholy poetry of that Irish dropout, rescued for posterity by his devoted brother, sounds like the mutterings of a half-drowned drunk in a roadside bog. As the wine began to work on me, and the violin leaned over the verse like a priest administering the last rites, I conjured up those narrow lanes between sodden fields, where Beckett's crumbling heroes stumble on in tetchy solitude, and every roadside house is both a pub and a funeral parlour. And it came vividly home to me that Kierkegaard's Jutland would have been a lot less ghoulish with a pub or two, and his own life a lot happier if, instead of tormenting Regina Olsen – whom the violinist more and more resembled as I drank – he had at last come home to his Regina and asked her to be his queen.

Nietzsche. Nietzsche's first work, *The Birth of Tragedy*, proclaimed the religious origins of art, and the rediscovery of Dionysus as the god of joy, dance and recurrence. Panned by the academic critics, the book effectively brought its author's precocious career as a professor of philology to an end. It is nevertheless the best thing that has ever been written on tragedy and, in my view, the work of Nietzsche's which is most clearly focused on intellectual questions – by which I mean questions that exist independently of the one who asks them, in this case independently of Nietzsche. It is also a tribute to Dionysus that deserves to be washed down with the god's greatest gift to us.

But then, there are the later writings, the *Problematik* of which is not independent of Nietzsche at all. Indeed they are the most egoistic writings ever to have been received as wisdom. Moreover, they seem progressively to lose sight of the real meaning of Dionysus. Towards the end of the sane portion of his life we find Nietzsche writing (*The Will to Power*, s. 252) 'Dionysus versus the "Crucified": there you have the antithesis'. As though Dionysus had not been taken up by the Crucified: as though the Eucharist had not shown what the god of wine is capable of!

And then there is his influence. *Thus Spake Zarathustra* was hailed by the Nazis, who saw its godless invocation of the Superman as foreshadowing their own pagan suprematism. Foucault took Nietzsche as authority for the view that power is the root of human society, and transgression the most liberating response to it. And all those who find themselves, for whatever reason, in antagonistic relation to *agape* in all its forms, can take comfort from Nietzsche, whose message, as currently understood, might be adapted from Shakespeare's Polonius: 'To thine own self be true, and the bigger the self the better'.

Nietzsche believed that you could undermine morality by giving a 'genealogy of morals'; morality demands that we fight back with a genealogy of Nietzsche – and what a pitiable creature then emerges. Nietzsche's writings are brilliant eruptions of a self-obsessed neurotic, and they appear, when set in their full biographical context, as so many exercises in self-deception. These invocations of life, health, cruelty and the will to power are the masks of a timid invalid, who lived a largely hermetic life, and who never achieved power over anything or anyone, let alone himself. Although we should drink to the author of *The Birth of Tragedy*, therefore, it should be with a thin, hypochondriac potion, maybe a finger of Beaujolais in a glass topped up with soda-water.

Russell. Russell's books must be sharply distinguished into two kinds, said Wittgenstein. Those on logic and the foundations of mathematics should be bound in blue, and everybody should be compelled to read them. Those on politics and popular philosophy should be bound in red and forbidden. Not being of Wittgenstein's imperious cast of mind I stop short of his conclusion. But his judgement was sound, and with a great work like *The Principles of Mathematics* only the very best claret will do – I suggest a Château Beychevelle or a Château Ducru-Beaucaillou from a superior vintage, such as 1988 or 1995.

Husserl. The contrast with Russell could not be greater. Like Russell Husserl began his philosophical career with an attempt to make sense of mathematics, and made nonsense of it. He went on to invent the science, or pseudo-science, of phenomenology, believing that there was a method whereby we could isolate what is essential in our mental contents by 'bracketing' the material world. The reams of inspissated prose that this produced ought to have alerted Husserl to the fact that he was describing nothing at all. But no: he merely invented a 'crisis of the European sciences' in order to explain it. Unknown to himself (and self-knowledge was the first victim of this obsessive study of the self) Husserl *was* that crisis. And it takes a strong stimulus to get through such a crisis and land on one's feet. I recommend three glasses of slivovitz from Husserl's native Moravia, one to give courage, one to swallow down the jargon, and one to pour over the page.

Sartre. The reputation of Jean-Paul Sartre has never stood higher than it did in 1964, the year in which he was awarded the Nobel

Prize for Literature, and in which he wrote what was perhaps his
most poignant and beautifully written work, the short account of
his early childhood entitled *Les Mots*. Sartre emphatically
declined to accept the Nobel Prize, just as he had declined the
Légion d'honneur, and just as he rejected, in *Les Mots*, his calling
as a writer. In fact 1964, the high point of Sartre's recognition by
the Establishment, was also the high point of his antagonism
towards establishments, and of his refusal to believe that he had
become one. For the remaining years of his life Sartre devoted his
literary energies to expanding and elaborating the Marxist
mumbo-jumbo of his *Critique de la raison dialectique* (1960)
and to writing an enormous unfinished biography of Flaubert
(*L'Idiot de la famille*), proving that Flaubert was really Sartre, or
Sartre Flaubert, and in any case that neither man existed, non-
existence being the writer's secret or not-so-secret goal.

Since achieving non-existence in 1980 Sartre's reputation has
suffered a steady decline, as people have come to understand the
damage inflicted by his teaching and example. Following the loud
excuses that he offered for the murder of the 11 Israeli team
members at the Munich Olympics in 1972, French intellectuals
had already placed a question mark over his previously
impregnable moral authority, and the publication in 1984 of
Marc-Antoine Burnier's *Le Testament de Sartre*, bringing
together the mind-boggling apologies for mass murder that had
issued from the philosopher's pen throughout his years of
influence, added an exclamation mark that will never be rubbed
out. Nevertheless, Sartre's commanding presence, like a black sun
at the centre of French culture, drew 30,000 people after his coffin
as it journeyed to Montparnasse, and his mesmerizing vision of
modern life, as a sphere of absolute freedom, in which choice is
the only value, and in which everything we choose returns to the
Nothingness from which we conjure it, underlies all the
philosophies which have issued from the Parisian intelligentsia
during the last three decades.

Sartre's great work of philosophy, *L'Être et le néant* (1943),
introduces the Nothingness that haunts all that he wrote and said.
Sartre was a kind of athlete of negation, able to wrestle Nothing
out of Something whatever the subject or the cause. He out-
satanized Baudelaire in his choice of heroes, discovered in the
professional thief Jean Genet the type of the modern saint (*Saint*

Genet, comédien et martyr, 1952), and advocated crime as a form of moral purity. He reinvented the class enemy of Marx and inspired a whole generation of young people to live in antagonism towards the 'bourgeoisie' – the class that jettisons freedom in favour of the 'bad faith' of customs, institutions and laws. Although he was at first a sharp critic of the Communist Party, having witnessed the Party's shameless collaboration with the Nazis, he was converted to Marxism in the 1950s, and afterwards refused to allow his anti-communist play, *Les mains sales*, to be performed, urging his readers 'to judge communism by its intentions and not by its actions' – a stance that he retained until the end of his life.

Sartre's anti-bourgeois rhetoric changed the language and the agenda of post-war French philosophy, and fired the revolutionary ambitions of students who had come to Paris from the former colonies. One of those students was later to return to his native Cambodia and put into practice the 'totalizing' doctrine (expressed in *Critique de la raison dialectique*, and in *Situations VIII and IX*, 1968) that has as its targets the 'seriality' and 'otherness' of the bourgeois class. And in the purifying rage of Pol Pot it is not unreasonable to see the contempt for the ordinary and the actual that is expressed in almost every line of Sartre's demonic prose. *'Ich bin der Geist, der stets verneint,'* says Mephistopheles – I am the spirit who always negates. The same can be said of Sartre, for whom *l'enfer, c'est les autres* – hell is other people, meaning that other people are hell (*Huis clos*, 1947). Like Milton's Satan, Sartre saw the world transfigured by his own pride – and it is this pride that caused him to refuse the Nobel Prize, since tributes originate in the Other and are therefore beneath the notice of the authentic Self.

For all his moral defects, however, there is no denying Sartre's stature as a thinker and a writer. If any work shows this it is *Les Mots*, a book written in reaction to the cult of Proust, and designed to rectify the growing misconception, as Sartre saw it, of the place of words in the life and growth of a child. Childhood for Sartre is not the lifelong refuge evoked by Proust, but the first of many mistakes, in which all subsequent mistakes have their premonition. He writes with a sardonic succinctness that is in itself a rebuke to Proust, and the result – strongly influenced by the surrealist Michel Leiris – is a masterpiece of autobiography, to be compared with De Quincey's *Confessions of an English Opium Eater* and Sir Edmund Gosse's *Father and Son*. Undoubtedly 1964 was a good year for Sartre, since it was the year that showed his true powers as a writer, and in which he temporarily emancipated himself from the grim, jargon-ridden prose of the *Critique de la raison dialectique*. *Les Mots* is written by a man who was capable of laughter – and who might have permitted himself to laugh, were laughter not a weapon in the hands of the Other.

Why am I saying all this? you ask. The answer is that Sartre is my excuse to return to 1964, not a great vintage, but one that is indelibly marked for me by the bottle of 1964 Chambertin Clos de Bèze that I drank in 1980, and which was my greatest insight into the depth and length of flavour that a real Burgundy can achieve in a second-best year. If ever I were to read Sartre again, I would look for a 1964 Burgundy to wash the poison down. Small chance of finding one, however, so there is one great writer whom I shall never again revisit – and I thank God for it.

Heidegger. What potion to complement the philosopher who told us that 'nothing noths'? To raise an empty glass to one's lips, and to feel it as it travels down – noth, noth, noth, the whole length of the tube: this surely is an experience to delight the real connoisseur.

Patočka. Socrates and Boethius were put to death, and Averroës and Maimonides exiled; but philosophers have got off pretty lightly in recent times, Sartre and Heidegger in particular skirting the edge of real criminal thinking without suffering the slightest personal loss. But modern philosophy does have one martyr, and that is Jan Patočka, first spokesman for the Czechoslovak Charter 77, who died under police interrogation in 1977. A pupil of Husserl, he was steeped in the same fruitless jargon as his master. But reality came to Patočka's rescue, when young people begged him to explain the sufferings of their country, and were rewarded with his wise and gentle underground lectures on the care of the soul. These lectures should be washed down with Czech wine, as my lectures so often were when (until my arrest in 1985) I tried to follow in the great man's footsteps. I say Czech wine, though of course, then as now, the real wines of what has become the Czech Republic are produced in Moravia.

In Patočka's day the best Moravian wine was not bottled at

source, not sold through chain stores, not made by Australians, not beefed up to moron-strength, not tainted by Chardonnay. The rumour of its existence was conveyed by word of mouth, and to be let into the secret you had first to show that you could be trusted: a difficult feat in a country where no one had been trusted by anyone since 1938. When you finally reached the cellar, dug into limestone hills beneath the vines; when you had been led down the dank and ill-lit avenues by the purple-gilled proprietor, sipping from each barrel through a glass pipette, and amplifying the taste with slices of smoked belly of pork (called *Anglická slanína*, in what is the only known compliment paid to English charcuterie by foreigners, a compliment based on an evident mistake); when you had made your choice and paid your dues, it was then up to you to get the stuff home. Some brought bottles, some jerry cans, some little barrels that they sealed with metal caps. And if you wanted to give the wine some bottle age, you must learn how to bottle it properly, with long corks and sealing wax. Best in my experience is the excellent red made from the local variety of Cabernet Franc. This grape is named, in central Europe, after St Lawrence. Don't ask me why, or why the name Lawrence should appear in Slavonic languages as Vavřinec. To wash down the lectures on Plato and Europe with a bottle of *Svaté Vavřinecké* will give you a clear vista into suffering and sacrifice.

You may well ask how things are today, when Czechoslovakia no longer exists, and the Czech lands have entered the global economy. The answer is contained in the Habsburg railway system, which proves that the country has not entered the global economy at all. The genial dust-flavoured trains take you rattling from village to village in a state of suitable discomfort, doing no more damage than if you had stayed at home. A day-long journey, chopping and changing, might cost no more than ten pounds. And while the train shakes and squeals past forests and gorges, by the banks of rivers and the backs of allotments, you can sip one of the local products, secure in the knowledge that, by supporting the wine trade, you are helping to break up the collective farms – the most ecologically disastrous of communism's many disastrous legacies. Small producers are springing up everywhere, hiving off sections of the eroded prairies, planting vines, trees and hedges, restoring rock-hewn cellars and abandoned cottages, and generally reclaiming the sod from the sods. And peering through one of those windows, all but opaque with dirt, sipping your *Svaté Vavřinecké*, your finger tracing that difficult argument about the 'solidarity of the shattered', you will know that suffering and sacrifice are sometimes worthwhile.

Wittgenstein. 'I don't care what I eat,' said Wittgenstein tetchily, responding to a kindly meant enquiry from his host, 'so long as it is always the same.' It is hard to understand the remark, except as a rude way of saying 'I am above all that'. Even the most ascetic monk needs a change of flavour from time to time, if only to be reminded of the variety and abundance of God's gifts. In the matter of drink, however, we are far more inclined to uniformity. Having discovered the brewer, grower or distiller of our choice, we place the same bottle on the table, day after day. This may be the only constancy in the lives of modern city dwellers, and therefore a compensation for their cheat-filled days. The moral serenity of marriage is recuperated in liquid form, and the true Penelope of the wandering wino is the house wine that awaits him on the table.

This constancy is in one sense the opposite of that proclaimed by Wittgenstein. It is not that we don't care what we drink, but on the contrary that we do care, very much. Still, the right way to wash down Wittgenstein is with the wine that you would ordinarily put on your table, the wine you like as your daily companion, the wine that is not for guests, still less for special guests, but for the daily and unassuming you. A bourgeois claret, perhaps, or a straightforward Beaujolais. And don't think of the taste, for fear of misconstruing it as a private object, like the beetle in the box of *Philosophical Investigations*, section 293.

Strauss. Among the many cultural figures who bear this name my favourite is Richard, the second act of whose *Rosenkavalier* I refuse to dismiss as kitsch, believing it to be musical art of the highest order. For consistency, however, though at a level of instinct rather than intellect, the laurels should go to Johann the Younger. Johann the Elder has his good moments too. As for David, let's just acknowledge his inexplicable influence before passing on to the equally inexplicable influence of Leo. If there is such a thing as a 'school' of academic political science surviving today, it is that of the Straussians. And because Leo Strauss, a central European refugee, came from the burning continent with a knapsack of rescued ideas, he was first of all warmly embraced for his invigorating message, and then roundly condemned as a reactionary, as his pupils stepped into positions of power and influence and reminded the Americans of their political rôle. One of these pupils was Warren Winiarski, the one who beat Mouton into second place with wine from a newly planted vineyard in California, and whose story is told by George M. Taber in *The Judgement of Paris*. Mr Winiarski gives a succinct summary of his philosophy in Fritz Allhoff's collection on *Wine and Philosophy*. Whatever you think of Strauss as a thinker (and I don't think much) his talents as a teacher have been fully proven, and it is with a glass of Winiarski's Stag's Leap that he should be swallowed.

Hamvas. Almost unknown in anglophone circles, the Hungarian philosopher Béla Hamvas, who died in 1968, deserves special mention in these pages not only for his resolute patriotism and staunch defence of the Hungarian ideal in difficult times – a defence that made him eventually unpublishable in his homeland and which condemned him, the most learned and imaginative thinker in post-war Hungary, to a life of manual labour – but also for his attempt to rescue philosophy from the two great negations: positivism and Marxism. Hamvas was dismissed from his position as a librarian by the evil György Lukács, who was censor in chief to the post-war communist government. His philosophy, dwelling upon man's spiritual need and inner freedom, and mounting an exemplary defence of the Christian vision, was thereafter recognized as a threat to the loathsome system that Lukács and his cronies had imposed on the Hungarian people. I could go on, but why mention this minor figure, you ask, when his mentor, Karl Jaspers, has no entry in this appendix, and when there are other and greater Bélas – Bartók, for instance – who could just as well be taken with a drink? The answer is simple: Hamvas is the only major philosopher, to my knowledge, to have written a book on the philosophy of wine. However reluctantly, I must raise a glass to that unknown, and I hope never to be translated book, and so reflect on the wines of Hungary as I have experienced them.

I acquired the taste for Hungarian wine in a dingy cellar in

Pest, where Chardonnay from Lake Balatón was served from a barrel. After a day delivering contraband to shaggy dissidents, I was in dire need of what the communists called 'normalisation', and this Chardonnay had a peasant-like shrewdness of attack that made the whole fraught day seem like a festival. For a brief hour or two I even had the illusion of understanding that absurd language and the strange people I would meet, for most of whom Hamvas was a hero. Lake Balatón Chardonnay is now exported under the Chapel Hill brand, and has acquired an American accent – even lipped bottles, the equivalent of baseball caps and Bermuda shorts. This may be why it no longer has the effect on my linguistic abilities that was observed on that memorable but unremembered evening.

Hungarian viticulture has greatly improved since then, and the 22 wine-growing regions have been meticulously mapped and delicately praised by Alex Liddell in *The Wines of Hungary*. Within a few minutes of the Buda suburbs – where once a week Hamvas would change his shirt and grab another book before returning to the distant power plant where he was worked to death – you are in vine-wreathed hillsides, scattered with allotments, summer-houses and the remains of old farms. Here delicate and fruity white wines are grown on limestone soil, and a recently sampled Budai Pinot Gris, with its elderflower aroma and leafy taste, was a wonderful reminder of those strange summer days in 1988, when the *Zeitgeist* seemed to be hovering with a deceptive made-in-America smile above the city, like the *fata morgana* known in Hungarian as a *délibab*, a word successively applied to nationalism, communism, socialism, capitalism, Habsburg nostalgia, folk culture – in short, to anything in which the Hungarians happen momentarily to believe.

By contrast with Budai, the wines of Villanyi and Szekszárd are ripe, rich and complex. The 1998 Pinot Noir from Villanyi is a creditable rival to the lesser burgundies, while a Szeksárdi Cabernet Franc 2000 (a good vintage for Hungarian reds) won the praise of my Romanian protégées, who have never before praised anything Hungarian. This wine is vinified by Vencel Garamvari in his labyrinthine cellars under Budapest; its deep blackcurrant colour, fine claret nose, and harmonious taste show the Cabernet Franc – the red grape of the Loire valley – at its most alluring. It is with a bottle of this robust concoction that I swallowed my grief on learning that I am not the first philosopher to have written a book on the philosophy of wine.

Sam the Horse. As the argument of this book makes clear, no horse can savour the things it eats or drinks, not even the things that it most enjoys. But still, Sam has his preferences, and they cut right across the oenological orthodoxies. In fact his oats are never more eagerly gobbled or fiercely guarded than when laced with rosé. It goes without saying that, on a warm summer evening, when day lingers and the old sap rises in limbs which have seen better days, rosé is irresistible. The fresh aroma of fruit, the colour recalling the favourite drinks of childhood, the ease with which the cool and refreshing draught runs with its light into the inner darkness: all these have a holiday quality, soothing away the stress of a working life and conjuring a world of lovers and comforters. This is the true, the blushful Hippocrene, and it bubbles in the mouth like a song of cherubs. Still, when all is said and done, what remains of the flavour? What depth, what complexity, what velvet allure? Would not a glass of raspberry cordial laced with industrial alcohol have the same effect? These deeply disturbing, even heretical, thoughts come creeping in behind the shallow ecstasies. It is pointless addressing those questions to Sam for, as Wittgenstein says, if a horse could speak, we would not understand him. (OK, the text says 'lion', but the point is just the same.)

Although there are no really great examples, however, we should take comfort in the fact that good rosé is cheap. Besides, for rosé to pretend to greatness would be an absurdity comparable to a pop song in pentameters, or a bikini made of mink. Rosés are drained from the must before the tannin has been extracted, and so will not, in general, keep for long, the great exception – the Tavel rosé from the Rhône – being distinguished by the fact that, if you tasted it blindfold, you would probably mistake it for a creamy Viognier-based white. And (like people) rosés are of two different kinds: those that want to be something, and those that would rather be nothing. Sam likes them both.

Among the harmless, drinkable nothings the rosé d'Anjou from the Loire is always welcome. So too is the lesser kind of *rosado* from Portugal and Spain; so too is my personal favourite – the Rosé de Provence, which should be drunk with oats, if you are a horse, otherwise with *saucisson sec* and black olives, while listening to birdsong in a messianic, or at any rate Messiaenic, frame of mind. Then there are the rosés with attitude, such as the Cabernet Sauvignon from Mas Oliveras – a whiff of old Catalonia that has the strength and conviction of so many Spanish rosés, which are wines to be drunk with food on a daily basis. Even stronger, and with a pale amber colour suggestive of the cask, is the Cabernet-Merlot mix from Nelson's Creek in South Africa. If there is such a thing as a complex rosé then this is it: hints of cigar-box on the nose and ... Rather than lapse into winespeak I will say that this is the wine with which Sam and I celebrated his greatest triumph, which was a day with the Duke of Beaufort's hounds, when he jumped all the hedges at Badminton.

But to my mind (and possibly to Sam's mind as well) the prize must go to the Amethystos rosé from Greece, imported by Oddbins. This, made from a local grape that imparts a deep hunting pink to the appearance and a full octave of flavours to the taste, fills the air with its perfume. Imaginary insects flutter above the glass, and if you put your ear to it you can, after a glass or two, hear the murmur of the wine-dark sea.

Index of Subjects

Index of Names

Index of Wines

209